Introduction to MATLAB® Programming

With an emphasis on Software Design through Numerical Examples

Jonathan H. Dorfman

Decagon Press, Inc.

Introduction to MATLAB® Programming
With an emphasis on Software Design through Numerical Examples
Jonathan H. Dorfman

Decagon Press, Inc.
1442A Walnut Street #312
Berkeley, CA 94709-1405
www.DecagonPress.com

Copyright © 2007 by Jonathan H. Dorfman

Cover Design: ©2007 Decagon Press, Inc.

Notice of Rights
All rights reserved. This work may not be translated, copied, transmitted, or reproduced in any way, in whole or in part, by any means, electronic, mechanical, photocopying, recording, or otherwise, or in any form of information storage or retrieval, without the express written permission of the publisher. For information on obtaining permission for reprints and excerpts, contact permissions@decagonpress.com.

Notice of Liability
The information in this book is distributed on an "As Is" basis, without warranty. Neither the author nor the publisher shall have any liability to any person or entity with respect to any loss or damage caused or alleged to be caused directly or indirectly by the instructions contained in this book, or by the software described in it.

Trademarks
The use in this work of trade names, trademarks, service marks, and similar terms, even if not identified as such, is not to be taken as an expression of opinion as to whether or not they are subject to proprietary rights.

MATLAB® is a trademark of The MathWorks, Inc. and is used with permission. The MathWorks does not warrant the accuracy of the text or exercises in this book. This book's use or discussion of MATLAB® software or related products does not constitute endorsement or sponsorship by The MathWorks of a particular pedagogical approach or particular use of the MATLAB® software.

For MATLAB® product information, please contact:
The MathWorks, Inc.
3 Apple Hill Drive
Natick, MA, 01760-2098 USA
Tel: 508-647-7000 Fax: 508-647-7001
E-mail: info@mathworks.com
Web: www.mathworks.com

To my Parents

Preface

Why another book on MATLAB

The present text evolved from courses taught by the author at U. C. Berkeley in 2005-2006. The class was designed as an elective for students taking the upper-division Numerical Analysis sequence which covered introductory topics such as root-finding and interpolation, followed by Numerical Linear Algebra, and concluding with numerical methods for initial-value problems for systems of Ordinary Differential Equations. Since all course assignments required some component of MATLAB programming, the need existed for an efficient path enabling novice students to write functional, albeit rudimentary, programs within a few weeks. This circumstance motivated one of the guiding premises on which this text is based - the need to quickly develop sufficient competency in MATLAB programming to code a numerical homework assignment.

As there are many excellent introductions to MATLAB, not the least of which are provided by the MathWorks online tutorials, the above consideration does not, by itself, justify writing this text. With some exceptions, however, these texts cover *elements* of the language, and do not undertake a single serious theme of evolving complexity. In my courses, on the other hand, because students were focused on completing their first assignment (on applying Newton's root-finding algorithm to compute the square root of five), we had the benefit of a concrete context and goal for writing our first program. This circumstance motivated the second guiding premise of the present text - to write functional programs, albeit awkward and limited, from the start. Over time and after many iterations, our basic program evolves to an intermediate version capable of generating formatted tables and plots (e.g. for analyzing rates and orders of convergence). Though still limited to computing the square root of five, thanks to function handles and MATLAB's impressive vectorization capability, this implementation is shown to be one line away from a *general purpose root-finder for solving a system of nonlinear equations in n unknowns*.

For many, this course was their first introduction to writing software. During office hours in the Computer Lab, I had the opportunity to observe many students who were of the "MATLAB? - how hard can it be..." school of programming. Armed with a for-loop and display-statement, some students approached their assignments by generating scores of pages of numbers, perhaps unaware that no one would ever take the time to read a single digit. Others would attempt to display a graph, but were at a loss when the plot resulted in a horizontal line with the y-axis labelled 10^{137}. With a little effort, these students could generate meaningful and self-documenting tables, quickly identify bugs in their code, and create professional looking plots with color and legends; they just needed someone to *show* them. And this brings us to the third guiding principle (and title) of this text, which I believe justifies its publication - beginning students should be taught the principles of *software design*. An experienced programmer learning MATLAB is likely to ask only two questions:

"Where's the Help Documentation, and how do I access the Debugger?",

but many students *never* learn to use the Debugger. These observations are not surprising to anyone who recalls the early days when Fortran ruled and programs were unstructured heaps of spaghetti code, with print statements sprinkled throughout for debugging.

In this spirit, the following principles of program design are developed throughout the course:

- Effectively using Help and Debugging tools
- Modularizing code into functional units, especially input, output, and algorithms
- Designing input functions which employ graphical user interfaces (GUI's)
- Designing output functions which generate professional quality figures
- Designing algorithms whose performance can be quantified
- Designing algorithms whose applicability can be generalized using function handles
- Making programs portable so they are executable as stand-alone applications by third parties, and usable as functional components by other programmers
- Writing readable code by adding comments and by judicious use of intermediate variables and auxiliary functions, whose names are meaningful and self-documenting

In view of the above, I believe this book could be profitably used for a Computer Science course entitled "An Introduction to Programming".

What is not covered

This is *not* a text for a course in Numerical Analysis. Indeed, many of the subtle issues that would make such a course scientifically challenging are intentionally ignored, for example the behavior of Newton's algorithm near a critical point. The fact that we work exclusively with the *absolute error*, rather than with the numerically more meaningful *relative error*, should clarify the point of view taken.

Though some exercises introduce multidimensional ($p \times q \times r$)-arrays and a few advanced matrix operations (e.g. `lu, qr, eig`), substantive treatments of multilinear algebra (e.g.

kron, reshape, repmat), and canonical forms (e.g. spdiags) have been omitted. We also have intentionally ignored MATLAB's symbolic toolbox, which we consider to be of secondary interest (for reasons of performance) to numerical applications.

Future directions

In the bibliography we recommend three books for future study. These are suggested for further reading on each of the three fundamental directions developed in the course: Linear Algebra, Differential Equations, and User Interface Design. Each of these texts will be accessible to the student completing the present text.

Acknowledgements

Finally, I wish to thank Barbara Peavy - the very existence of the MATLAB course offered at Berkeley owes much to her commitment to the quality of the Mathematics Department's curriculum, not to mention her administrative wizardry. I also acknowledge with gratitude helpful feedback from Max Trokhimtchouk, who taught the MATLAB course over the Summer of 2007, and whose critical reading of early drafts is greatly appreciated. Additionally, I thank Robert Lyons and Professors Craig Evans and Beresford Parlett for their encouragement while I undertook this project.

Contents

Preface   1

1 Introduction   1
   1.1 Goals of the course 1
   1.2 Suggestions to students 1
   1.3 Structure of the text 2
   1.4 Notation and conventions 3
   1.5 Topics covered in the course 5
   1.6 Principles of program design 6

I The MATLAB programming environment   7

2 The Command Window   9
   2.1 Configuration Preferences 9
   2.2 Command-line session in the Command Window 10
   2.3 Computing $\sqrt{5}$ using Newton's algorithm 11
   2.4 Manually iterating Newton algorithm 12
   2.5 What the current implementation accomplishes 15
   2.6 Shortcomings of the current implementation 15
   2.7 Topics covered in this chapter 15

3 The Edit Window   17
   3.1 Creating an M-file in the Edit Window (NewtonAlg2.m) 17
   3.2 Introduction to the Debugger 21
   3.3 An improved version (NewtonAlg3.m) 24
   3.4 What the current implementation accomplishes 28
   3.5 Shortcomings of the current implementation 29
   3.6 Topics covered in this chapter 29

4 The Help Browser and Command/Edit Windows revisited   31
   4.1 Navigating the MATLAB documentation 31
   4.2 Script Files: The Command Window is dead; Long live the Edit Window . . . 33

4.3 Debugging: The Command Window still lives 36
   4.4 Topics covered in this chapter 37

II Writing a simple MATLAB program 39

5 Displaying Output 41
   5.1 Formatting numeric output (NewtonAlg4.m) 41
   5.2 Elimination of the hardwired values (NewtonAlg5.m) 47
   5.3 Formatting table output (NewtonAlg6.m) 48
   5.4 What the current implementation accomplishes 49
   5.5 Shortcomings of the current implementation 49
   5.6 Topics covered in this chapter 49

6 Conditionals and Flow control 51
   6.1 Logical (Boolean) expressions 52
   6.2 Conditional statements 53
   6.3 The full-blown if-elseif-else-end statement 58
   6.4 More control: for-loops and while-loops 60
   6.5 Topics covered in this chapter 63

7 Arrays I 65
   7.1 Using arrays for storage (NewtonAlg7.m) 65
   7.2 What the current implementation accomplishes 71
   7.3 Shortcomings of the current implementation 71
   7.4 Topics covered in this chapter 71

8 Arrays II 73
   8.1 Array initialization 73
   8.2 Array operations 76
   8.3 Performance: for-loop vs. array-operation vs. built-in implementations . . . 78
   8.4 Topics covered in this chapter 85

9 Arrays III 87
   9.1 Accessing array elements 87
   9.2 Using arrays to represent mathematical functions 89
   9.3 Topics covered in this chapter 93

10 Plotting I 95
   10.1 Plotting a collection of data points in the plane 95
   10.2 Controlling the appearance of plots 99
   10.3 Plotting parametric curves in the plane 105
   10.4 Topics covered in this chapter 108

11 Computing $\sqrt{5}$: NewtonAlg.m — **109**
   11.1 The order of convergence of iterative numerical algorithms 109
   11.2 Applying plotting techniques to numerical investigations 111
   11.3 Topics covered in this chapter 114

III Writing a complex MATLAB program — **115**

12 Functions I — **117**
   12.1 A simple example of a user-defined function 118
   12.2 Passing arguments and returning values 120
   12.3 Implementing NewtonAlg as a function (NewtonAlg10.m) 126
   12.4 Topics covered in this chapter 128

13 Functions II — **129**
   13.1 Tolerance as a terminating condition (NewtonAlg12.m) 129
   13.2 A complex program (Main.m, Tabulate.m, NewtonAlg13.m) 134
   13.3 Topics covered in this chapter 141

14 Functions III — **143**
   14.1 Calling functions indirectly using function handles 145
   14.2 Adapting NewtonAlg to any equation (ScalarNewton.m) 147
   14.3 Subfunctions (RootFinder.m) 149
   14.4 Topics covered in this chapter 153

15 Arrays IV — **155**
   15.1 Multi-dimensional arrays and Matrix Algebra 155
   15.2 Topics covered in this chapter 166

16 Arrays V — **167**
   16.1 The empty array and dynamic allocation 167
   16.2 Cell arrays 170
   16.3 Topics covered in this chapter 173

17 Sharing Data I — **175**
   17.1 Global variables and callbacks (OdeMain.m) 175
   17.2 GUI programming (OdeGui.m) 178
   17.3 Structures 184
   17.4 Topics covered in this chapter 188

18 Sharing Data II — **189**
   18.1 MAT-files (CompareAXeqB.m) 189
   18.2 Lookup tables (Pascal.m) 195
   18.3 Topics covered in this chapter 199

19 Plotting II — **201**
- 19.1 Plotting parameterized curves in three dimensions 201
- 19.2 Rotations and Projections (HelixMain.m) 203
- 19.3 Object-oriented programming (SliderGui.m) 206
- 19.4 Topics covered in this chapter 211

20 Plotting III — **213**
- 20.1 Graphing the function $z = F(x, y)$ (GraphZ.m) 214
- 20.2 Plotting surfaces in three dimensions (Paraboloid.m) 217
- 20.3 Plotting trajectories of a constrained dynamical system (Gravity.m) 227
- 20.4 Topics covered in this chapter 234

21 Systems of nonlinear equations — **235**
- 21.1 Generalizing scalar equations 235
- 21.2 Vectorizing the Newton algorithm for systems (VectorNewton.m) 237
- 21.3 A root-finder for two dimensional systems (Nonlinear2dSolver.m) 240
- 21.4 Topics covered in this chapter 245

Chapter 1

Introduction

1.1 Goals of the course

This course emphasizes writing complete programs from the beginning. Just as in a foreign language class it is more effective to speak in complete sentences from the beginning, as opposed to spending several weeks studying vocabulary books, we will start by writing awkward and primitive programs which will be improved over the course of each chapter.

Some of the skills we will develop throughout the course are:

1. Programming fundamentals. This includes commenting code, utilizing the Help Browser, naming variables, and avoiding "magic numbers."

2. Debugging techniques. Setting breakpoints, inspecting variables, and single-stepping code are introduced in the early chapters, and used throughout the text.

3. Program organization. Particular attention will be devoted to the design of functions, and the use of function handles, parameter passing and global variables.

4. Performance evaluation. This includes timing program execution, isolating algorithmic computations from user interactions, and determining the best built-in function when several are available.

5. Array manipulation: In addition to working with systems of linear equations, using arrays to store data and represent mathematical functions will be described in detail.

6. User input and output. Techniques for creating formatted tables, self-documenting plots, and graphical user interfaces are explained and utilized throughout the text.

1.2 Suggestions to students

Readers who may legitimately purchase the Student Version of MATLAB are strongly encouraged to do so. Even in a university environment where one may have access to a server installation, using a stand-alone copy of MATLAB installed on your personal computer has many advantages. In particular, there are no limitations on access, or dependence on authentication servers being 'up'. Though the Student Version may lack some of the packages (like splines or wavelets or optimization) included with some university installations, this will not be an issue for beginning students. The cost of the Student Version (at the time of this writing) is roughly $100, which is less than the cost of many textbooks. Your Student Version should be useful to you for many years in the future, especially if you are pursuing an engineering or other scientific course of study.

1.3 Structure of the text

Each chapter conforms to a general format in which we introduce the main topic, then explain the mathematical background or programming motivation, followed by a description of the relevant MATLAB commands.

The chapters in Parts I and II of the text include a section on the "Shortcomings of the current implementation", which serves as motivation for developing techniques covered in subsequent chapters. Part II culminates in a polished version of NewtonAlg.m, which computes the square root of five using the same algorithm described in Chapter 2, but as a well-designed program capable of formatted tabular output and professional looking plots. The obvious shortcoming of NewtonAlg.m is that it should be good for finding roots of more general functions, and this is addressed in the first three chapters of Part III which cover the subject of Functions.

Part III, entitled "Writing a Complex MATLAB Program", is where we graduate from cobbling together sentences in order to communicate a thought, to composing essays that integrate many ideas. As alluded to above, the ability to organize tasks into Functions, and the related mechanism of a Callback Function, enable us to achieve this new level of complexity, unattainable with the methods of Part II. Once functions have been added to our repertoire, we write a general purpose root-finder for scalar equations in Chapter 14 by making a small modification to NewtonAlg.m. In the remainder of Part III the chapter format changes slightly in that the progression of subjects becomes less linear, and a section on the shortcomings of the current implementation is no longer appropriate. Instead, more diverse mathematical and scientific applications are explored, and sections are devoted to specific program implementations, for example "Lookup tables (Pascal.m)".

Finally, each chapter concludes with a section entitled "Topics covered in this chapter", which should be helpful for review and later reference.

Throughout the text we conduct tutorial sessions in which elements of the language are introduced, and the behavior of specific commands is explored. Needless to say, the reader is presumed to follow these sessions by interacting directly with MATLAB at their computer. In addition to describing the MATLAB language, much of the text is devoted to motivating principles of program design. In this regard, we have included the complete source code for all of the programs developed; it is hoped that the reader will devote as much attention to studying these program listings (some of which occupy several pages) as the other parts of the text.

For the most part the text proceeds logically, being mindful to *define* each element of the language before *using* it in a program, but there are a few exceptions. In particular, we introduce the for-loop and the formatted print-statement in the early chapters, giving their precise definitions only later when we describe arrays. In some instances we introduce a new MATLAB construct in the sample code (e.g. the empty array), ask the reader to consult the documentation for its definition, and then provide an exercise to elucidate its use.

Exercises in engineering textbooks typically fall into one of three categories:

1. Those designed to give students practice exploring the techniques discussed in the text;

2. Those designed to introduce new material which could not be included, presumably for lack of space;

3. Those designed to pose challenging questions for the student to solve, possibly at the level of undertaking a "project", or writing a stand-alone program.

There are over one hundred exercises in the book, none of which fall into the third category. Part I and Part II of the text contain somewhat more exercises of the first category, asking the student to experiment using a new command in various contexts, thereby clarifying its behavior. The exercises in Part III tend to fall into the second category, often asking the student to lookup a new command in the Help documentation, and then apply it by modifying the sample code. In a few cases we have provided solutions, but for most questions (like "what happens when you enter the statement ...") MATLAB itself will provide the answer. On account of their integral role in developing the course material, we believe that all of the exercises should be attempted.

1.4 Notation and conventions

We use courier mono-spaced typeface for fragments of executable code; this includes MATLAB commands (e.g. `who`), keywords (e.g. `return`), and built-in functions (e.g. `abs()`), as well as the text and names of our own user-defined variables and functions (e.g. `VectorNewton()`).

As is standard practice in mathematical texts, we use boldface type for vectors (e.g. $\mathbf{x} \in \mathbb{R}^n$), as well as vector-valued functions (e.g. $\mathbf{F} : \mathbb{R}^n \to \mathbb{R}^n$). Vectors will generally be assumed to be column vectors, thus

$$\mathbf{x} = \begin{bmatrix} x_1 \\ \vdots \\ x_n \end{bmatrix}.$$

The distinction between row vectors and column vectors is not so critical for the mathematical discussions, as the context is usually sufficient to resolve any ambiguities. For example, $\mathbf{x}\cdot\mathbf{y}$ will always means $\sum_{k=1}^{n} x_k y_k$, whether one views this as an inner-product of two column vectors

$$\mathbf{x}\cdot\mathbf{y} = \begin{bmatrix} x_1 \\ \vdots \\ x_n \end{bmatrix} \cdot \begin{bmatrix} y_1 \\ \vdots \\ y_n \end{bmatrix},$$

or performing matrix multiplication of a row vector by a column vector[1]

$$\mathbf{x}\cdot\mathbf{y} = \begin{bmatrix} x_1 & \cdots & x_n \end{bmatrix} \cdot \begin{bmatrix} y_1 \\ \vdots \\ y_n \end{bmatrix}.$$

In contrast, the distinction between row and column vectors in MATLAB programming is a matter of *critical* importance; being sloppy when it comes to distinguishing between row and column vectors can be the source of many needless bugs in MATLAB, and we will be fastidious in respecting the distinction. In particular, we use arrays as row vectors of the type [1,2,...,n] early on in Chapter 3, but we intentionally do not introduce column vectors or matrices until much later in Chapter 8. Lest the reader have the impression that Linear Algebra applications are neglected, be assured this is not the case: By the end of Chapter 15 we will be familiar with manipulating outer-products and rotation matrices in arbitrary dimensions. Also, we prefer explicit versions of built-in functions, and avoid MATLAB's short-cut notation of using zeros(dim), ones(dim), eye(dim), rand(dim) for creating the arrays zeros(dim,dim), etc.

Our mathematical notation for the entries of an $m \times n$ matrix is standard:

$$A = \begin{pmatrix} a_{1,1} & \cdots & a_{1,n} \\ \cdots & a_{i,j} & \cdots \\ a_{m,1} & \cdots & a_{m,n} \end{pmatrix}, \qquad 1 \leq i \leq m, \ 1 \leq j \leq n.$$

This convention for the entries $a_{i,j}$ of A is consistent with that employed by MATLAB, where A(i,j) is used to access the entry at the ith-row and j^{th}-column.

MATLAB's notation for the transpose of an $m \times n$ matrix A uses the single-quote A'. Our convention for the mathematical transpose uses the lower-case t, as in A^t.

Another standard mathematical notation we employ is the symbol := to indicate that the left hand side is *defined* by the expression on the right hand side.

---

[1] The former interpretation is viewed by mathematicians as a $(2,0)$-tensor, or bilinear form on $\mathbb{R}^n$, whereas the latter interpretation is the natural pairing between a vector and a covector, or a $(1,1)$-tensor. These distinctions disappear in Euclidean space, which will be our point of view when discussing mathematical motivation.

As for Calculus conventions, we prefer the $f'(a)$ notation to $\left.\dfrac{df}{dx}\right|_a$, but are completely comfortable manipulating the quantities Δx (or $\Delta \mathbf{x}$) as one finds in Physics and Engineering texts. With regard to several variables, if $f : \mathbb{R}^n \to \mathbb{R}$ is a scalar-valued function of several variables, then the gradient of f is written

$$\nabla f(\mathbf{a}) = \left[\frac{\partial f}{\partial x_1}(\mathbf{a}), \ldots, \frac{\partial f}{\partial x_n}(\mathbf{a})\right].$$

For vector-valued functions $\mathbf{F} : \mathbb{R}^n \to \mathbb{R}^m$ given by $\mathbf{F}(\mathbf{x}) = [f_1(\mathbf{x}), \ldots, f_m(\mathbf{x})]^t$, we represent the Jacobian matrix as

$$D\mathbf{F}(\mathbf{a}) = \begin{bmatrix} \nabla f_1 \\ \vdots \\ \nabla f_m \end{bmatrix} = \begin{bmatrix} \dfrac{\partial f_1}{\partial x_1}(\mathbf{a}) & \cdots & \dfrac{\partial f_m}{\partial x_n}(\mathbf{a}) \\ \vdots & \dfrac{\partial f_i}{\partial x_j}(\mathbf{a}) & \vdots \\ \dfrac{\partial f_m}{\partial x_1}(\mathbf{a}) & \cdots & \dfrac{\partial f_m}{\partial x_n}(\mathbf{a}) \end{bmatrix}.$$

Conventions related to the programming environment are as follows: This text was developed using Version 7.0.4 Release 2007a of MATLAB in the Microsoft Windows® XP environment. On the other hand, a student with a version of MATLAB as early as Release 12 (circa 2001) will find no obstacles to learning from the text, although some screen-shots of menus and help windows may appear unfamiliar. The only topics in which users of an earlier version are at a disadvantage is with respect to including secondary functions in a source file, and also invoking functions indirectly through "anonymous function handles." In this regard, we explain both the older (obsolete, yet functional) techniques, as well as the more recent and preferred techniques.

When we refer to menu items, we use colons to separate the levels of hierarchy. For example "File:Preferences:Help menu" indicates the Help menu which can be selected as a sub-menu of the Preferences menu, which itself is a sub-menu of the File menu.

As for operating system conventions, we assume the user has a two-button mouse. When we refer to "clicking" with the mouse, we will always mean left-clicking. In those instances when right-clicking is required, we will be careful to identify the distinction.

1.5 Topics covered in the course

The major topics of the text are easily discerned from a cursory glance at the Table Of Contents:
- Arrays
- Plotting
- Functions
- Sharing Data

The topics of Arrays and Plotting are somewhat specific to MATLAB, whereas the topics of Functions and Sharing Data are integral to any programming language.

1.6 Principles of program design

As mentioned in the Preface, our emphasis on program design is, in our opinion, a distinguishing feature of the text. Below we identify these core principles, summarized according to the context in which they are applicable.

Programming principles relating to portability

1. Create Functions with clearly defined input, code-body, and output
2. Document Functions with comments and meaningful variable names
3. Provide Functions with default inputs so they can be executed without arguments
4. Make Functions general by passing function handles
5. Avoid global variables
6. Consider passing structures when argument lists become too clumsy

Programming principles relating to output

1. Use `fprintf` to make tables
2. Use `plot` to display graphical data
3. Use the `text` command to embed explanations within plots
4. Embellish output by using color with graphics, and LaTeX with text

Programming principles relating to performance

1. Isolate algorithms from I/O
2. Avoid dynamic memory allocation (always pre-allocate arrays)
3. Static data should be pre-computed and loaded from MAT-files
4. Avoid recursion, except to validate a more efficient (even if less elegant) implementation

Part I

The MATLAB programming environment

Chapter 2

The Command Window

2.1 Configuration Preferences

MATLAB can be invoked on a Windows platform by navigating to the Start:Programs:MATLAB menu from the TaskBar. When MATLAB launches, you choose to display any combination of five basic windows: Command Window, Command History, Current Directory, Workspace, and Help Browser. The appearance of any of these windows can be toggled using the View menu (note the check-mark next to each window currently displayed).

The Command Window is critical for most MATLAB programming. Initially, we will use the Command Window to interact with MATLAB as a programmable calculator, but this use will be short-lived. In Chapter 3 we will introduce script files, and thereafter all source code will be executed from files. On the other hand, more than fifty percent of program development occurs in the Debugger, and this requires constant interaction with the Command Window. For this reason, the Command Window should always be displayed in your MATLAB environment.

Programs of any complexity will involve multiple files, and even if the current project uses only one script file, you will often want to consult source code written for earlier projects. For this reason, we suggest that the Current Directory window always be displayed.

Finally, the Help Window, which uses its own window and does not share real-estate with the Command Window and Current Directory window, should always be displayed[1].

Though obviously a personal preference based on how best to use the available real estate, the remaining two windows (Command History and Workspace), will never be used in this course.

A snapshot of our MATLAB window is shown below:

---

[1] If you use an older version of MATLAB, the Help files should be copied to your hard-disk. See the location options in the File:Preferences:Help menu.

10   Chapter 2. The Command Window

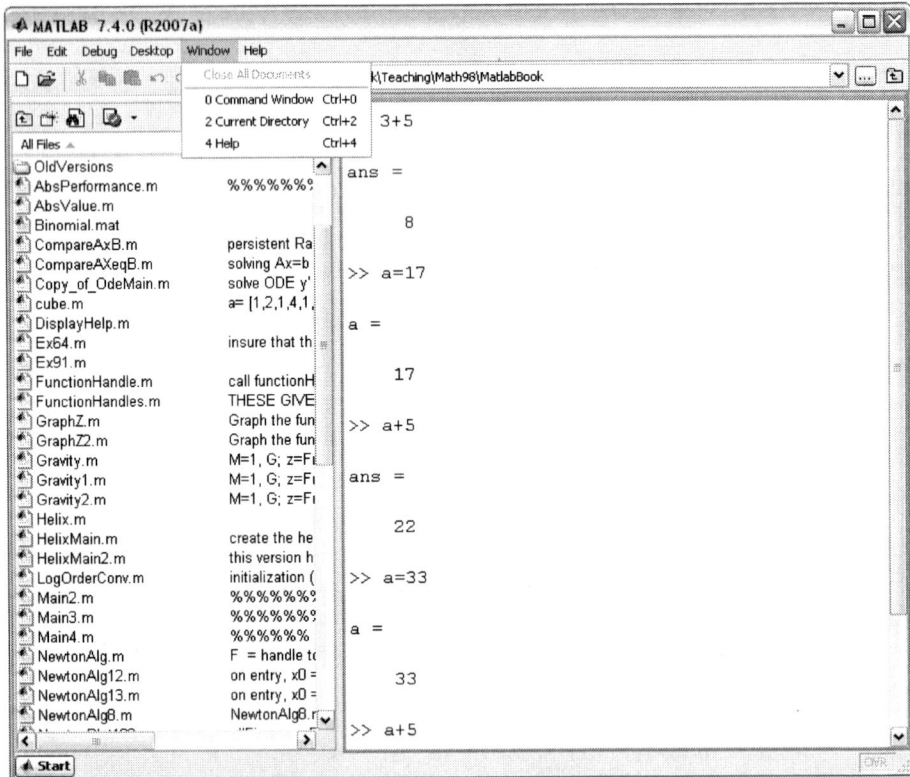

2.2   Command-line session in the Command Window

With these configuration preferences out of the way, we explore the basics of the MATLAB language by issuing commands in the Command Window. In what follows, we present the commands typed and the responses from MATLAB in the left panel of a two-panel display. Comments and observations are provided in the right panel. MATLAB keywords which refer to newly introduced commands are displayed in the left margin; as our vocabulary grows, this should be helpful in referring back to the context in which the commands were introduced. As mentioned in the Introduction, in order to proceed with the following "tutorial session", you will need to interact with MATLAB at the computer.

Command Window as a calculator

```
1  17+5
2  ans =
3      22
4
```

Command Window can be used as a calculator

assignment operator =

```
5  a=17
6  a =
7      17
```

a is a variable
= is the assignment operator
a will "come into existence" when it appears on the left hand side of = for the first time

```
 8 a+5
 9 ans =
10     22
11
12 a=33
13 a =
14     33
15
16 a+5
17 ans =
18     38
```
can add 5 to a (just like adding 5 to 17)

this assignment does not cause a new variable a to "come into existence"; it just changes the *value* of the variable a (created on line 5) from 17 to 33

use up-arrow twice to quickly recall two commands-ago (see line 8)

2.3 Computing $\sqrt{5}$ using Newton's algorithm

In this section we will compute (or, at least approximate) the square root of five using an elementary numerical algorithm. First, recall that the square root of five is defined to be the positive solution to the equation $x^2 = 5$. Given a function $f(x)$, one says that "x is a root of f" if it solves the equation $f(x) = 0$, and therefore evaluating $\sqrt{5}$ amounts to determining the positive root of the quadratic function

$$f(x) = x^2 - 5.$$

The subject of "root-finding algorithms" is fundamental to Numerical Analysis. A fairly straightforward method which employs the derivative $f'(x)$ is due to Isaac Newton. Newton's root-finding algorithm[2] works by starting with an initial guess at a root, called x_0, and then repeatedly applies the formula

$$x_{n+1} = x_n - \frac{f(x_n)}{f'(x_n)}$$

to obtain a sequence of iterates. Under favorable circumstances, these x_n will converge to a root $\hat{x}$:

$$x_n \longrightarrow \hat{x}, \quad \text{where} \quad f(\hat{x}) = 0.$$

In the present case, we approximate $\sqrt{5}$ by applying the above formula to $f(x) = x^2 - 5$. Since $f'(x) = 2x$, Newton's iterative algorithm takes the form

$$x_{n+1} = x_n - \frac{x_n^2 - 5}{2x_n}.$$

With an initial guess of

$$x_0 = 2,$$

we proceed to compute successive approximations to $\sqrt{5}$.

---

[2]For more information on Newton's method, see http://en.wikipedia.org/wiki/Newton's_method.

2.4 Manually iterating Newton algorithm

Since we have already been introduced to using MATLAB's Command Window as a calculator, we will implement Newton's algorithm by manually calculating the successive approximations x_1, x_2, x_3, and so on.

```
x0 =
    2

x1=x0 - (x0^2-5)/2x0
??? x1=x0 - (x0^2-5)/2x0
                      |
Error:Missing operator, comma,
              or semicolon.
x1=x0 - (x0^2-5)/2*x0
x1 =
    3

x2=x1 - (x1^2-5)/2*x1
x2 =
    -3

x1=x0 - (x0^2-5)/(2*x0)
x1 =
    2.2500

x2=x1 - (x1^2-5)/(2*x1)
x2 =
    2.2361

x3=x2 - (x2^2-5)/(2*x2)
x3 =
    2.2361
```

power operator ∧ (lines 4, 5)

multiplication operator * (line 9)

MATLAB thinks 2x0 is a variable, which is invalid since variable names cannot start with a number

Use 2*x0 to indicate multiplication by 2

Producing -3 as an approximation to $\sqrt{5}$, is suspicious: on lines 9 and 13, one must use parentheses around the denominator 2*x0

Note that it is not enough to recompute x2, since it depended on the incorrectly computed x1 - we must recompute x1 first!

Now recompute x2

...and also recompute x3

At this point, we might draw the conclusion that the algorithm has converged after three iterations to the stable value `2.2361`. In fact, the apparent convergence is due to the limited number of digits which are displayed in the Command Window. We correct this by telling MATLAB to display more digits using the `format` command.

2.4. Manually iterating Newton algorithm

format command	`1 format long`	tell Command Window to display fourteen digits
	`2 x3`	
	`3 x3 =`	
	`4     2.23606797791580`	recall x3 with new format
	`5`	
	`6 x4=x3 - (x3^2-5)/(2*x3)`	displaying 10 more digits shows algorithm has not stabilized at x3
	`7 x4 =`	
	`8     2.23606797749979`	
	`9`	or even at x4
	`10 x5=x4 - (x4^2-5)/(2*x4)`	
	`11 x5 =`	x4 and x5 agree
	`12     2.23606797749979`	
	`13`	
sqrt function	`14 sqrt(5)`	compare to MATLAB's built-in square-root function sqrt
	`15 ans =`	
	`16     2.23606797749979`	
	`17`	
	`18 5^(1/2)`	another way to compute $\sqrt{5}$
	`19 ans =`	
	`20     2.23606797749979`	
	`21`	
	`22 5^0.5`	and yet another way
	`23 ans =`	
	`24     2.23606797749979`	
	`25`	
	`26 5^0.5 - x5`	let MATLAB do the comparison
	`27 ans =`	
	`28        0`	
	`29`	
	`30 x5^2-5`	another measure of the accuracy of x5 without knowing $\sqrt{5}$
	`31 ans =`	
	`32     8.881784197001252e-016`	...a pretty small number
eps	`33 eps`	
	`34 ans =`	compare the difference x5^2-5 with the relative accuracy of MATLAB arithmetic
	`35     2.2204e-016`	
	`36`	
realmin	`37 realmin`	...which should not be confused with the smallest number MATLAB will handle
	`38 ans =`	
	`39     2.2251e-308`	

Since one normally does not have an independent means (such as MATLAB's `sqrt(5)` function) to compute roots of equations, another approach to quantifying the accuracy of the

14   Chapter 2. The Command Window

approximations x_n is to study the quantities

$$|x_n - x_{n-1}|, \quad \text{or} \quad \left|\frac{x_n - x_{n-1}}{x_n}\right|.$$

For our present purposes, we simply consider whether the $\{x_n\}$ *appear* to converge by virtue of $|x_n - x_{n-1}| \longrightarrow 0$.

Exercise 1

Give an example to show that it is theoretically possible for the successive differences in a sequence x_n to get smaller (i.e. $|x_n - x_{n-1}| \to 0$), and yet the sequence is not convergent, i.e. there is *no* $\hat{x}$ for which $|x_n - \hat{x}| \to 0$.

---

abs function

```
1  abs(x1-x0)
2  ans =
3      0.25000000000000
4
5  abs(x2-x1)
6  ans =
7      0.01388888888889
8
9  abs(x3-x2)
10 ans =
11     4.313319530702131e-005
12
13 abs(x4-x3)
14 ans =
15     4.160143340925515e-010
16
17 abs(x5-x4)
18 ans =
19     0
20
21 x3=x4
22 x3 =
23     2.23606797749979
24
25 x4=x3 - (x3^2-5)/(2*x3)
26 x4 =
27     2.23606797749979
```

looks like x_1, x_2, x_3, x_4 is forming convergent sequence

another technique to get the fifth iterate x_5 without creating a new variable x5 is to reuse line 6 of previous screen after resetting the variable x3 to x4

recall an earlier command in history with up-arrow key (can also use Command History window)

Notice that our efforts to save some typing at the end of the last session is at the expense of clarity; namely, the variables x3 and x4 no longer hold the iterates corresponding to their names, which is misleading.

2.5 What the current implementation accomplishes

Our "current implementation", which is to say our manual interaction with MATLAB through its command-line interface, has accomplished the following:

1. computed four iterations of the Newton algorithm to approximate $\sqrt{5}$

2. crudely quantified the accuracy of the approximation x5

3. in principle, more iterates could be computed to improve accuracy, though at the expense of more typing, or at the expense of easily tracking the iteration number by attaching it to a meaningful variable name like x1,x2,...

2.6 Shortcomings of the current implementation

The principal drawback of the present command-line approach is that it makes the following tasks awkward, or impossible:

1. inserting comments in order to document each step

2. debugging

3. editing

4. saving work

2.7 Topics covered in this chapter

Using the Command Window as a programmable calculator, we executed the first few iterations of Newton's algorithm to compute the square root of five to fourteen significant digits. We became acquainted with MATLAB's Command Window environment, and learned how to use the arrow-keys to navigate the command history. The following elements of the MATLAB language were introduced:

1. Arithmetic operators: +, -, *, /, ^

2. Assignment operators: =

3. Naming variables: x0,...,x5

4. Controlling how numbers are displayed: `format long`

5. Built-in functions: `sqrt()`, `abs()`, `eps`, `realmin`

Chapter 3

The Edit Window

In this chapter we address the flaws intrinsic to our first "program" computing $\sqrt{5}$. Recall the shortcomings observed from Chapter 2:

1. Code is not easily debugged.

2. Code is not documented; our marginal comments are not integrated into the sequence of commands.

3. Code is awkward to modify; editing is limited to recalling one-line commands and changing an X1 to X2; for example, how do we enter multi-line commands when a for-loop is required?

4. Code is not portable; how do we "package" the code to be reproducible for use by another person, or for integration into another program?

Any one of these flaws is sufficiently serious to necessitate a new approach which is not "straight-jacketed" by the command-line interface; happily, it turns out that they have a common solution, namely the creation of a "Script File". Henceforth, *every* program we write, even code-fragments, will reside in script files, also referred to as "M-files".

To be sure, there are work-arounds for each of the itemized flaws, and we will describe these at the end of Chapter 4. We hope our discussion of these work-arounds will convince the reader even further that the Command Window is a hopelessly Neanderthal environment for programming!

3.1 Creating an M-file in the Edit Window (NewtonAlg2.m)

In what follows we will explain in a tutorial fashion how to create, edit, and save a script file. Single-click[1] on the "File" icon in the Toolbar, which is located on the far left directly below the File menu in the main menubar. Alternatively, one may:

---

[1] Unless specified as "right-click", clicking with the left button will be assumed.

Chapter 3. The Edit Window

- Select File:New:M-File.

- Right-click in the pane of the Current Directory Window, and select New:M-file. After the file "Untitled1.m" appears, double-click on it.

Each of these techniques is illustrated here:

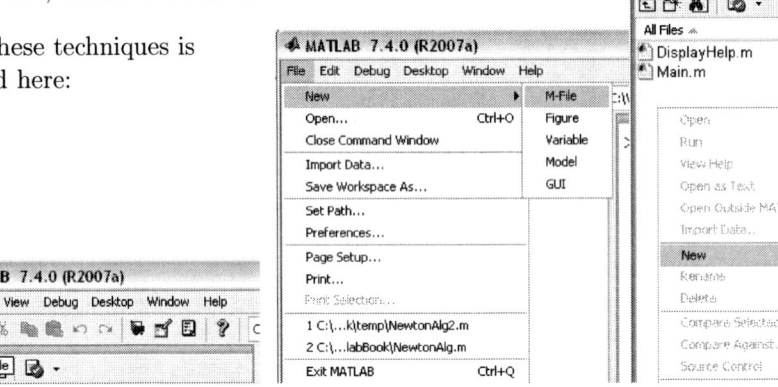

A new window appears, called the Edit Window. Note that the File menu (and most other menu options familiar from the Command Window) are equally available from the Edit Window, as well as some additional ones (e.g. Text and Debug[2]). Not only has the Edit Window appeared, but it presents to you an empty file. The close-box in the far upper right corner will terminate the Editor, close the Edit Window, and all files currently being edited; the close-box positioned a little lower down is for closing the frontmost displayed file, i.e. the file currently being edited. Type the following text into the new M-file:

```
%%%%%%%%%%%%%%%%%%%%%%%%%%%
%%%% Newton Algorithm Version2:
% in this program we will introduce %, ; and breakpoints
%Description of program:
%X0 is initial guess
X0   = 2;

%does 4 iterations, displays X4
%Xnp1 = Xn - f(Xn)/f'(Xn)
%f(X) = X^2 - 5

X1   = X0 - (X0^2 - 5)/(2*X0);

X2   = X1 - (X1^2 - 5)/(2*X1);

X3   = X2 - (X2^2 - 5)/(2*X2);
```

---

[2] In older versions, one will find the menu Breakpoints.

```
17
18 X4  = X3 - (X3^2 - 5)/(2*X3);
19 %by leaving off trailing semicolon,
20 % this next line will display the result
21 %  of four iterations of algorithm
22 X4        %comments can also appear at the end of a line of executable code
```

Notice the file has been temporarily named "Untitled", and that an asterisk follows its name in the titlebar, indicating that the file has been modified since the last save. Save the file as "NewtonAlg2.m" by any of the following methods:

- Click the "Disk" icon in the Toolbar (third from left, below the Main menu bar).
- Select File:Save As...
- Select File:Save (you will be prompted to name the untitled file).
- Use the keyboard shortcut ctrl-S.

The first two methods are illustrated here:

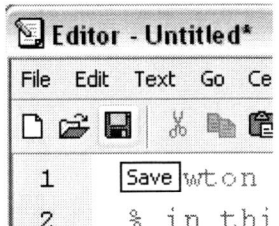
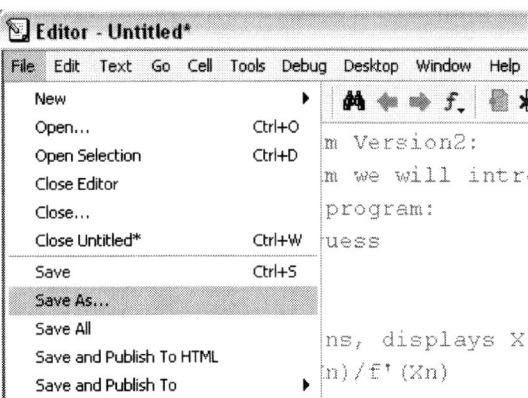

Also, the file name NewtonAlg2.m should now appear in the Directory Window[3], and the new name, with the asterisk removed, will appear in the Edit Window.

> **Exercise 2**
>
> Determine the File menu-selection, Toolbar icon, and keyboard-shortcut you would use for Printing the file being edited. How about for opening an existing file?

---

[3]If NewtonAlg2.m does not appear, then right-click in the Directory Window and select Refresh.

20   Chapter 3. The Edit Window

Run the program NewtonAlg2.m using each of the following techniques:

- Click the "File icon with the Down-arrow" located in the Toolbar
- Select Debug:Run from the Debug menu.
- Use the keyboard shortcut F5.
- From the Command Window, type `NewtonAlg2`.

These methods are illustrated in the the following illustrations.

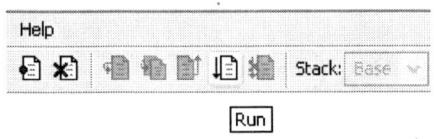

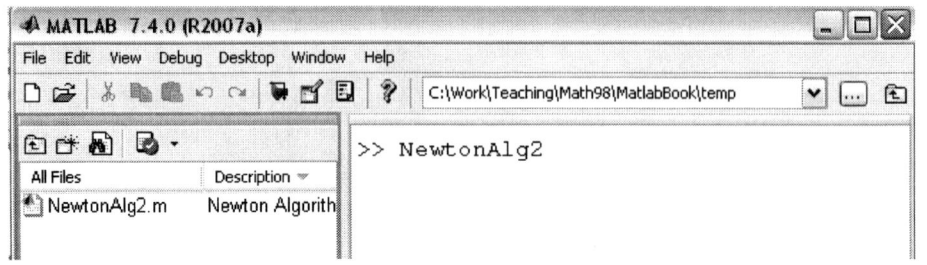

Not surprisingly, running NewtonAlg2.m produces the same result we saw in Chapter 2. What are some of the differences?

First, we have introduced a new special character, the percent symbol (%), which indicates to MATLAB that all remaining text on that line should be ignored. In other words, we have a mechanism for documenting our code with comments.

Secondly, we have introduced the semicolon (;) character which can be appended to commands whose output to the Command Window we wish to suppress. In other words, by appending or not appending semicolons to each line of executable code, we can control which runtime data is displayed to the Command Window. Recall that in our first command-line implementation of Newton Algorithm in Chapter 2, *all* of the intermediate calculations were displayed in the Command Window. In NetwonAlg2.m, we have arranged for only X4, the result of the fourth iteration, to be displayed (by *not* using a semicolon). This is only a temporary solution to the problem of displaying output. We will soon see that rarely should data be output to the Command Window in this way.

> **Exercise 3**
>
> Explain why using the Command Window to output data during the execution of a program is undesirable. How about upon the termination of a program? Hint: See Section 3.5.

> **Exercise 4**
>
> Of the four shortcomings of the command-line approach of Chapter 2, namely lack of portability and inability to debug, edit, and document, which flaws have already been addressed by creating the script file NewtonAlg2.m?

3.2 Introduction to the Debugger

In this section we give a tutorial introduction to MATLAB's built-in Debugger. Though one may occasionally choose to execute debugging steps from the Command Window, debugging is normally performed from the Edit Window where one can easily view the source file and observe individual lines of codes as they execute.

From within the Edit Window, display the file NewtonAlg2.m. Set a breakpoint at the first executable instruction (line 5) X0 = 2 by clicking in the narrow column between the line-number column in the left margin, and the text (a horizontal dash should already be visible at each executable line). Alternatively, click anywhere on the line to select it (the flashing insertion caret should be visible), and then use any of the following methods:

- Click in the "File icon with the Red dot" located in the Toolbar.
- Select Debug:Set/Clear Breakpoints from the Debug menu.
- Use the keyboard shortcut F12.

The first method is illustrated below:

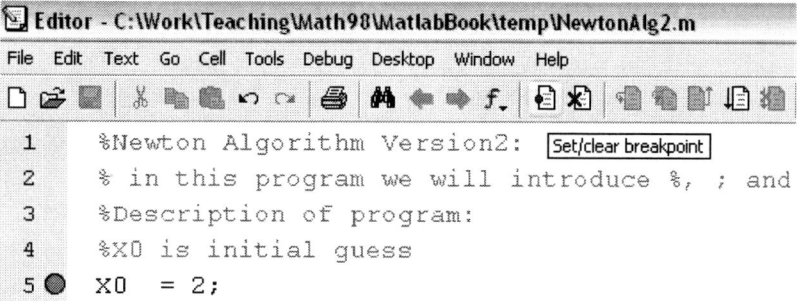

Exercise 5

Explain why some lines of the source code do not display a horizontal dash.

Exercise 6

Passing the arrow cursor over each of the icons on the Toolbar, identify the Toolbar icon, menu selection, and keyboard-shortcut for each of the seven Debug functions.

Use each of the above techniques to set another breakpoint at the instruction X4 (line 22). Now execute the program NewtonAlg2.m by any of the techniques from the previous section. Observe that the program stops at the first line at which we had set a breakpoint.

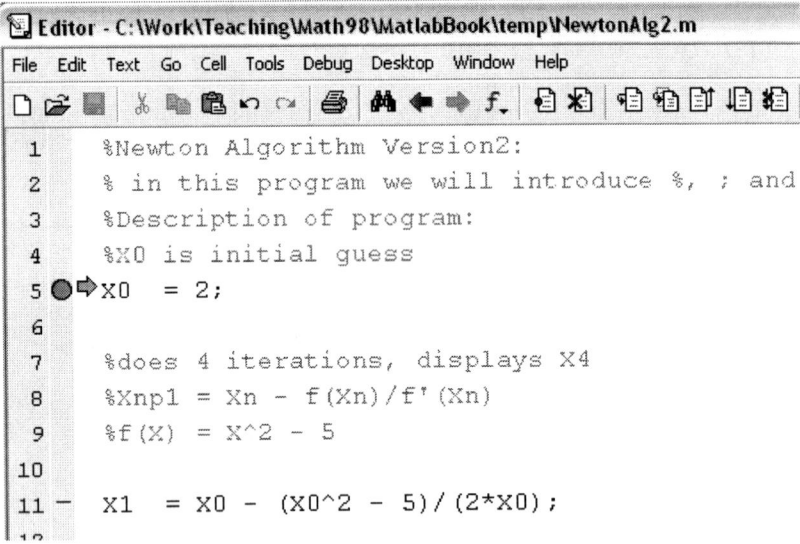

Additionally, observe the following:

1. A green arrow appears at the line *about to be executed*.

2. The prompt in the Command Window has changed from >> to K>>, indicating that we may execute Debugger commands in addition to the normal commands.

Next, we will see how the Command Window is most effectively put to use, namely, when it is used in conjunction with the Debugger.

3.2. Introduction to the Debugger

`K>> X0`	Type `X0` in the Command Window. We have not *yet* executed the line in the source file at which `X0` is assigned the value 2, so `X0` is as-yet undefined.
`??? Undefined function or variable 'X0'`	

who command

`K>> who`	Display the variables to which MATLAB has currently assigned values using the `who` command.

dbstep command

`K>> dbstep`	Type `dbstep` at the `K>>` prompt to tell the Debugger to "single step" into the source code and execute the line `X0=2`. Observe how the green arrow advances.
`11   X1  = X0 - (X0^2 - 5)/(2*X0);`	

`K>> X0`	Now retype `X0`, or use the up-arrow key to recall the previous command.
`X0 =`	
`     2`	

`K>> who`	Similarly, retype or recall the `who` command.
`Your variables are:`	Notice `X0` has now "come into existence". Observe how "hovering" with the cursor over the text `X0` in the source file also displays its value.
`X0`	

`K>> dbstep`	Type `dbstep` again, or use the "Step" icon in the Toolbar. Observe the green arrow advance to the next executable instruction.
`13   X2  = X1 - (X1^2 - 5)/(2*X1);`	

dbcont command

`K>> dbcont`	Type `dbcont` to continue execution until the second breakpoint (line 22).
`22   X4        %comments can also ...`	
	Can we set new (or clear old) breakpoints while paused in the Debugger? What happens when we hover over `X4` in the source file?
`X4 =`	
`    2.2361`	Single-step the instruction `X4`. Explain why the value is displayed in the Command Window.

dbquit command

`K>> dbquit`	Type `dbquit` to abort execution. Since we're already at the last executable line of the file, is this any different from `dbstep` or `dbcont`?
`>>`	

Exercise 7

Follow up on Exercise 6 by completing the following table:

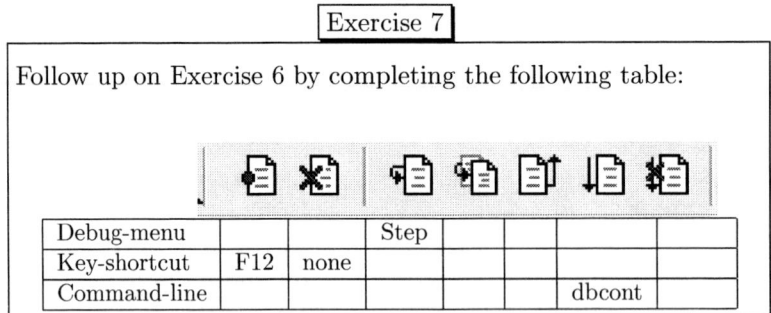

Debug-menu			Step				
Key-shortcut	F12	none					
Command-line					dbcont		

We have seen two ways of inspecting the values of runtime variables, namely hovering over the text of the variable in the Edit Window, and typing the variable name into the Command Window. A third way, which will never be used, is provided by invoking the View:Workspace Window. As programs become more complex they will inevitably require inspecting variables which represent large arrays and matrices; consequently, using the Command Window to inspect variables is the only practical method. In fact, much of the skill of debugging will require efficient techniques for "looking inside" large data variables by inspecting their sub-arrays and sub-structures. For example, to verify that code which creates a 1000 × 1000 tridiagonal matrix is "doing the right thing", one may want to inspect just a section of the diagonal band.

3.3 An improved version (NewtonAlg3.m)

While there is more to say about debugging and editing script files than what was described in the previous two sections, we have certainly covered the essential techniques. Our use of these techniques will improve with practice as we pursue the immediate business at hand, namely writing MATLAB programs. Thus, we now return to the implementation of our Newton square root algorithm in NewtonAlg2.m.

Let's first identify some flaws with the current implementation:

(1) The input is hardwired in line 5 (`X0 = 2;`).

(2) The algorithm is not adaptable to increasing the number of iterations from 4 to 50000.

(3) The output is inadequate in line 22 (`X4 %no semicolon`).

In computer programming, the term *hardwired* refers to values (usually assigned to variables for initialization, or to upper or lower thresholds of a counter, or to the size dimensions of an array), which are buried in code, and therefore can be changed only by editing the source file. The most extreme example of hardwired numbers are the so-called "magic numbers," which are encountered when reading someone's source code and coming across a line like

```
minThreshold = 1.0243e-13;     or     contour(Z,[-0.34,-0.12,1.45,6.67]);
```

3.3. An improved version (NewtonAlg3.m)

One imagines that these numbers have a special significance, yet finds that they are completely unexplained. In some cases one may even find that changing a magic number will break the program! In general, hardwired values are discouraged. It is preferable to pass such values to the code as input parameters, or at a minimum to identify these values clearly in an "initialization section" at the beginning of the source file.

In the present case, the Newton algorithm requires an "initial guess", which we have called X0, and which is set with the statement X0 = 2 in line 5. This is an example of a hardwired value since changing our initial guess requires *editing* the file NewtonAlg2.m. We will ultimately correct this design flaw when we introduce input arguments, but for now we will be content to have identified the defect, and to document clearly in the source file that the initial guess has been hardwired.

As for the second flaw, that the current implementation commits four assignment statements for each of the four iterations of the algorithm, suggests that we would need to generate 50,000 additional lines of code should we desire 50,000 iterations. We will address this design flaw by introducing a new instruction called the *for-loop*.

As for the third problem associated with the form of the output, we will again be content to have identified the defect, and defer its solution to a later chapter.

At this point we comment that all of our programs will share a fundamental structure:

Structure of any program
Input
Body of Algorithm
Output

Indeed, at this stage our program is so simplistic that these three components, present in any program, are especially visible in the NewtonAlg2.m implementation. In this context, the three design flaws described above consist of a flaw in each of the three elemental components.

We first attack the defect identified in (2) above. Consider mimicking the sequence of instructions

```
1 X1 = X0 - (X0^2 - 5)/(2*X0);
2 X2 = X1 - (X1^2 - 5)/(2*X1);
3 X3 = X2 - (X2^2 - 5)/(2*X2);
```

with the following sequence:

```
1 X1 = X0 - (X0^2 - 5)/(2*X0);
2 X0 = X1;
3 X1 = X0 - (X0^2 - 5)/(2*X0);
```

```
4  X0  = X1;
5  X1  = X0 - (X0^2 - 5)/(2*X0);
6  X0  = X1;
```

The only difference between these computations is that the result of the third iteration is misleadingly assigned to a variable named X0. Assuming we can track the iteration by some other means (this will be accomplished with a *loop-counter*) the naming of the variables is immaterial. On the other hand, the second implementation suggests the introduction of a new programming construct called the *for-loop*, which has the critical advantage of being adaptable to any number of iterations.

Motivated by the above discussion, we propose the following code for our next version of the Newton Algorithm, which should be entered into a new M-file:

```
1  %%%%%%%%%%%%%%%%%%%%%%%%%%%%
2  %%%% NewtonAlg3.m
3  %%%%%%%%%%%%%%%%%%%%%%%%%%%%
4  % this version consolidates blocks that are structured alike into loops
5  % hardwired quantities like X0 are clearly identified
6  %   in initialization section
7  % introduce variables Xnew, Xold, keep track of iteration
8  %%%%%%%%%%%%%%%%%%%%%%%%%%%%
9  %initialization (hardwired variables)
10 X0  = 2;
11 %%%%%%%%%%%%%%%%%%%%%%%%%%%%
12 % compute Xnew in terms of Xold,
13 % then copy Xnew to Xold
14 %%%%%%%%%%%%%%%%%%%%%%%%%%%%
15 Xold    = X0;    %initial value of Xold
16 %%%%%%% A New Construct: the for-loop %%%%%%%%%
17 for i=1:4
18     Xnew    = Xold - (Xold^2 - 5)/(2*Xold);
19     Xold    = Xnew;
20 end
21 %display final result of 4 iterations by omitting semicolon
22 Xnew
```

> **Exercise 8**
>
> Can you explain the rationale for assigning to the variable X0 the value 2 at the beginning (initialization) portion of the code, rather than directly assigning it to Xold as we have done in line 15, and skipping the variable X0 altogether?

3.3. An improved version (NewtonAlg3.m)

We do not *define* the for-loop construct at this point, as this will be done in a more comprehensive context in Section 6.4. On the other hand, by using the Debugger techniques of the previous section we will see how the for-loop works in practice, and thereby arrive at a "functional understanding" of this important instruction.

Set a breakpoint at line 15. Click the "Save and Run" icon in the Toolbar.

Exercise 9

Explain why the icon says "Save and Run" rather than "Run" when applied to an as-yet-unsaved file.

Name the file "NewtonAlg3.m" when prompted. Upon breaking into the Debugger at line 15, use the "Step" icon in the Toolbar to single-step through each instruction until the program terminates. Furthermore, after the execution of each line of code, inspect the values of the three variables

```
Xold, Xnew, i
```

Exercise 10

Explain how the for-loop works. If you are familiar with other programming languages, explain how the sequence of values of i differs from the auto-incrementing behavior common to other for-loop constructs. For example, try changing i to 1000 after the third iteration - does it increment to 1001 in the next iteration? Upon falling through the **end** statement on the fifth iteration, what is the value of i?

In order to fully understand the behavior of the loop-counter in MATLAB's for-loops, it is necessary to first understand arrays and the 1:n construction. This too will be covered in a later chapter.

At this point we have addressed the second defect enumerated at the beginning of the chapter. NewtonAlg3.m is now adaptable to an arbitrarily large number of iterations. On the other hand, by solving one problem, we have introduced another, namely the hardwired value 4 has appeared! Actually, the previous version NewtonAlg2.m already manifested something much worse than a hardwired value like 4: the fact of using four individual lines of code, each with its own corresponding variable X1, X2, X3, X4, is itself (conceptually) an extreme form of hardwired coding. We will revisit the hardwired nature of the number of loop iterations in Section 5.2, and again in Section 12.3 when we explain functions, but for now we will be satisfied that the problem of adaptability has elegantly been overcome by introducing the for-loop.

> **Exercise 11**
>
> Consider replacing the lines
> ```
> for i=1:4
>    Xnew = Xold - (Xold^2 - 5)/(2*Xold);
>    Xold = Xnew;
> end
> ```
> with the lines
> ```
> for i=1:4
>    Xold = Xold - (Xold^2 - 5)/(2*Xold);
> end
> ```
> What are the advantages and disadvantages of these implementations?

> **Solution 11**
>
> The second implementation has a performance advantage in that it omits the overhead of executing the assignment `Xold = Xnew`. On the other hand, should we wish to track (for convergence reasons) the difference between successive approximations, the first implementation is required.

3.4 What the current implementation accomplishes

The virtues of the current implementation of NewtonAlg3.m are quite significant, and substantially address the drawbacks of our first implementation identified in Chapter 2:

1. The code is documented: Comments describing functionality of code, as well as explanatory remarks, appear alongside the executable commands.

2. The code is portable: NewtonAlg.m can be printed or emailed to another person.

3. The code is easily modifiable: All the functionality of the Editor can be utilized in copying, pasting, and rearranging blocks of code and other text.

4. The code can be debugged: All the functionality of the Debugger can be utilized to set breakpoints, single-step code, and inspect runtime values of variables.

5. The code is adaptable: One line of code can be modified to execute 50,000 iterations of the algorithm.

6. The code is clearly organized into its fundamental components: Input, Body of Algorithm, Output.

3.5 Shortcomings of the current implementation

The drawbacks of the present implementation of NewtonAlg3.m are as follows:

1. Input is hardwired. Assignment of variables like X0 for the initial guess should ultimately be achieved by passing input arguments. On the positive side, this hardwired variable is clearly identified in the initialization portion of the source file.

2. The loop-counter is hardwired: The loop-counter specifying 4 iterations of the for-loop is hardwired. On the negative side, this hardwired value is buried in the code body.

3. Output is unacceptable: Blasting a number into the impermanent Command Window during program execution is unacceptable because there is no description of its meaning, nor mechanism to "capture" it in a form that can be analyzed or input into another program. In fact, if we display a variable from within a for-loop, it is likely that nothing but screens full of unintelligible data will fly across the Command Window. In the next chapter we will see how to make a table of output values with labelled rows and columns; ultimately, we will discuss generating output in graphical form, and also as a MAT-file.

3.6 Topics covered in this chapter

Using the Edit Window and Debugger we wrote and single-stepped our first MATLAB program. We introduced a new programming statement from the MATLAB language, the for-loop, whose precise definition will be described in detail in Chapter 6.4. The topics covered in this chapter are summarized below; they are fundamental to mastering the practical skills used throughout the course.

1. File commands issued from the Directory Window: New M-file, Open, Refresh

2. File commands issued from the Command Window or Edit Window: New M-file, Open, Save, Save As, Print

3. Debugger commands issued from the Edit Window: Run, Continue, Step, Set/Clear Breakpoint, Exit Debug Mode

4. Debugger commands issued from the Command Window: `dbstep`, `dbcont`, `dbquit`

5. Control statements: `for`

6. Miscellaneous Commands: `who`

7. Special characters for adding comments and suppressing output: `%`, `;`

Chapter 4

The Help Browser and Command/Edit Windows revisited

In this chapter we will become acquainted with MATLAB's Help Browser. In addition to learning the Debugger, knowing how to use the Help facility of a language is an indispensable skill for all future programming.

4.1 Navigating the MATLAB documentation

From either the Command Window or the Edit Window, select the "Help:MATLAB Help" item from the Help menu located on the far right of the main menubar. Each time Help is invoked it may take some time for it to initialize its database. For this reason, we recommend never closing the Help Browser, but rather keeping it minimized when it is not being used. From within the Help Browser, select "Help:Using the Help Browser" item from the Help menu. The "Help Browser Overview:Help for Using MATLAB" section[1] of the MATLAB documentation will appear, which provides a comprehensive description of the Help functionality. It is important to read enough of this documentation to feel competent in using the Help facility.

Effectively using Help is a skill not unlike that of using a dictionary, whereby you have a guess of some functionality you expect to be supported by MATLAB, but you don't know the exact word to search. For our purposes, we will make some observations emphasizing the most important features of Help. Notice that in the Navigation pane on the left of the window[2] there appear four tabs: Contents, Index, Search, and Favorites.

Contents: As you can see there are *many* chapters to the documentation. The chapter titled MATLAB describes everything relevant to this course. Many of the other chapters describe modules that may not be included with your installation of MATLAB, and even some (like the Symbolic Math Toolbox) that are installed but will never be used in our numerically

---

[1] Formerly "Development Environment:Getting Help:Using the Help Browser" in older versions.
[2] If the Navigation pane is not visible, select the menu item "View:Help Navigator".

oriented applications. Needless to say, there is always value in perusing the documentation, as this is a good way to become exposed to topics and ideas that might otherwise never occur to you. However, during the process of *writing* programs, the Contents tab is rarely used.

Index: This is the dictionary-like interface to the documentation. The first column gives an alphabetical listing of keywords in the index. The second column is titled Product. If an indexed keyword does not indicate that it is part of the "MATLAB" Product[3] then it is probably not relevant to us. For example, if we performed an indexed search on the keyword `input`, we would ignore those instances which referred to the Financial or Control Systems Toolboxes, and select only the one linked to the MATLAB Function Reference. While some keywords belong to several products, others may even have distinct usages within a given product. Those keywords which are discussed in several parts of the documentation are marked with a [1][2],.., such as

>　`for[1][2]`

which has entries in both the MATLAB Function Reference and the MATLAB Programming documentation. Since this course proceeds by methodically introducing instructions of known syntax, our use of Help will be more targeted at clarifying usage and collecting examples. For this reason, we find that most of the time spent in the Help Browser will be using the Index tab.

Search: This capability is generally more useful for reading up on a topic in the documentation, rather than looking up the usage of a keyword already known to us. These searches will often lead one to overviews, tutorials, and demos, while in some instances these searches may give an even more direct entry into the documentation than provided by an Index lookup. As we will illustrate in some exercises, one should be mindful to consult the Search tab in addition to the Index tab when researching the usage of specific MATLAB commands.

Demos[4]: This feature is not needed for our subsequent work.

Exercise 12

Using the Index tab in the Help Browser, lookup the *for* instruction and verify your solution to Exercise 10.

Exercise 13

Using both the Index tab and the Search tab, lookup the commands "dbquit" and "debug".
Can you find a click-able link to the `Editor/Debugger`? How does this compare with directly searching "Editor/Debugger" in the Search tab?

---

[3] Earlier versions identify the Product as MATLAB " Reference", "Programming", "Graphics", etc.
[4] In older versions this tab was replaced with **Features**.

MATLAB also provides "command-line Help", which can be accessed by simply typing `help` followed by the name of the topic. For example, one can type

```
help for
help hsv
help view
```

There are few advantages of this method compared to the visual documentation of the Help Browser. The most serious shortcoming of this method is that it is not *contextual* like the Search tab; the command-line Help requires one to know the *exact* topic on which to search. On the positive side, it produces click-able links to other documentation, both visual and command-line, which can be more expedient than consulting the Help Browser straight out. In practice, command-line Help is most useful when one already knows the particular command to use (e.g. `view()`), but wants to do a quick check on some detail of its usage (e.g. is it `view(az,el)` or `view(el,az)`?).

Finally, let's not overlook the value of using Google® on the internet!

Exercise 14

Find the MATLAB function for graphing a function `z=F(x,y)` in three dimensions.

Solution 14

Google "graph three dimension MATLAB", and follow the link www.mathworks.com/academia/student_center/tutorials/visualizing_data.html. Read (or jump) to the end to learn about the `mesh` command. Lookup `mesh` using the Index tab in the Help Browser, being careful to select the one belonging to the MATLAB product. Follow the links to the `mesh` and `surf` commands. Also type `help mesh` at the command-line, and follow the links in the section labelled "See also."

4.2 Script Files: The Command Window is dead; Long live the Edit Window

In this section we describe some work-arounds to the flaws itemized at the beginning of the chapter. Our purpose here is three-fold:

1. Convince the reader even further that all programming should be done in script files.

2. Introduce the `diary` command.

3. Illustrate some new techniques, like copy & paste between the Help, Command, and Edit Windows.

First, let's recall a comment made at the beginning of the chapter with respect to the awkwardness of editing code in the command-line environment of the Command Window. Specifically, we raised the question of how to incorporate multi-line commands when a for-loop (or other code block) is required. There are a few solutions to this problem. One technique is to gang up the elements of a multi-line construct into a single line using the comma (,) as a separator. For example, the code block

```
for i=1:nIter
    Xnew    = Xold - (Xold^2 - 5)/(2*Xold);
    Xold    = Xnew;
end
```

could be entered as:

```
for i=1:nIter, Xnew = Xold - (Xold^2 - 5)/(2*Xold), Xold = Xnew, end
```

A second solution is to type

```
for i=1:nIter
```

followed by Shift-Enter instead of the usual Enter key[5] This technique gives you a new line with which to work in the Command Window, without telling MATLAB to terminate the line being typed. Neither of these "solutions" is a reason to continue programming from within the Command Window - in fact, they are practically never used, and no matter how effectively they serve as a work-around, they are no substitute for bringing to bear the full functionality of a visual editor.

Exercise 15

In the "ganging up" technique, how would the addition of a comment be handled, for example, if the third line read
`Xold = Xnew;      %clobber old with new.`

Recall, further, that the command-line approach used in Chapter 2 lacked portability - we were unable to "memorialize" our program for use by others, or even by ourselves at a later time. To overcome this problem, we introduce the `diary` command which serves to "capture into a file" all text being displayed in the Command Window. Along the way, we will demonstrate a third way of forcing multi-line commands into the Command Window.

From the Command Window type the line

---

[5] The current version of MATLAB specifically recognizes code-blocks (including those belonging to for-loops), and allows them to be entered at the command-line directly. Nonetheless, this example helps illustrate our larger point which is nonetheless valid.

4.2. Script Files: The Command Window is dead; Long live the Edit Window

```
diary QuestionableProgram.m
```

Next, go to the Help Browser and using the Search tab lookup the keyword `surf`, or use the Index tab and click on the link labelled `surf`. Scroll toward the end of the documentation in the right pane, and by pressing the left button with the cursor positioned to the left of the text [X,Y,Z], followed by dragging the cursor to the end of the text a few lines below, select the four lines of sample code. See the figure below:

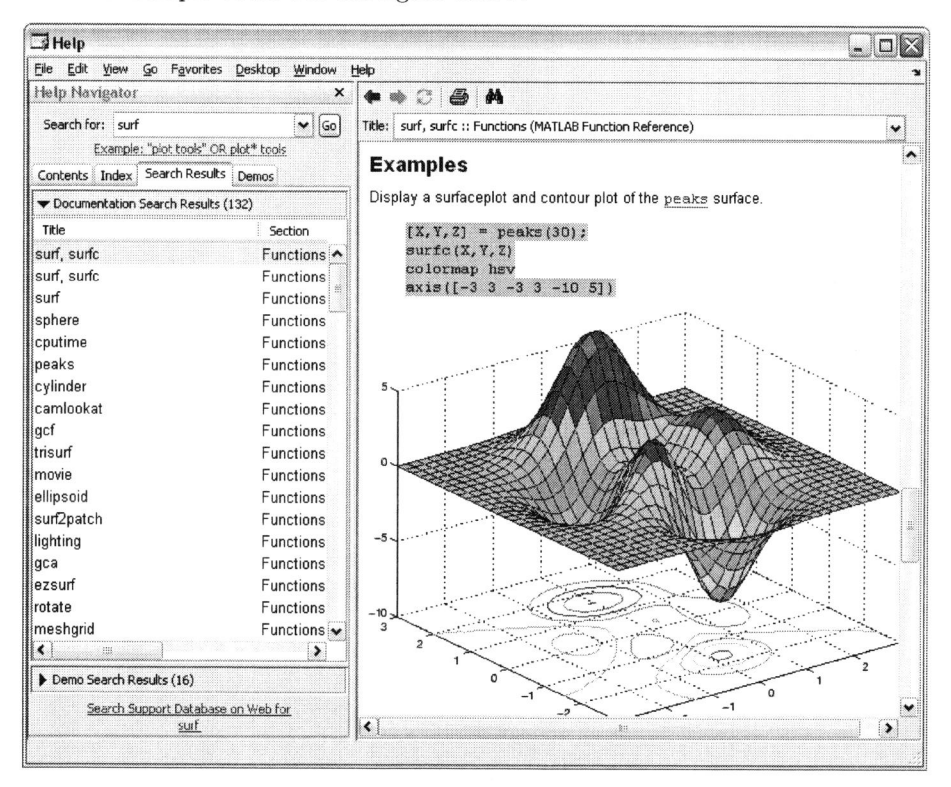

Right-click on the body of the selected text (in black) and select Copy from the popup menu. Alternatively, one can use ctrl-C (at least in a Windows environment). Next, click back on the Command Window, right-click and select Paste (or use ctrl-V) to paste into the command line the copied text of sample code. Press Enter. The demo code should execute and a new figure window showing the surface plot will pop up. Finally, type

```
diary off
```

Close the figure window. Notice that a file with the name QuestionableProgram.m appears in the Directory Window. Double-click on the filename and verify that the contents appears as follows:

```
1 [X,Y,Z] = peaks(30);
2 surfc(X,Y,Z)
```

```
3 colormap hsv
4 axis([-3 3 -3 3 -10 5])
5 diary off
```

Exercise 16

Remove the last line (`diary off`) from QuestionableProgram, and rerun it by clicking the "Save-and-Run" icon.

Exercise 17

Is there any reason to have created QuestionableProgram using the diary method rather than the Edit Window?

4.3 Debugging: The Command Window still lives

Hopefully we have made a compelling case for creating all your programs in files from the Edit Window. This does not mean that the Command Window is entirely dead. In fact, when it comes to debugging, it is indispensable. To see this, perform the following steps:

- Open the file QuestionableProgram.m in the Edit Window.

- Set a breakpoint at the the line `colormap hsv`.

- Execute to the breakpoint by clicking the Run icon.

- Observe a surface plot appear in its own figure window.

- Single-step the `colormap` command. You should see colors set as in the `surf` documentation.

- From the Command Window, type `help hsv`.
  (one of those rare occasions when using command-line help is convenient :)

- Notice the following nine pre-defined colormaps provided by MATLAB:
  GRAY, HOT, COOL, BONE, COPPER, PINK, FLAG, PRISM, JET.

- From the Command Window, type `colormap GRAY`. What do you observe about the surface plot?

- Explore the appearance of the other colormaps.

- Using the Help Browser, explore any additional pre-defined colormaps.

- Terminate your debug session by either typing `dbquit` at the command-line, or clicking the "Exit Debug Mode" icon.

4.4 Topics covered in this chapter

In addition to describing the command-line functions `help` and `diary`, we have demonstrated through sample Help, Edit, and Debug sessions the following three principles:

Rarely use `help` in the Command Window.
Use Help Browser for visual, cross-referenced, hyperlinked help.

Do not use the Command Window for programming.
Always use the Edit Window to create an M-file
(even for a fragment of sample code).

Do use the Command Window for debugging.
This may include capturing results with the `diary` command.

Part II

Writing a simple MATLAB program

Chapter 5

Displaying Output

Let's now return to developing our program NewtonAlg.m by first recalling the drawbacks of its last implementation in Chapter 3:

1. Input is hardwired: Assignment of variables like X0 for the initial guess should ultimately be achieved by passing input arguments.

2. The loop-counter is hardwired: The loop-counter specifying 4 iterations of the for-loop is hardwired, and unlike the input variable X0, this hardwired value is buried in the code body.

3. Output is unacceptable: We need to display more than just 2.23606797749979 for our output to be meaningfully communicated to others.

This chapter is devoted to addressing the third of these drawbacks related to output.

5.1 Formatting numeric output (NewtonAlg4.m)

After completing four iterations of Newton's square root algorithm, our program dumps a 15-digit number to the screen. When we want to "communicate" this result to the world at large, whether in a homework assignment or a scholarly publication, it is essential that the number be formatted with accompanying text to explain precisely what it signifies.

One may have the impression that displaying the 15-digit number on the screen is sufficient, since any explanatory text can be added after the number has been copied into a word processing program. The truth of the matter is that, by utilizing MATLAB's formidable capabilities for displaying data, one may generate formatted output *programmatically* which is so coherently presented and self-contained that the formatting capabilities of a word-processor are unneeded. In the following sections we will illustrate some of these formatting capabilities, ultimately arriving at the following output:

```
 -----------------------------------------------------------
 Newton's algorithm applied to F(X) = X^2-5 = 0
 -----------------------------------------------------------
 iteration      Xn           |Xn - Xn-1|        Xn^2-5
 -----------------------------------------------------------
 0            2.0000000          ---           1.0000000
 1            2.2500000       0.2500000        0.0625000
 2            2.2361111       0.0138889        0.0001929
 3            2.2360680       0.0000431        0.0000000
 4            2.2360680       0.0000000        0.0000000
```

> **Exercise 18**
>
> If the fourteen numbers appearing in the table above were sequentially blasted into the Command Window during program execution, how easy would it be to transfer the data into your word-processor (no matter how wonderful your word processor is at creating tables)? How about if there were fourteen hundred numbers?

At this point we mention five methods of communicating a program's output:

(1) Omit the semicolon (;) after an expression (or an assignment statement which assigns a value to a variable), thereby displaying its value in the Command Window when the instruction executes.

(2) Use the `disp` and `num2str` functions to display variables in the Command Window accompanied with some unformatted text.

(3) Use the `fprintf` and `sprintf` functions to output variables, accompanied with *formatted* text, to either the Command Window, a file, or a string variable.

(4) Use the plotting functions to create graphs.

(5) Return the variable so it can be used by a calling function.

Only (1)-(4) apply to outputting data in human-readable form, and only (1)-(3) apply to outputting data in textual form (though plots can also be embellished with elaborate textual information). We have already seen method (1) employed in NewtonAlg3.m, and decided it needs to be replaced with something better. For the sake of completeness we will describe (2), but after discussing (3) we will see that there is no reason to ever use (2). Using (1) for *debugging* purposes is occasionally appropriate[1]. The conclusion is that (3) and (4) are the

---
[1] There was a time when methods (1) and (2) were the predominant technique used for debugging, namely, sprinkling print statements throughout the code to provide feedback on the "state" of runtime variables. In this age of sophisticated debuggers, this technique has thankfully been rendered obsolete.

5.1. Formatting numeric output (NewtonAlg4.m)

predominant methods for communicating data in human-readable form.

Finally, to properly understand formatted text, and the `disp` and `fprintf` instructions in particular, one must have an understanding of *string variables*, which in turn requires some understanding of *arrays*! The subject of arrays in MATLAB is fundamental and extensive, and a comprehensive treatment of this topic will begin in Chapter 7. Thus, as when we encountered the for-loop in an earlier chapter, we again ask the reader to indulge this logical inconsistency, and to simply mimic the manipulations we perform on string variables. We feel the benefit of adding the powerful `fprintf` statement to our vocabulary at this early stage outweighs the disadvantage of an incomplete understanding of strings[2]. Hopefully, this early exposure to manipulating strings may be a profitable path to understanding them.

What is the significance of the NewtonAlg3.m program's output 2.23606797749979? Precisely, it is the result of four iterations of Newton's algorithm applied to $x^2 - 5$ with the initial guess $x_0 = 2$. At a minimum, even if we are content with just the result 2.23606797749979, when we display this output we must also provide some explanatory text to that effect.

Below is a version of NewtonAlg4.m which uses each of the methods (1)-(3) mentioned in the previous section. Note that on line 21 there appear three periods ... where one would expect the text of line 22 to appear. These three periods are used to tell MATLAB to treat the text which appears on the next line as if it had been added to the current line. For this reason, the three periods ... are called a "line-continuation character".

```
1  %%%%%%%%%%%%%%%%%%%%%%%%%%%%%%
2  %%%%%%%%% NewtonAlg4.m %%%%%%%%
3  %initialization (hardwired variables)
4  X0  = 2;                    %initial guess at square root of 5
5  %%%%%%%%%%%%%%%%%%%%%%%%%%%%%%
6  %update X from last iteration,
7  % so no need to copy old->new (see Exercise 11)
8  X   = X0;
9  for i=1:4
10     X = X - (X^2 - 5)/(2*X);
11 end
12
13 %Method (1)
14 %display final result of 4 iterations by making
15 % assignment to Xfinal and omitting semicolon
16 Xfinal = X
17
18 %Method (2)
19 %print using disp and num2str -
```

---

[2] See, for example, Exercise 55.

```
20 % compose pieces of string and concatenate them together
21 str = ['after 4 iterations, approximate square root of 5 is ',...
22         num2str(Xfinal)];
23 disp(str);
24
25 %Method (3)
26 %print using fprintf - better for controlling precision displayed
27 fprintf('\nafter 4 iterations, approximate square root of 5 is %6.4f',...
28         Xfinal);
```

Run NewtonAlg4.m and verify the output appears as:

```
1 Xfinal =
2     2.2361
3
4 after 4 iterations, approximate square root of 5 is 2.2361
5
6 after 4 iterations, approximate square root of 5 is 2.2361
```

Type `format long` and verify the output appears as:

```
1 Xfinal =
2     2.23606797749979
3
4 after 4 iterations, approximate square root of 5 is 2.2361
5
6 after 4 iterations, approximate square root of 5 is 2.2361
```

Change the %6.4f to %15.13f in line 14 and verify the output appears as:

```
1 Xfinal =
2     2.23606797749979
3
4 after 4 iterations, approximate square root of 5 is 2.2361
5
6 after 4 iterations, approximate square root of 5 is 2.2360679774998
```

Exercise 19

Justify the assertion that anything you can do with method (1) or method (2), can be equally (or better) achieved with method (3).

5.1. Formatting numeric output (NewtonAlg4.m)

Exercise 20

Are there any limitations on the use of the line-continuation character ...?
In particular, how would MATLAB handle the following rewrite of line 21:
`str = ['after 4 iterations,...`
or line 27:
`fprintf('\nafter 4 iterations,...`

A brief description of the `fprintf()` function is that it prints its first argument, which is a string (called the *format string*), onto the Command Window. If all the text that one wants to print is *static*, i.e. known at the time the program is written before it executes, then passing this pre-composed string is sufficient. If, on the other hand, one wants to display *dynamic* data, i.e. quantities whose values are known only at execution time, then one

(1) inserts "placeholders" into the format string indicated by the symbols `%d`, `%e`, `%f`, `%g`,

(2) and adds to the argument list of parameters passed to `fprintf` the corresponding runtime variable.

Additionally, we will see in the next section on hardwired variables that one may also want to print variables whose value does not change during execution, but nonetheless are maintained in the code as a variable.

Exercise 21

In line 27 replace the `%f` with `%d`, `%e`, and `%g`, and make a guess as to how these symbols determine the output format. Verify your guess by consulting the Help documentation.

Exercise 22

Suppose `X = 3` and `Y = 5`.
Explain why each of these lines produces the same output.
`disp('3 + 5 = 8');`
`str = '3 + 5 = 8'; disp(str);`
`str = ['3','+','5','=','8']; disp(str);`
`str = [num2str(X),'+',num2str(Y),'=',num2str(X+Y)]; disp(str);`
`str1 = [num2str(X),'+',num2str(Y)];`
`str2 = num2str(X+Y); disp([str1, str2]);`

Chapter 5. Displaying Output

Exercise 23

Show that in each of the lines in Exercise 22 above, one may substitute `fprintf` for `disp` with equivalent results.

Exercise 24

Continuing with the previous exercises, show that the `fprintf` function provides the additional method: `fprintf('%d + %d = %d',X,Y,X+Y);`

The MATLAB function `sprintf` is similar to `fprintf`; the only difference is that, instead of printing the resulting formatted string to the Command Window, it is returned so that it can then be assigned to a string variable in the program.

Exercise 25

Lookup `sprintf` and `%s` and explain how the following lines of code work:
```
str = sprintf('%d + %d = %d',X,Y,X+Y); fprintf(str);
str = sprintf('%d + %d = %d',X,Y,X+Y); fprintf('%s',str);
str = '%d + %d = %d'; fprintf(str,X,Y,X+Y);
```

Exercise 26

Lookup the special `fprintf` symbols `\n` (newline) and `\t` (tab), and modify NewtonAlg4.m so that its output using methods (2) and (3) reads:
```
after 4 iterations,
approximate square root of 5 is 2.2361
```

Solution 26

```
Method (2):
cr = sprintf('\n');
...
str = ['after 4 iterations,',cr,'approximate square root of 5
       is ', num2str(Xfinal)];
Method (3):
fprintf('\nafter 4 iterations, \napproximate square root of 5
       is %6.4f', Xfinal);
```

5.2 Elimination of the hardwired values (NewtonAlg5.m)

We intentionally chose to address the issue of displaying formatted output before attacking the problem of the hardwired loop-counter. The reason is that now the hardwired value 4 assigned to the loop-counter appears separately in the `fprintf` statement, and this motivates an important programming principle:

> Hardwired values should be assigned to a variable *once* in the initialization section of the program.

In this way, a modification to the hardwired value can be made in a single, clearly identified line of code, and the change will automatically propagate throughout the rest of the program to other instances of the hardwired value[3].

In NewtonAlg3.m, if we change the number of iterations, say from 4 to 14, this necessitates changing *all* occurrences of 4 throughout the code. Our solution is to introduce a new variable 'nIter' which will be substituted for the two occurrences of 4 in the program, and which will be assigned the hardwired value of 4 in the initialization portion of the code. This leads us to propose the following improvement to the code for NewtonAlg4.m in which a placehoder (%d) is included in the format string, and the variable `nIter` is added to `fprintf`'s list of arguments.

```
%%%%%%%%%%%%%%%%%%%%%%%%%%%%%%
%%%%%%%%% NewtonAlg5.m %%%%%%%%
% make number of iterations a variable
%initialization (hardwired variables)
X0      = 2;
nIter   = 4;
%%%%%%%%%%%%%%%%%%%%%%%%%%%%%%
X       = X0;
for i=1:nIter
    X   = X - (X^2 - 5)/(2*X);
end
Xfinal  = X;

%print using fprintf - better for controlling precision displayed
fprintf('\nafter %d iterations,...
         \napproximate square root of 5 is %6.4f', nIter, Xfinal);
```

This version takes advantage of `fprintf`'s ability to print the value of the number of iterations as the variable `nIter`. Notice also that we treat the assignment `nIter = 4` in the same manner as the hardwired initialization of `X0`.

---
[3]In other languages these hardwired variables are sometimes referred to as variables of *constant* type.

48   Chapter 5. Displaying Output

To be sure, our program still contains a hardwired value, but it is no longer sprinkled throughout the code as it was in the previous version. Changing the number of iterations from 4 to 14 in NewtonAlg4.m would necessitate tracking down both occurrences of the hardwired value, whereas in NewtonAlg5.m it requires modifying only the line `nIter = 4` at the beginning of the file.

The seemingly silly question of whether the numbers (-5, ^2) are hardwired magic numbers (no less so than `X0` and `nIter`) will have significant implications for the ultimate design of NewtonAlg.

5.3   Formatting table output (NewtonAlg6.m)

In this section we will output the formatted table displayed at the beginning of the chapter. The reason for displaying the quantities $|X_n - X_{n-1}|$, the differences between the approximation generated at the current iteration and the previous iteration, is theoretically significant; if the algorithm is converging to a final value, then these differences will get closer to zero. Finally, we display another quantity more reliably indicative of convergence, namely $|X_n^2 - 5|$, which will also converge to zero as X_n converges to a solution of $X^2 - 5 = 0$.

In NewtonAlg5.m above, the statement which appears inside the for-loop:

```
10      X = X - (X^2 - 5)/(2*X);
```

is appealingly compact (see Exercise 11), but we will need to revisit the NewtonAlg3.m implementation which uses `Xold` and `Xnew` in order to calculate $|X_n - X_{n-1}|$. Notice that this version utilizes the special fprintf symbols for newline (\n), and tab (\t), in order to lineup the columns when formatting the table.

```
1 %%%%%%%%%%%%%%%%%%%%%%%%%%%%%%%
2 %%%%%%%%%% NewtonAlg6.m %%%%%%%%%%
3 %using fprintf we output a formatted table displaying columns
4 %iteration, value of Xn,  difference |Xn - Xn-1|, residual Xn^2-5
5 % first iteration is X0=initial guess
6 %%%%%%%%%%%%%%%%%%%%%%%%%%%%%%%
7 X0       = 2;
8 nIter    = 4;
9
10 %initial fprintf statements for top three rows of table
11 fprintf('\n----------------------------------------');
12 fprintf('\nNewton''s algorithm applied to F(X) = X^2-5 = 0');
13 fprintf('\n----------------------------------------');
14 fprintf('\niteration \t Xn \t\t |Xn - Xn-1| \t Xn^2-5');
15 fprintf('\n----------------------------------------');
16 fprintf('\n0 \t\t\t %9.7f \t\t --- \t\t %9.7f',X0,abs(X0^2 - 5));
```

```
17
18 Xnew      = X0;
19 for i=1:nIter
20     Xold       = Xnew;
21     Xnew       = Xold - (Xold^2 - 5)/(2*Xold);
22     residual   = abs(Xnew^2 - 5);
23     succDiff   = abs(Xnew - Xold);
24     %each loop iteration, print Xn, |Xn - Xn-1|, and Xn^2-5
25     fprintf('\n%d \t\t\t %9.7f \t %9.7f \t\t %9.7f',...
26                 i,Xnew, succDiff, residual);
27 end
```

5.4 What the current implementation accomplishes

1. Instead of dumping a lonely 15-digit number to the screen, a self-explanatory table is output giving meaningful information on the execution of the Newton algorithm.

2. The hardwired value for the number of iterations has been consolidated into the single variable `nIter`. The benefit of this approach is that changing the number of iterations requires one simple change to the assignment `nIter = 4` in the initialization portion of the code. The change will automatically propagate to the two other places in the code, namely the for-loop and the fprintf statement, where this value is used.

5.5 Shortcomings of the current implementation

The drawbacks of the present implementation of NewtonAlg6.m are as follows:

1. Outputting the formatted table occurs *as* the algorithm is executed. If someone wanted to use our code as the fastest $\sqrt{5}$-calculator in the world, they would be hampered by:

   - the unwanted display of intermediate calculations;
   - the performance degradation due to the print statements;

   In other words, we need to isolate the formatted output from the algorithm.

2. The initial guess `X0` and number of iterations `nIter` are still hardwired.

5.6 Topics covered in this chapter

In this chapter we explained how to create well-documented, formatted tables to communicate data generated during a program's execution. We also explained the importance of creating a variable to consolidate multiple instances of a hardwired constant. Such variables should be assigned the hardwired value in the initialization portion of the code. Additionally, we described the following functions and elements of the MATLAB language:

1. Functions which compose and output text: `display()`, `num2str()`, `fprintf()`, `sprintf()`
2. `fprintf` placeholder characters: `%d`, `%e`, `%f`, `%g`, `%s`
3. `fprintf` special characters: `\n`, `\t`
4. Line-continuation character: ...

Chapter 6

Conditionals and Flow control

At this point we have made great progress in creating a program which implements an algorithm for computing $\sqrt{5}$. Recall that we have cheated when it comes to using for-loops and `fprintf`, since we have deferred defining arrays and strings to a later chapter. In spite of these shortcuts, it has still taken us four chapters to produce the rather simplistic NewtonAlg6.m, and this has been due to our excessive attention to design considerations. In this chapter we take a break from this strong emphasis on program design and "hit the vocabulary books", which is to say that we will add substantially to our repertoire of MATLAB instructions.

It will be seen in the coming sections that we need our programs to execute different blocks of instructions depending on the values of variables *which are not known until the program executes*. Thus, as in all programming languages, we require a mechanism for *controlling* the flow of program execution - *while* the program is executing. In this chapter we will learn how to form conditional expressions and use them to control the execution flow of a program.

We remark that in the early evolution of programming languages, a "goto" instruction was employed to jump around the code between different blocks of instructions. This capability, when abused, led to a proliferation of "spaghetti code" which software developers found to be error-prone, difficult to debug, and costly to maintain[1]. This state of affairs motivated the design of "goto-less" programming languages, Algol, Pascal, and C being among the first of a generation of structured languages. By eliminating the goto instruction from the programmer's vocabulary, one was prevented from committing the sin of writing spaghetti code. Needless to say, MATLAB is a structured language. To be sure, like C, MATLAB does support three instructions that can abruptly jump to another place in the code - these are the `break`, `continue`, and `return` statements - which we intentionally omit from this chapter.

---

[1] In the context of software, the term "maintain" refers to modifying the code to fix existing problems, or to implement additional features (often by someone other than the original author).

6.1 Logical (Boolean) expressions

For now, we define an *expression* as any syntactically valid combination of variables, constants, and operators[2]. When the operations (and function invocations) are executed in an expression, the expression is said to "evaluate" to a numerical value[3].

Unsurprisingly, an expression like 4 evaluates to 4. An example employing the "assignment operator =" shows that the expression x = 4 also evaluates to 4. Given that x has been assigned the value 4, employing the "arithmetic operator +" (which takes two arguments), what can you say about the expression x + 3? As expected, it will evaluate to 7. What about the expression x > 1? After all, the comparison symbol > is a legitimate operator (a "logical operator" which takes two arguments). Let's try some experimentation in the Command Window:

```
x = 4
ans =
    4

x + 3
ans =
    7

x > 1
ans =
    1

x < 1
ans =
    0

x == 4
ans =
    1
```

Notice that when comparing x with a numerical value like 4 and testing for equality, the two-character symbol == (double-equals) is used, since = is reserved to indicate assignment. To test for inequality, the two-character symbol ~= is used.

Expressions which contain symbols like the comparison operators

$$<, >, <=, >=, ==, \sim=$$

are typically thought of as evaluating to a "Boolean" quantity: True or False. Now MATLAB does not have a Boolean data-type, and as we saw above with the expressions (x < 4) and

---
[2] Later, this definition will need to include function-call invocations.
[3] Later, this definition will need to include strings and arrays.

($x == 4$), the numeric value 1 is assigned to a Boolean expression which is True, while a numeric value of 0 is assigned to a Boolean expression which is False. For this reason, MATLAB refers to these True/False expressions as "Logical" (1/0) quantities. Though we will freely use the equivalent terminologies of Boolean and Logical when describing certain expressions, values, operations, etc., be aware that the MATLAB documentation uses the "Logical" terminology exclusively.

In addition, the Boolean operations of logical AND (indicated by the ampersand symbol &), logical OR (indicated by the vertical-bar symbol |), and negation (indicated by the tilde symbol ~) can be used to combine the results of several intermediate Boolean expressions. For example:

```
x = 4
ans =
    4

y = (x < 6)
ans =
    1

z = (x > 2)
ans =
    1

xGreater2AndLess6 = y & z
ans =
    1
```

There is an important point to be made concerning Booleans and expressions. Namely, almost[4] *any expression*, (whether or not it contains arithmetic/logical-operators like > or &), can be treated as a Boolean, since numerical expressions are considered True if they evaluate to a non-zero value!

> **Exercise 27**
>
> After making the assignment $x = 4$, what does the Boolean expression ~x evaluate to? What about ~~x?

6.2 Conditional statements

We see from the previous section that the Command Window is a convenient environment for doing one-line experiments, e.g. when we need to clarify how a given expression is evaluated.

---
[4]Nested assignment operations, for example, are excluded.

As emphasized in earlier chapters, its best use is when debugging code that runs from a file in the Edit Window. We now discuss this subject. Using the Edit Window, create a new file named "Chapter6.m", and type in the following code:

```
1 x    = -7;
2 %this replaces x with abs(x)
3 if (x < 0)
4     x    = -x;
5 end
6 %if x > 0, do nothing
7 x
```

Set a breakpoint at line 1 and run the program. As you single-step the code notice that the instruction x = -x at line 4 gets executed. Let the program run to completion and notice the new value of x is displayed in the Command Window by virtue of the absence of semicolon at end of line 7. Next, rerun the program, and again, after breaking at line 1, single-step to line 3. Now, using the Command Window, type x = 12. With x assigned the value 12 (overriding the previous instruction which assigned to x the negative value -7), single-step the `if` statement at line 3. You should observe that the next line of code executed is the `end` statement, leaving x with the value 12. Run the program to completion and notice that 12 is displayed.

The general form of the `if` statement is:

```
1 if (Boolean expression)
2     (statement)
3 end
```

As we observed, `(statement)` gets executed only when `(Boolean expression)` evaluates to True. One can embellish the above construct to execute a block of several statements instead of just one, as well as executing a different set of statements in case the Boolean expression evaluates to False:

```
1 if (Boolean expression)
2     (statement)
3     ...
4     (statement)
5 else
6     (statement)
7     ...
8     (statement)
9 end
```

In other words, the statements between the `else` and the `end` are executed precisely when the the statements between the `if` and the `else` are NOT executed.

6.2. Conditional statements

We illustrate this by an example which calculates the absolute value of a number, thereby mimicking MATLAB's built-in abs() function. First, add the following lines of code to the file Chapter6.m:

```matlab
x    = -7;
%this assigns to variable y the abs(x)
if (x < 0)
    y    = -x;
else
    y    = x;
end
fprintf('\nabs(%f) is %f\n', x, y);
```

When we run the code in Chapter6.m from the Edit Window, the experiment from the previous section will also execute. To avoid this, let's first comment out those unwanted lines by inserting percent characters as the first character in each line. A nice editing shortcut to accomplish this task is to select the block of code from line 1 to line 7, right-click with the cursor positioned over the highlighted text, and then select Comment from the popup menu. See the figure below:

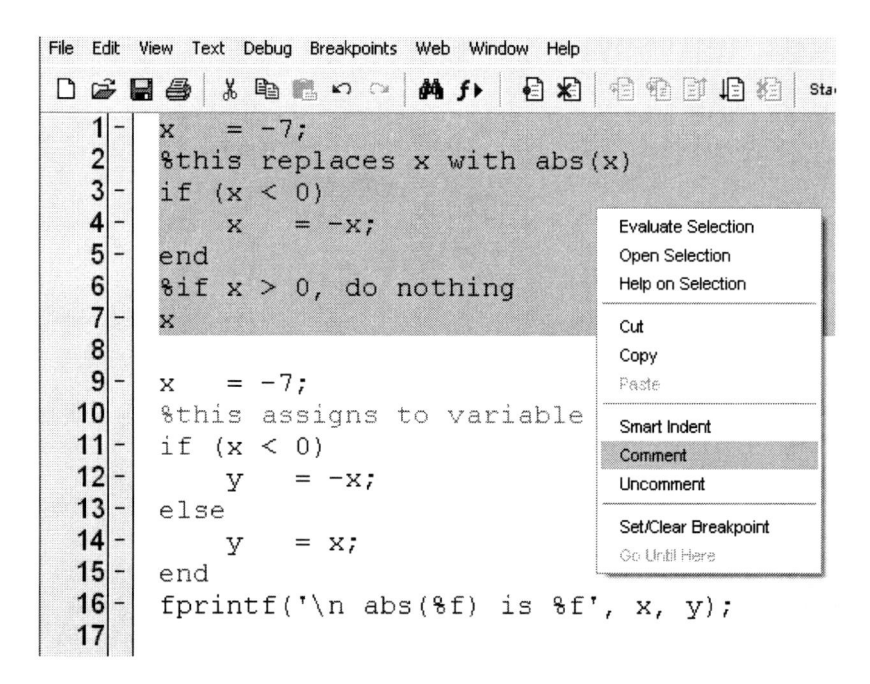

Set a breakpoint at the first executable statement at line 9 and single-step to observe how the if-statement works. Run this experiment again, but this time change the value of x from -7 to 12 before executing the if-statement.

Chapter 6. Conditionals and Flow control

Exercise 28

Explain why the following two code fragments are equivalent.
Fragment One:
```
if (x < 0)
else
    y = 1;
end
```
Fragment Two:
```
if (x >= 0)
    y = 1;
end
```
Note that (`statement`) is allowed to be the "empty" statement.

Exercise 29

Determine if the following are always equivalent.
Fragment One:
```
if (x < 0)
    (statement one)
else
    (statement two)
end
```
Fragment Two:
```
if (x < 0)
    (statement one)
end
if (x >= 0)
    (statement two)
end
```

Solution 29

No. Suppose (`statement one`) read x = -x.

This next code fragment "verifies" that our if-else-end implementation of the absolute value agrees with MATLAB's built-in `abs()` function.

```
1 %% code to 'verify' our implementation of abs(x)
2 for i=1:1000
```

6.2. Conditional statements

```
3      x   = (rand - 0.5);       %-0.5 <= x <= +0.5
4      if (x < 0.0)
5          y   = -x;
6      else
7          y   = x;
8      end
9      if (abs(x) ~= y)
10         beep
11         fprintf('\n something''s wrong with our homegrown abs()');
12     end
13 end
```

> **Exercise 30**
>
> Lookup the `rand` and `beep` commands in the Help Browser. Then explain how the above code works, and why we've put the word "verify" in quotes.

We now explore some more examples of the if-else-end construction. Recall that the "indicator function" of a set A[5] is defined as

$$\mathbf{1}_A(x) := \begin{cases} 1 & x \in A, \\ 0 & x \notin A. \end{cases}$$

Thus, $\mathbf{1}_{(0,\infty)}(x)$, also called the Heaviside function and denoted $H(x)$, takes the value one when x is positive, and zero otherwise. Here is an implementation of the Heaviside function $y = H(x)$:

```
1 %Heaviside function y = H(x)
2 if (x <= 0)
3     y   = 0;
4 else
5     y   = 1;
6 end
7 fprintf('\n%f = H(%f)', x, y);
```

Next, consider the following two code fragments implementing $y = \mathbf{1}_{[-2,2]}(x)$:

```
1 %characteristic function on [-2,2] using logical AND operator
2 if (x >= -2) & (x <= 2)
3     y   = 1;
4 else
5     y   = 0;
6 end
```

---
[5]Also called the "characteristic function", and sometimes denoted χ.

```
%characteristic function on [-2,2] using logical OR operator
if (x < -2) | (x > 2)
    y   = 0;
else
    y   = 1;
end
```

> **Exercise 31**
>
> Explain why each of the above two code fragments implements $1_{[-2,2]}$.
> How about the one-liner
> y = (x >= -2) & (x <= 2)?

6.3 The full-blown if-elseif-else-end statement

The "signum" function is defined as follows:

$$\text{sgn}(x) := \begin{cases} 1 & x > 0, \\ 0 & x = 0, \\ -1 & x < 0. \end{cases}$$

Here is an implementation of $y = \text{sgn}(x)$:

```
%%signum function
if (x < 0)
    y   = -1;
else
    %the following if-statement executes when x >= 0
    if (x > 0)
        y   = 1;
    else
        y   = 0;
    end
end
```

> **Exercise 32**
>
> Using Help, determine how to use MATLAB's built-in signum function. Mimicking the code we wrote to verify our absolute value function, use MATLAB's `sign()` function to similarly verify our implementation of the signum function above.

6.3. The full-blown if-elseif-else-end statement

Suppose we deleted all the text between the first `else` and the second `if`, so that the two keywords combined to form `elseif`? We would end up with:

```
1 %%signum function
2 if (x < 0)
3     y   = -1;
4 elseif (x > 0)
5         y   = 1;
6     else
7         y   = 0;
8     end
9 end
```

It turns out that this code is almost legitimate; `elseif` is a valid keyword just like `if` and `else`, but there's one too many `end` statements! MATLAB can help resolve valid groupings in `if-elseif-else-end` blocks: Select the text above, right-click on the highlighted text and then select Smart-Indent on the popup menu. See the figures below:

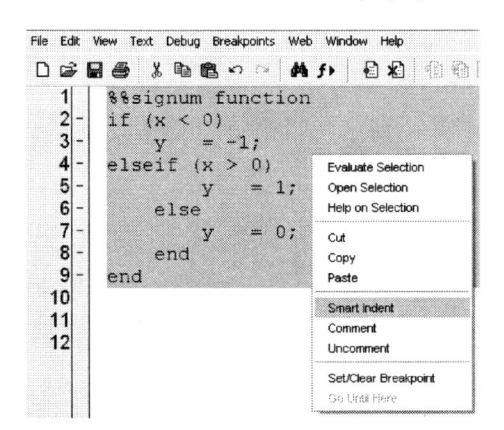

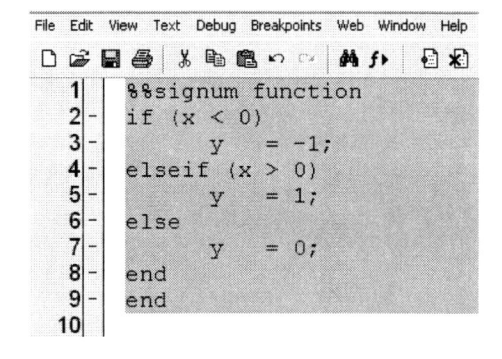

The correct use of the `elseif` is as follows:

```
1 if (Boolean expression)
2     (statement)
3     ...
4     (statement)
5 elseif (Boolean expression)
6     (statement)
7     ...
8     (statement)
9 ...
10 elseif (Boolean expression)
11     (statement)
12     ...
```

```
13      (statement)
14 else      %captures all remaining cases
15      (statement)
16      ...
17      (statement)
18 end
```

In our case, the following code gives an equivalent implementation of the signum function:

```
1 %%signum function
2 if (x < 0)
3     y    = -1;
4 elseif (x > 0)
5     y    = 1;
6 else
7     y    = 0;
8 end
```

It may seem that the status of the last `else` has been confused; in the first version the last `else` was grouped within an `if-else-end` block which itself was subordinate to the first `else`, whereas here each of the conditionals (`if`, `elseif`, `else`) appears to be on an equal footing. This confusion is superficial, as you can see by convincing yourself that in either implementation the statement attached to the last `else` (namely y=0) is executed *only* if each of the other tests (x < 0 and x > 0) has failed!

It is important to keep in mind that the order of the sequence of `elseif` tests is important.

```
1 %if-elseif-elseif-else-end statements are evaluated sequentially
2 x    = -100;
3 if (x < 0)
4     y    = 1;
5     fprintf('x less than 0 is handled here');
6 elseif (x < -2)
7     %the following will never execute
8     y    = 999;
9     fprintf('x is less than -2, but also NOT less than 0 - impossible!');
10 end
```

6.4 More control: for-loops and while-loops

In this section we discuss two statements which control the execution of a block of statements which need to be repeated multiple times. We first consider the *while-loop*, and then revisit the *for-loop* first introduced in Chapter 3.

If the language supported a "goto" statement, the following method would be appropriate for repeatedly executing a block of statements until some condition (`Boolean expression`) failed:

```
1 if (Boolean expression)
2     (statement)
3     goto line 1
4 end
```

Since we have eliminated goto from the language, the following construct is used to accomplish the same effect.

```
1 while (Boolean expression)
2     (statement)
3 end
```

> **Exercise 33**
>
> Using just the `if-end` and fictitious `goto` statements, give an equivalent description of the `if-elseif-elseif-else-end` construct. Keep in mind Exercise 29.

Adding to our experimental file Chapter6.m, type in the following code:

```
1 i   = 1;
2 while (i <=10)
3     fprintf('\n%d''th iteration of while loop',i)
4     i = i + 1;
5 end
```

Notice how two consecutive single-quotes ('') are used to force a single quote to appear in the output string. Set a breakpoint at the first executable line, run to the breakpoint, and single-step every instruction of the program until it terminates. Being careful to inspect the value of i with each debug step, confirm that the `while` instruction works as advertised.

Since it turns out that the above use of the while-loop is so common, the for-loop is often utilized since it will accomplish the same effect more succinctly:

```
1 for i=1:10
2     fprintf('\n%d''th iteration through for-loop',i)
3 end
```

Be aware that in this particular example the for-loop behaves like the while-loop, yet its definition is actually different - recall Exercise 10! Again, we defer the full explanation until our discussion of arrays.

Exercise 34

Rewrite the for-loop and print statement so that the following output is produced:

```
1'st iteration through for loop
2'nd iteration through for loop
3'rd iteration through for loop
4'th iteration through for loop
5'th iteration through for loop
6'th iteration through for loop
7'th iteration through for loop
8'th iteration through for loop
9'th iteration through for loop
10'th iteration through for loop
```

Exercise 35

Lookup the built-in MATLAB function `mod()`. Write a code fragment to extract the ten's digit from a positive integer.

Exercise 36

Lookup `&&` and `||` in the Help Browser and familiarize yourself with the "short-circuited" version of the logical operators `&` and `|`. Note that the Editor (in the R2007 release) will inform you when these short-circuited versions are recommended.

Exercise 37

Rewrite the loop in Exercise 34 so it displays the first hundred numbers 1'st, 2'nd,...,100'th.

Solution 37

```
for i=1:100
  onesDigit = mod(i,10);
  if (onesDigit == 1) & (i ~= 11)
    str = 'st';
  elseif (onesDigit == 2) & (i ~= 12)
    str = 'nd';
  elseif (onesDigit == 3) & (i ~= 13)
    str = 'rd';
  else
    str = 'th';
  end
  fprintf('\n%d''%s iteration through for-loop',i,str)
end
```

6.5 Topics covered in this chapter

This chapter introduced Boolean expressions, typically constructed from arithmetic and logical combinations of a program's variables. Additionally, several MATLAB commands have been introduced which can evaluate a Boolean expression (using the runtime values of the variables), and then transfer control to a specified block of executable statements in the program. We described the following MATLAB statements:

1. Arithmetic comparison operators: <, >, <=, >=, ==, ~=

2. Logical operators: &, |, ~, &&, ||

3. Conditional control statements: if-elseif-else-end

4. Looping control statements: for, while

5. Built-in functions: rand, beep, sign(), mod()

Chapter 7

Arrays I

Arrays, which include vectors, matrices, and strings, are important structures in most every programming language, particularly in those with scientific applications. In MATLAB, however, arrays have an especially prominent role as *the* fundamental data structure around which the language was designed. It is an impressive fact that most MATLAB code involving an iterated evaluation of a scalar function can be *vectorized* in such a way that a for-loop is replaced with a single instruction!

In this course we encounter the following three fundamental contexts in which arrays arise:

1. Saving a sequence of values of a runtime variable for subsequent retrieval and analysis

2. Representing mathematical functions (scalar and vector-valued)

3. Matrix algebra

7.1 Using arrays for storage (NewtonAlg7.m)

In Chapter 6 we extended our repertoire of MATLAB instructions and also got around to explaining the for-loop construct that had been heavy-handedly introduced into NewtonAlg4.m. In this section we will return to the task of improving NewtonAlg6.m, and on the way we will motivate the use of arrays for storing data. In particular, we demonstrate how arrays can be used to store a sequence of values generated during the runtime execution of a program. Currently, if our NewtownAlg6.m is to be useful as a tool for understanding the numerical analysis of computing the square-root of five, we will need to embellish it with exactly this kind of "storage" functionality.

Let's first recall the shortcomings of NewtonAlg6.m itemized in Chapter 5:

1. Outputting the formatted table occurs *as* the algorithm executes. If someone wants to use our code solely as the fastest $\sqrt{5}$ calculator in the world, they will be hampered by:
   - the unwanted display of intermediate calculations;

- the performance degradation due to the print statements;

In other words, we need to isolate the formatted output from the algorithm.

2. The initial guess X0 and number of iterations nIter are still hardwired.

In a later chapter we will discuss MATLAB *functions*, and in some sense each of the above issues is properly addressed in that context, namely passing input arguments (like X0 and nIter) and returning output (like a table of data which can be printed externally from the algorithm). However, this only means that the ultimate resolution of items (1) and (2) must wait for an implementation of NewtonAlg as a function. In the meantime, concerning the output issue described in (1), we still need to discuss what constitutes a "table of data" in our MATLAB code. Additionally, concerning the input issue described in (2), it may not be mathematically appropriate for nIter to be designated as an input parameter[1] since "when to stop iterating the algorithm" is not known ahead of time! In fact, it is more appropriate to terminate the iteration process when no further "progress" is being achieved, which is to say convergence within some desired tolerance. By introducing arrays for storage in NewtonAlg6.m, we will go a long way towards attacking the flaws in (1) and (2) itemized above.

As a warmup to modifying NewtonAlg6.m to track convergence, let's introduce a variable residual whose significance is simply that it is identically zero when a solution has been found, and is *close* to zero when a solution is *close* to being found. We choose the quantity $|x_n^2 - 5|$ to serve these requirements.

Another quantity of mathematical interest, and indeed one which will converge to zero whenever x_n converges, is the difference between successive iterations $|x_n - x_{n-1}|$. We will assign this difference to a variable named succDiff[2], since these differences going to zero[3] is a *necessary* condition for the sequence x_n to converge.

```
%%%%%%%%%%%%%%%%%%%%%%%%%%%%%%%%
%%%%%% warmup to NewtonAlg7.m %%%
%initialization (hardwired variables)
x0      = 2;
nIter   = 5;    %still hardwired!

%initial fprintf statements for top row of table
fprintf('\n----------------------------------------');
fprintf('\niteration \t Xn \t\t |Xn - Xn-1| \t |Xn^2-5|');
xnew    = x0;
for i=1:nIter
```

---

[1] Unlike X0, which most certainly has the status of an input parameter.
[2] Since the word diff is the name of a built-in MATLAB function, it should not be used as a variable name.
[3] Of course, $|x_n - x_{n-1}| \to 0$ is not a *sufficient* condition for convergence of x_n, as the partial sums of the series $x_n = \sum_{k=1}^n k^{-1}$ illustrates. Also, the successive differences may ultimately go to zero (i.e. in the limit as $n \to \infty$), while at the same time manifesting an unpredictable behavior for all n less than some large N.

7.1. Using arrays for storage (NewtonAlg7.m)

```
12     xold       = xnew;
13     xnew       = xold - (xold^2 - 5)/(2*xold);
14     residual   = abs(xnew^2 - 5);
15     succDiff   = abs(xnew - xold);
16     %each loop iteration, print Xn, |Xn - Xn-1|, and |Xn^2-5|
17     fprintf('\n%d \t\t\t %9.7f \t %9.7f \t\t %9.7f',...
18                i,xnew, succDiff, residual);
19 end
```

Now we are in a position to attack the flaws (1) and (2) in NewtonAlg6.m. In particular, NewtonAlg7.m will utilize an array to store, for each iteration where i takes the successive values $1, 2, \ldots,$ nIter, the values of the approximation x_n, the residual $|x_n^2 - 5|$ and the difference $|x_n - x_{n-1}|$. With these values collected into the "array variables"

   x(1),..,x(nIter)

and

   residual(1),..,residual(nIter)

and

   succDiff(1),..,succDiff(nIter)

we can subsequently display them in a table in the output section of the program.

Exercise 38

Explain two benefits of having the history of approximations x_n available subsequent to the execution of the algorithm portion of the code.

Solution 38

In order to understand the mathematical theory associated with Newton's algorithm, we need to have the sequence x_n available for a more detailed numerical analysis. Also, the high overhead associated with the `fprintf` statement buried within the algorithmic section of the code will interfere with any attempt to improve (or even measure) the performance of our algorithm.

```
1 %%%%%%%%%%%%%%%%%%%%%%%%%%%%%%%%%
2 %%%%%%%%%%%% NewtownAlg7.m %%%%%%%%
3 %%%% initialization section %%%%%
```

```matlab
4 %initialization (hardwired variables)
5 x0          = 2;
6 nIter       = 5;
7 %initialization (not hardwired)
8 z           = zeros(1,nIter);
9 x           = z;
10 residual   = z;
11 succDiff   = z;
12
13 %%%%%%%%%%%%%%%%%%%%%%%%%%%%%%%%
14 %%%% algorithm section %%%%%%%%%%
15 x(1)       = x0;
16 for i=2:nIter
17     xold       = x(i-1);
18     x(i)       = xold - (xold^2 - 5)/(2*xold);
19     succDiff(i) = abs(x(i) - xold);
20     residual(i) = abs(x(i)^2 - 5);
21 end
22
23 %%%%%%%%%%%%%%%%%%%%%%%%%%%%%%%%
24 %%%%%%% output section %%%%%%%%%%
25 %all printing done here
26 %printing the first few rows is now where it belongs
27 % - in the printing section!
28 fprintf('\niteration \t Xn \t\t |Xn - Xn-1| \t |Xn^2-5|');
29 fprintf('\n--------------------------------------------------');
30 %repeat the above for-loop
31 % note that all the data we print has been saved
32 %  in arrays x, succDiff, residual
33 for i=1:nIter
34     fprintf('\n%d \t\t %f \t\t%f \t\t%f',...
35                 i,x(i), succDiff(i), residual(i));
36 end
```

After creating the file NewtonAlg7.m and entering in the above code, set a breakpoint at the first instruction and single-step the entire program. After each single-step operation, inspect the values of the arrays by typing `x, residual, succDiff` into the Command Window.

The result of examining the variables `x, residual, succDiff` after the initialization section and after each iteration in NewtonAlg7.m should be as follows:

```
1 format long
2 K>> x, residual, succDiff
3 x =
```

7.1. Using arrays for storage (NewtonAlg7.m)

```
 4       0         0         0         0         0    0    0
 5 residual =
 6       0         0         0         0         0    0    0
 7 succDiff =
 8       0         0         0         0         0    0    0
 9 K>> x, residual, succDiff
10 x =
11       2.00000000000000      2.25000000000000    0    0    0
12 residual =
13       0    0.06250000000000    0         0         0
14 succDiff =
15       0    0.25000000000000    0         0         0
16 K>> x, residual, succDiff
17 x =
18       2.00000000000000      2.25000000000000    2.23611111111111    0    0
19 residual =
20       0    0.06250000000000    0.00019290123457    0         0
21 succDiff =
22       0    0.25000000000000    0.01388888888889    0         0
23 K>> x, residual, succDiff
24 x =
25       2.00000000000000      2.25000000000000    2.23611111111111
26       2.23606797791580    0
27 residual =
28       0    0.06250000000000    0.00019290123457    0.00000000186047    0
29 succDiff =
30       0    0.25000000000000    0.01388888888889    0.00004313319531    0
31 K>> x, residual, succDiff
32 x =
33       2.00000000000000      2.25000000000000    2.23611111111111
34       2.23606797791580      2.23606797749979
35 residual =
36       0    0.06250000000000    0.00019290123457    0.00000000186047
37       0.00000000000000
38 succDiff =
39       0    0.25000000000000    0.01388888888889    0.00004313319531
40       0.00000000041601
```

Next, we make the observation that having the x_n available outside the algorithmic section of the code obviates the need to calculate the residuals $|x_n^2 - 5|$, and successive differences $|x_n - x_{n-1}|$ within the for-loop. In other words, we can simply save x_n in an array, and with these values available to us in the output section of the code we can beat out the quantities $|x_n^2 - 5|$ and $|x_n - x_{n-1}|$.

```matlab
%%%%%%%%%%%%%%%%%%%%%%%%%%%%%%%%
%%%%%%%%%%% NewtownAlg8.m %%%%%%
%%%% initialization section %%%%%
%initialization (hardwired variables)
x0      = 2;
nIter   = 5;
%initialization (not hardwired)
x       = zeros(1,nIter);

%%%%%%%%%%%%%%%%%%%%%%%%%%%%%%%%
%%%% algorithm section %%%%%%%%%%
x(1)    = x0;
for i=2:nIter
    x(i)    = x(i-1) - (x(i-1)^2 - 5)/(2*x(i-1));
end
%%%%%%%%%%%%%%%%%%%%%%%%%%%%%%%%
%%%%%%% output section %%%%%%%%%%
fprintf('\niteration \t Xn \t\t |Xn - Xn-1| \t |Xn^2-5|');
fprintf('\n--------------------------------------------------');
for i=2:nIter
    succDiff    = abs(x(i) - x(i-1));
    residual    = abs(x(i)^2 - 5);
    fprintf('\n%d \t\t \%f \t\t%f \t\t%f',i,x(i), succDiff, residual);
end
```

Although we have yet to explain the constructs (1:nIter), (2:end) and [...;...;...], not to mention multi-dimensional arrays, we cannot resist showing off the following variant of the implementation in NewtionAlg8.m:

```matlab
%%%%%%%%%%%%%%%%%%%%%%%%%%%%%%%%
%%%% initialization section %%%%%
%initialization (hardwired variables)
x0      = 2;
nIter   = 5;
%initialization (not hardwired)
x       = zeros(1,nIter);

%%%%%%%%%%%%%%%%%%%%%%%%%%%%%%%%
%%%% algorithm section %%%%%%%%%%
x(1)    = x0;
for i=2:nIter
    x(i)    = x(i-1)- (x(i-1)^2 - 5)/(2*x(i-1));
end
```

```
16 %%%%%%%%%%%%%%%%%%%%%%%%%%%%%%%
17 %%%%%%% output section %%%%%%%%%%
18 fprintf('\n--------------------------------------');
19 fprintf('\niteration \t Xn \t\t |Xn - Xn-1| \t |Xn^2-5|');
20 fprintf('\n%d \t\t %f \t\t%f \t\t%f',...
21         [1:nIter; x; [0, abs(x(2:end) - x(1:end-1))]; abs(x.^2 - 5)]);
```

> **Exercise 39**
>
> Read about fprintf in the Help documentation and see if you can make sense out of the above implementation.

At this point, we have a very respectable implementation of Newton's algorithm for computing the square root of five.

7.2 What the current implementation accomplishes

After a detour in Chapter 6, we have returned to evolving our program to overcome the shortcomings identified in NewtonAlg6.m.

1. The input section of the code isolates and clearly identifies the hardwired variables X0 and nIter.

2. The algorithmic section of the code is streamlined to compute the iterates x_n efficiently in a tight for-loop. This time-critical operation is unhindered by non-algorithmic operations like formatting and displaying output.

3. The output section of the code beats out of the x_n data several quantities of numerical interest, and displays them in a formatted table.

7.3 Shortcomings of the current implementation

The drawbacks of the present implementation of NewtonAlg8.m are as follows:

1. The initial guess X0 is hardwired.

2. The number of iterations nIter is not only hardwired, but should be replaced with more mathematically appropriate criteria for terminating the for-loop. This will be addressed when we discuss the notion of "tolerance" in Chapter 13.

7.4 Topics covered in this chapter

In this first of five chapters on the fundamental topic of arrays, we introduced the elementary use of arrays for storing and retrieving runtime data.

Chapter 8

Arrays II

We now proceed to give a methodical treatment of arrays. First, we consider only one-dimensional arrays, which is to say row-vectors ($1 \times n$) and column-vectors ($n \times 1$). Even if your code never involves calculations with Linear Algebra, one-dimensional arrays (which include strings, loop-counters and interval domains for math functions) are indispensable to MATLAB programming.

8.1 Array initialization

Most high-level programming languages make a distinction between a variable "declaration" and a variable "definition". Indeed, compiled languages like C++ require that the "data type" of a variable be specified in a *declaration* statement in order that syntactical consistency be enforced at compile-time. On the other hand, simply declaring a variable does not make the variable "come into existence"; variables come into existence by virtue of memory being allocated for them, whether at load-time or execution-time, and this is accomplished by the *definition* statement. Since MATLAB is not a compiled language, but rather an interpreted (or scripted) language, there is no data-type enforcement, and therefore no declaration of variables. Memory allocation, on the other hand, is a necessary fact of every program, whether compiled or interpreted.

How does one make variables "come into existence" in MATLAB? Recalling our experiments with the `who` command from Chapter 3, we have seen how simple assignment statements like `x0 = 2` and `str='some text'` will result in these variables coming into existence. Finally, we have seen in NewtonAlg7.m, that the statement `x = zeros(1,nIter)` results in x coming into existence as an array of five zeros. In what follows we conduct a tutorial session in the Command Window where we will perform many one-line experiments to discover how the array works in MATLAB.

```
 1  >> clear
 2
 3  >> who
 4
 5  >> z    = zeros(1,6)
 6  z =
 7       0     0     0     0     0     0
 8
 9  >> z    = ones(1,6)
10  z =
11       1     1     1     1     1     1
12
13  >> z    = rand(1,4)
14  z =
15       0.1509    0.6979    0.3784    0.8600
16
17  >> z    = linspace(1,6,6)
18  z =
19       1     2     3     4     5     6
20
21  >> z    = linspace(1,6,3)
22  z =
23       1.0000    3.5000    6.0000
24
25  >> z    = linspace(1,6)
26  z =
27    Columns 1 through 4
28       1.0000    1.0505    1.1010    1.1515
29       ...
30    Columns 97 through 100
31       5.8485    5.8990    5.9495    6.0000
32
33  >> z    = 1:6
34  z =
35       1     2     3     4     5     6
36
37  >> z    = 1:2:10
38  z =
39       1     3     5     7     9
```

Annotations (left margin):
- **zeros function** (line 5)
- **ones function** (line 9)
- **rand function** (line 13)
- **linspace function** (line 17)
- **a:b** (line 33)
- **a:h:b** (line 37)

Annotations (right column):
- just in case any variables (like z) were previously assigned values earlier in the session
- verify variables are removed from workspace
- make z come into existence as (1×6)-array consisting of 6 zeros (row vector)
- assign to z the (1×6)-array consisting of 6 ones (row vector)
- assign to z the (1×4)-array of 4 random numbers, each uniformly distributed between 0 and 1
- assign to z the (1×6)-array consisting of 6 numbers equally spaced from 1 to 6 (inclusive, which is to say including the endpoints 1 and 6)
- assign to z the (1×3)-array consisting of 3 numbers equally spaced from 1 to 6 (inclusive)
- assign to z the (1×100)-array consisting of 100 numbers equally spaced from 1 to 6 (inclusive); observe that the count defaults to 100 when no third parameter is specified
- assign to z the (1×6)-array consisting of the numbers *starting* at 1, continuing by *counting up* by 1's, and stopping when a number *greater than* 6 (in this case 7) is reached
- assign to z the (1×5)-array consisting of the numbers *starting* at 1, continuing by *counting up* by 2's, and stopping when a number *greater than* 10 (in this case 11) is reached

8.1. Array initialization

```
1 >> z     = 6:-1:1
2 z =
3      6     5     4     3     2     1
4
5 >> h=0.05; 0:h:1
6 ans =
7   Columns 1 through 4
8        0    0.0500    0.1000    0.1500
9   ...
10  Columns 18 through 21
11   0.8500    0.9000    0.9500    1.0000
12
13 >> z = [exp(1), -atan(1.0)/pi, 1.23e-1]
14 ans =
15   2.7183   -0.2500    0.1230
```

assign to z the (1×6)-array consisting of the numbers *starting* at 6, continuing by *counting down* by 1's, and stopping when a number *less than* 1 (in this case 0) is reached

assign to z the (1×21)-array consisting of the numbers *starting* at 0, continuing by *counting up* in increments of 0.05, and stopping when a number *greater than* 1 (in this case 1.05) is reached

$[x_1, .., x_n]$ assign to z the (1×3)-array whose three components are explicitly given by the numbers e, $\frac{-\arctan(1.0)}{\pi}$, and 1.23×10^{-1}

It may appear strange that only in the last of the above examples did we demonstrate the method of defining an array by explicitly giving each of its components. In practice, however, arrays rarely start out with known data; rather, they start life as one of the basic arrays of the correct size, and then acquire different values as components are generated, or as matrix or other functions are applied to it. Sometimes the arrays resulting from the above operations are used as input to another program, in which case the secondary program would consider these arrays to be *starting life* with known data. On the other hand, even in this case we will learn programmatic techniques for making such an array available to the second program while avoiding the need to explicitly type out each of its components in an initialization statement. Note that the commas are not required as separators when specifying the components of an array (spaces are sufficient, as observed in MATLAB's own output), but using commas is less error prone and a good habit to adopt from the outset.

Exercise 40

Assume $a < b$. Does the assignment `z = a:h:b` guarantee that b is included in the array z? How about a? Give an example to illustrate your answer.

Exercise 41

Consider implementing the assignment `z = linspace(a,b,N)` using the construct `z = a:h:b`. How must h be defined in terms of a,b,N? Give a quick way of determining the size of the increments from z.

> **Solution 41**
>
> The formula is `h = (b-a)/(N-1)`. Given z, use `h = z(2) - z(1)`.

> **Exercise 42**
>
> Consider implementing the assignment `z = a:h:b` using the construct `linspace(a,c,N)`. How must `c,N` be defined in terms of `a,b,h`? Also, give an example showing that `N = ceil((b-a)/h)` is incorrect.

> **Exercise 43**
>
> If you are asked to create an array which discretizes the interval $[a,b]$ with N equally distributed *data points*, which construct is most appropriate? How about N equally distributed *intervals*?

> **Exercise 44**
>
> If you are asked to create an array which discretizes the interval $[a,b]$ with sub-intervals of size h, where h is so small relative to $(b-a)$ that we are comfortable with the right endpoint landing within h of b, which construct is most appropriate?

8.2 Array operations

In earlier chapters we've encountered three types of operations which can be performed on scalar quantities; arithmetic, logical, and built-in operations. In this section we discuss how all of these operations can equally well be performed on the elements of an array. In other words, to the extent that an array is a collection of scalar quantities (its components), we can apply scalar operations to an array by applying them *component-wise* on each of the array's entries. To be sure, MATLAB provides functions for performing array-specific operations like summing the components of an array, but since these have no scalar counterpart we defer their discussion to a later section on matrix algebra.

8.2. Array operations

```
1 >> x     = rand(1,4)
2 x =
3    0.9501    0.2311    0.6068    0.4860
4
5 >> y     = 2*x
6 y =
7    1.9003    0.4623    1.2137    0.9720
8
9 >> alltwos = 2*ones(1,4)
10 y =        2    2    2    2
11
12 >> y    = alltwos.*x
13 y =
14   1.9003    0.4623    1.2137    0.9720
15
16 >> y    = x.^2
17 y =
18    0.9027    0.0534    0.3683    0.2362
19
20 >> y    = x.*x
21 y =
22    0.9027    0.0534    0.3683    0.2362
23
24 >> y    = 5 + x
25 y =
26    5.9501    5.2311    5.6068    5.4860
27
28 >> y    = x + 5*ones(1,4)
29 y =
30    5.9501    5.2311    5.6068    5.4860
31
32 >> x    = linspace(0,1,5)
33 x =
34    0    0.2500    0.5000    0.7500    1.0000
35
36 >> y    = x > 0.4
37 y =    0    0    1    1    1
38
39 >> y    = x > [0.3, 0.1, 0.6, 0.9, 0.2]
40 y =    0    1    0    0    1
```

array operator *

array operator .*

array operator .^

array operator +

array operator >

assign to x the (1×4)-array of 4 random numbers each lying in $[0,1]$

arithmetic operations on arrays using scalars: multiplying the array x by the scalar 2 will multiply each component of x by 2
$$2 * [x_1, \ldots, x_n] \longrightarrow [2x_1, \ldots, 2x_n]$$
multiplying the (1×4)-array of four 1's by the scalar 2 will multiply each component by 2, creating an array all of whose entries are 2

component-wise operations on arrays: multiplying the array x by the array consisting of 2's will multiply each component of x by 2
$$[2, \ldots, 2] .* [x_1, \ldots, x_n] \longrightarrow [2x_1, \ldots, 2x_n]$$

exponentiating the array x to power 2 will square each component
$$[x_1, \ldots, x_n] .\hat{\ } 2 \longrightarrow [x_1^2, \ldots, x_n^2]$$

multiplying the array x by itself is equivalent to squaring each component of x
$$[x_1, \ldots, x_n] .* [x_1, \ldots, x_n] \longrightarrow [x_1^2, \ldots, x_n^2]$$

adding the scalar 5 to array x will add 5 to each component of the array
$$5 + [x_1, \ldots, x_n] \longrightarrow [5 + x_1, \ldots, 5 + x_n]$$

adding to x the array consisting of all 5's will add 5 to each component of x
$$[x_1, \ldots, x_n] + [5, \ldots, 5] \rightarrow [x_1+5, \ldots, x_n+5]$$

logical operations on arrays:
comparing the array x to the scalar 0.4 will compare each component of the array to 0.4
$$[x_1, ., x_n] > 0.4 \longrightarrow [x_1 > 0.4, \ldots, x_n > 0.4]$$

comparing the array x to another array will compare each component
$$[x_1, ., x_n] > [.3, ., .2] \rightarrow [x_1 > .3, ., x_n > .2]$$

From the above session in the Command Window, we observe how arithmetic and logical operations can be performed on all the components of an array in one expression.

Exercise 45

Is there are any difference between the following four constructs?
```
5 + x
5 .+ x
x + 5
x .+ 5
```
Will one ever use .+ in an expression? How about .> ?

Exercise 46

Explain the behavior of the expression [1 2 3] .* [4 5 6].
How about [1 2 3] .^ [4 5 6]?

8.3 Performance: for-loop vs. array-operation vs. built-in implementations

In order to become more familiar with the use of array operations, and the performance trade-offs implied by their use, we now revisit our home-grown implementation of the absolute value (abs) function. In the following code we show how this function can be used to operate on arrays instead of scalars.

First, we recall the implementation of absolute value from Chapter 6.2.

```
%arbitrary initial value for x for demonstration
x    = -7;

%following will assign to variable y the abs(x)
if (x < 0)
    y    = -x;
else
    y    = x;
end
```

Based on what we learned from Chapter 6.4, we adapt the above code to return the absolute value of an array, by which, of course, we mean the component-wise absolute value of the array entries. An implementation along these lines goes as follows:

8.3. Performance: for-loop vs. array-operation vs. built-in implementations

```
1 %arbitrary initial value for xarray for demonstration
2 xarray  = [-7 3 -2 4];
3
4 %yarray will receive absolute values of xarray entries
5 yarray  = zeros(1,4);
6
7 for i=1:4
8     x   = xarray(i);
9     if (x < 0)
10        y   = -x;
11    else
12        y   = x;
13    end
14    yarray(i)   = y;
15 end
```

We will henceforth refer to an implementation in the spirit of the above code as a "for-loop implementation". On the other hand, using the operations discussed in the previous section, we can also come up with an "array-operation" implementation.

```
1 %arbitrary initial value for xarray for demonstration
2 xarray  = [-7 3 -2 4];
3
4 %yarray will receive absolute values of xarray entries
5 yarray = (xarray > 0).* xarray + (xarray < 0) .* (-xarray);
```

Note: The above is a particularly obtuse method of computing absolute value of an array, but it serves well our purpose of illustrating array operations.

Exercise 47

Explain how the above code works by single-stepping the following instructions:
```
xPos = (xarray > 0);
xWhenPosElseZero = xPos .* xarray;
xNeg = (xarray < 0);
minusxWhenNegElseZero = xNeg .* (-xarray);
xarrayAbsVal = xWhenPosElseZero + minusxWhenNegElseZero;
```

Finally, let's not forget MATLAB's built-in function `abs`, which we used with a scalar argument in Chapter 6.2, and now use with the array argument `xarray`.

```
%arbitrary initial value for xarray for demonstration
xarray   = [-7 3 -2 4];

%yarray will receive absolute values of xarray entries
yarray   = abs(xarray);
```

There are several considerations when choosing one implementation over another. One obvious consideration is counting the number of lines of code. For example, the first implementation could be done using two fewer lines:

```
%arbitrary initial value for xarray for demonstration
xarray   = [-7 3 -2 4];

%yarray will receive absolute values of xarray entries
yarray   = zeros(4);

for i=1:4
    if (xarray(i) < 0)
        yarray(i)   = -xarray(i);
    else
        yarray(i)   = xarray(i);
    end
end
```

We prefer the first implementation over this one because it highlights the fact that we pluck each entry out of `xarray`, inspect its value in the `if-statement`, and then assign the result to `yarray`. In this version, without examining each of the if-else-end conditions, it is not so clear as in the first implementation that `yarray(i)` is assigned a value each iteration through the loop. Additionally, if for some reason the index `i` needed to be changed to `i+1`, then this version requires we catch each of the occurrences buried deeper in the for-if-else-end-end nesting. Finally, since the if-else-end part of the code had already been verified to be correct for the scalar case, it is safer to reuse it as-is in the array version; one always risks introducing errors when modifying code!

In addition to the issues of increasing readability and decreasing exposure to errors, there is the fundamentally important consideration of "performance". Put simply, performance refers to the speed of execution, and because of its quantitative nature it is not subject to the same stylistic debates that often accompany the issues discussed in the previous paragraph. Since MATLAB provides a mechanism to measure the execution time of a fragment of code, the question of how efficiently one implementation performs compared to another can thankfully

8.3. Performance: for-loop vs. array-operation vs. built-in implementations

be answered by a completely objective procedure[1]. On the other hand, since performance is not always the *only* consideration, qualitative considerations must still be evaluated. Presumably, code that is unreadable and error-prone, even if it executes 5% faster in 20% of the cases, should be rejected!

MATLAB's mechanism for timing execution is provided by the tic and toc instructions. An internal timer is reset to start "ticking" when the tic instruction executes, and the value of the internal timer can be read by executing the toc instruction. We illustrate the use of tic and toc by comparing the execution time of each of the three implementations of the absolute value of an array.

```
%initialize the size of xarray
n       = 10;

%initialize yarray to receive n values,
yarray  = zeros(1,n);

%initialize xarray with roughly (on average) half its entries positive,
% and half its entries negative
xarray  = rand(1,n) - 0.5*ones(1,n);

%start the timer with tic-instruction
tic
for i=1:n
    x       = xarray(i);
    if (x < 0)
        yarray(i)   = -x;
    else
        yarray(i)   = x;
    end
end
%stop the timer with toc-instruction, display timing output to screen
timer   = toc
```

After running the above code, we discover that the displayed execution time is 0! Of course, the execution time is some non-zero number, but if it is smaller than the minimum time increment MATLAB uses in its internal tic-toc timing (one says it "exceeds the resolution" of MATLAB's stopwatch timer), then it cannot be deduced directly. On the other, there is a trick to indirectly deduce its value. If one puts the code whose execution time is to be measured *inside a loop*, then a sufficient number of repetitions will eventually be measurable; dividing this measured

---

[1]Needless to say, there are subtleties associated with performance evaluation, in spite of its quantitative nature. For example, since performance is often dependent on the initial data, one might have to quantify "worst-case", "average-case", and "best-case" behavior.

time by the number of repetitions will give the execution time of an individual instance of the code. The following variant of the above implementation incorporates this timing trick.

```
%initialize the size of xarray
n       = 10;
%initialize the number of repetitions of code fragment to be timed
nTicToc = 10000;

%initialize array with roughly (on average) half its entries positive,
% and half its entries negative
xarray = rand(1,n) - 0.5*ones(1,n);
yarray = zeros(1,n);

%start the timer with tic-instruction
tic
for j=1:nTicToc
    for i=1:n
        if (xarray(i) < 0)
            yarray(i)   = -xarray(i);
        else
            yarray(i)   = xarray(i);
        end
    end
end
%stop the timer with toc-instruction, display timing output to screen
timer   = toc/nTicToc
```

Exercise 48

One might argue that the encapsulation of the code by the for-statement introduces some overhead that will distort the timing. How valid is this objection when the number of repetitions is large? In particular, suggest a method for determining an acceptable value of the counter nTicToc.

Exercise 49

Why do we not start the timing by placing the tic instruction before the n = 10 statement?

8.3. Performance: for-loop vs. array-operation vs. built-in implementations

---

Exercise 50

Do you suppose that using `xarray = rand(1,n)` or `xarray = randn(1,n)` could affect the timing calculation? Verify your guess.

Exercise 51

How does the performance of the following code compare with the three implementations given above?
```
for i=1:n
   xarray(i) = abs(xarray(i));
end
```
How is the performance affected if we remove the trailing semi-colon so that `xarray(i)` is displayed to the screen? How about if we use the code fragment from Exercise 47?

Needless to say, all things being equal one should always use the most efficient implementation. But how do we "verify" that all things are, in fact, "equal"? One strategy is to keep both implementations in your program running side-by-side and always compare their results for equality; when the time comes to release your code in final form simply remove (or comment out) the less efficient implementation. One can use the MATLAB instruction `isequal` to compare two arrays (of the same size) for equality. In the code below we consolidate all of the ideas discussed in this section.

```
1  %%%%%%%%%%%%%%%%%%%%%%%%%%%%%%%%%%%%%%%%%
2  %%   AbsPerformanceTest.m
3  %%%%%%%%%% Initialization %%%%%%%%%%
4  n         = 10;             %size of xarray
5  nTicToc   = 10000;          %number of repetitions of instructions being timed
6  randArray = randn(1,n);     %randomize test data (normally distributed)
7  xarray    = randArray;      %create copy for for-loop implementation
8  yarray    = randArray;      %create copy for array-operation implementation
9  zarray    = randArray;      %create copy for built-in abs() implementation
10 Xarray    = zeros(1,n);     %create repository for abs(xarray)
11 Yarray    = zeros(1,n);     %create repository for abs(yarray)
12 Zarray    = zeros(1,n);     %create repository for abs(zarray)
13 %%%%%%%%%%%%%%%%%%%%%%%%%%%%%%%%%%%%%%%%%%
14 %% Performance Analysis of three implementations of abs(randArray)
15 %%%%%%%%%%%%%%%%%%%%%%%%%%%%%%%%%%%%%%%%%%
16 %%%%%%% for-loop implementation %%%%%%%
17 tic              %start timer
```

```
18 for j=1:nTicToc
19     for i=1:n
20         if (xarray(i) < 0)
21             Xarray(i)   = -xarray(i);
22         else
23             Xarray(i)   = xarray(i);
24         end
25     end
26 end
27 timer   = toc/nTicToc;  %stop timer, account for number repetitions
28 str     = sprintf('for-loop');
29 fprintf('\nExecution time of %s implementation:\n\t%e seconds\n',str, timer);
30
31 %%%%%%% array-operation implementation %%%%%%%
32 tic           %restart timer
33 for j=1:nTicToc
34     Yarray = (yarray > 0).*yarray + (yarray < 0) .* (-yarray);
35 end
36 timer   = toc/nTicToc;  %stop timer, account for number repetitions
37 str     = sprintf('array-operation');
38 fprintf('\nExecution time of %s implementation:\n\t%e seconds\n',str, timer);
39
40 %%%%%%% built-in abs() implementation %%%%%%%
41 tic           %restart timer
42 for j=1:nTicToc
43     Zarray = abs(zarray);
44 end
45 timer   = toc/nTicToc;  %stop timer, account for number repetitions
46 str     = sprintf('built-in abs()');
47 fprintf('\nExecution time of %s implementation:\n\t%e seconds\n',str, timer);
48
49 %%%%%%% check for accuracy of implementations %%%%%%%
50 %use logical function isequal()
51 % to test if two arrays agree in all components
52 if isequal(Xarray,Zarray)
53     fprintf('\nfor-loop implementation agrees with abs()\n');
54 else
55     fprintf('\nfor-loop implementation disagrees with abs()\n');
56 end
57
58 if isequal(Yarray,Zarray)
59     fprintf('\narray-operation implementation agrees with abs()\n');
60 else
```

```
61      fprintf('\narray-operation implementation disagrees with abs()\n');
62 end
```

Executing AbsPerformanceTest.m results in the following output:

```
Execution time of for-loop implementation:
    4.407543e-007 seconds

Execution time of array-operation implementation:
    6.926299e-006 seconds

Execution time of built-in abs() implementation:
    2.685537e-007 seconds

for-loop implementation agrees with abs()
array-operation implementation agrees with abs()
```

> **Exercise 52**
>
> Give two explanations for why your results may differ from those above. Rerun AbsPerformanceTest and comment on the consistency of the output. Change the `randn` instruction in line 6 to `rand` and explain why some implementations perform better.

8.4 Topics covered in this chapter

In this chapter we presented a comprehensive description of $(1 \times n)$ arrays, the so-called row vectors. We will see in Chapter 15 that the row vectors considered here are a special case of more general arrays called matrices. Nonetheless, row vectors are by themselves of paramount importance; their utility in storing data and representing strings would alone justify our devoting this chapter to them. We also introduced the topic of *performance*, and explained techniques for measuring and comparing the execution times of several code implementations. The following MATLAB operations and commands have been described:

1. Array initialization: `zeros()`, `ones()`, `rand()`, `randn()`, `linspace()`

2. Component-wise operations with arrays: `+`, `-`, `.*`, `./`, `.^`, `<`, `>`

3. Algebraic operations on arrays by scalars: `+`, `-`, `*`, `/`

4. Boolean functions of arrays: `isequal()`

5. Performance-related commands: `tic`, `toc`

Chapter 9

Arrays III

9.1 Accessing array elements

In this section we explain how individual elements of an array may be extracted. The simplest case is to extract a single component entry of an array as a scalar, which we've already employed in earlier implementations of NewtonAlg.m and some examples of the previous chapter. For example, if x = linspace(0,1,5), then the third element can be obtained as x(3) giving the value 0.5. We illustrate in the following Command Window session the rich variety of techniques for extracting a single component, a sub-array of contiguous elements, or even an array formed from arbitrary subsets of array elements.

```
 1 >> x   = linspace(0,1,5)
 2 x = 0   0.2500   0.5000   0.7500   1.0000
 3
 4 >> z = x(2)
 5 z = 0.2500
 6
 7 >> z = x(5)
 8 z = 1
 9
10 >> z = x(end)
11 z = 1
12
13 >> z = x(6)
14 ???  Index exceeds matrix dimensions.
```

x(k) — line 4

x(end) — line 10

create array x which is initialized to 5 equally spaced points between 0 and 1 (inclusive)

assign to z the scalar which is the 2nd element of the array x

assign to z the scalar which is the 5th element of the array x

assign to z the scalar which is the last element of the array x

assign to z the scalar which is the 6th element of the array x - but since there is no 6th element of the 5-element array x, this results in an error

87

x(i:j)
```
1 >> z = x(1:3)
2 z = 0      0.2500    0.5000
3
4 >> z = x(3:5)
5 z = 0.5000    0.7500    1.0000
6
```
assign to z the 3-element array consisting of the first 3 entries x(1), x(2), x(3)

assign to z the 3-element array consisting of the elements x(3), x(4), x(5)

x(i:end)
```
7 >> z = x(3:end)
8 z =
9      0.5000    0.7500    1.0000
10
11 >> z = x(3:end) - x(1:end-2)
12 z = 0.5000    0.5000    0.5000
13
```
assign to z the 3-element array consisting of the entries in x beginning with x(3) through the last element x(end)=x(5)

assign to z the 3-element array of the differences x(3)-x(1), x(4)-x(2), x(5) - x(3)

length function
```
14 >> n = length(x)
15 n =   5
16
17 >> nOneThird  = ceil(n/3)
18 nOneThird =
19        2
20
21 >> nTwoThird  = ceil(2*n/3)
22 nTwoThird =
23        4
24
25 >> z = x(nOneThird:nTwoThird)
26 z = 0.2500    0.5000    0.7500
27
```
assign to n the number of elements in x

assign to nOneThird the index corresponding to a position one-third into the array x

assign to nTwoThird the index corresponding to a position two-thirds into the array x

assign to z the 3-element array consisting of the middle-third sub-array of x

x([i,j,...,k])
```
28 >> z = x([1,2,5,2])
29 z = 0      0.2500    1.0000    0.2500
```
assign to z the 4-element array consisting of the entries x(1), x(2), x(5), x(2)

Exercise 53

Which of the examples above are special cases of the following rule:
$$x(y) := [x(y(1)), x(y(2)), \ldots, x(y(end-1)), x(y(end))]$$
What assumptions must be made on the entries of y in order for the above expression x(y) to be legitimate? Also, what is the length of x(y)?

> **Exercise 54**
>
> Lookup the built-in functions `diff` and `fliplr`. Give an equivalent implementation of each of these functions using the constructs introduced above.

> **Solution 54**
>
> ```
> diff(x)   := x(2:end) - x(1:end-1)
> fliplr(x) := x(length(x):-1:1)
> ```

> **Exercise 55**
>
> A *string* in MATLAB is nothing more than an array of characters. Explain how the following constructs work:
> ```
> str1 = ['H','e','l','l','o']
> str2 = ['W','o','r','l','d']
> str3 = [str1, str2]
> str4 = [str1, ' ', str2]
> str5 = fliplr([fliplr(str1),fliplr(str2)])
> str6 = str5([length(str2)+1:end,1:length(str1)])
> str7 = isequal(str1,'Hello')
> str8 = isequal(str3,str6)
> ```

9.2 Using arrays to represent mathematical functions

Mathematical functions are usually first introduced to students in Calculus courses, where one needs to understand how dependent variables (like the position of a projectile) "depend on" or "vary with respect to" an independent variable (like time). For example, one may recall Galileo's discovery that the height of a ball rolling down a plane inclined at the angle α obeys the law:
$$h(t) = (\tfrac{1}{2}g \sin \alpha)t^2 + h_0.$$
Here, $g = 32$ ft/sec^2 is the gravitational constant at the surface of the Earth, and h_0 indicates the initial height of the ball when it is released with no initial velocity. It is easily verified that the function $h(t)$ satisfies the following three necessary properties:
$$h(0) = h_0, \qquad h'(0) = 0, \qquad h''(t) = g \sin \alpha.$$
Mathematicians, physicists, and other scientists routinely treat physical quantities as belonging to a *continuum*: time and frequency ($\mathbb{R} = (-\infty, \infty)$), space and electric fields ($\mathbb{R}^3$), mass and

electrical resistance ($\mathbb{R}^+ = [0, \infty)$), acoustic and optical phase ($\mathbb{T}^1 = [-\pi, \pi]$), to name a few. In the example above, h assigns to each time after the ball is released the value of the height above the ground; thus, h assigns to each element of its "domain" $t \in \mathbb{R}^+$ a corresponding element in its "range" $h(t) \in \mathbb{R}^+$. On the other hand, experimentalists who deal with the world of measurement are always mindful (regardless of the philosophical question of whether continuum models are idealizations of reality) of the necessity of representing physical quantities by numerical data. In this context it is both natural and necessary to treat the domains and ranges of these mathematical functions as finite collections of numeric values. This discussion is meant to justify, indeed motivate, the transition from the mathematical description of a function

$$f : [a, b] \longrightarrow [c, d]$$

to its MATLAB description:

$$[x_0 = a, x_1, \ldots, x_{n-1}, x_n = b] \longrightarrow [y_0 = c, y_1, \ldots, y_{n-1}, y_n = d].$$

In this way, arrays make an appearance in MATLAB as representations of the (interval) domains of mathematical functions.

It is interesting to recall that in theoretical math classes the concept of a *function*

$$f : X \to Y,$$

and more generally that of a *relation*, are abstractly defined as subsets of $X \times Y$. Surprisingly, although this definition is often confusing to beginning students who consider it unduly abstract, it is quite natural and appropriate from the MATLAB point of view! For example, we will see later that when MATLAB plots a function with the command `plot(x,y)`, where $x = [x_1, \ldots, x_n]$ and $y = [y_1, \ldots, y_n]$, it is not necessarily productive to view y being graphed as a function depending on the independent variable x, as suggested by the mathematical notation

$$y = y(x);$$

it is enough to understand that what is plotted is the collection of (x, y)-pairs

$$(x_1, y_1), \ldots, (x_n, y_n),$$

or

$$[\mathtt{x(1)},\mathtt{y(1)}], \ldots, [\mathtt{x(end)},\mathtt{y(end)}].$$

In other words, mathematical functions $f : \mathbb{R} \to \mathbb{R}$ are represented in MATLAB as nothing more than a collection of (x, y)-pairs, which is to say a *pair of arrays*. More precisely, we should say a *pair of row-vectors of the same size*.

9.2. Using arrays to represent mathematical functions

Exercise 56

The operation $x \to x^{0.5}$ on $[0,1]$ is an example of a *relation* that is not a *function*, since both positive and negative square roots are "assigned" to the same positive number. Mathematically, one prefers to consider the set (y^2, y) rather than the set $(x, x^{0.5})$ when describing this relation. If we crudely represent the interval $[0,1]$ by [0, 0.25, 0.64, 1], then specify arrays x and y to use in the plot(x,y) command for plotting this relation (without connecting data points with line segments).

Solution 56

One possible solution is
   x = [0,.25,.25,.64,.64,1,1], y = [0,.5,-.5,.8,-.8,1,-1].
Another solution is given by
   x = [1,.64,.25,0,.25,.64,1], y = [-1,-.8,-.5,0,.5,.8,1].

We already saw in the previous section how a certain function originally introduced in the context of scalar functions, namely abs, can be used to operate on arrays. Specifically, abs acts on the array x by the rule

$$\text{abs(x)} := [\text{abs(x(1))}, \text{abs(x(2))}, \ldots, \text{abs(x(end))}]$$

This property allows abs to be applied to an array of numbers representing the discretization of an interval domain, thereby producing a corresponding array of absolute values representing a discretization of its range. For example, if we represent the interval $[-1,1]$ by the array x = linspace(-1,1,100), then the mathematical function $x \to |x|$ is represented by the pair of arrays

$$\text{x, abs(x)}$$

As explained in our earlier discussion on relations, this is consistent with the mathematical viewpoint in which $x \to |x|$ *is* the set

$$\{(x, |x|) \mid x \in \mathbb{R}\} \subset \mathbb{R}^2.$$

We emphasize that the mathematical function $x \to |x|$ remains a *scalar* function; it is only its representation by the pair x, abs(x) that utilizes the vectorized incarnation of abs(). This discussion can similarly be applied to other scalar functions like sin() and exp(). Though we defer to the next chapter a full discussion of MATLAB's plot command, we introduce it here in its simplest form as a way of graphically displaying a set of (x,y)-pairs. Just as we freely used the fprintf command in an earlier chapter before properly giving its definition, we now indulge in utilizing the plot command to help illustrate the use of arrays as mathematical functions.

Chapter 9. Arrays III

`>> x    = linspace(-pi,pi,5)`
`x =`
`   -3.1416  -1.5708   0   1.5708   3.1416`
	crudely represent the interval $[-\pi, \pi]$ with the 5-element array `x`

sin function `>> y1   = sin(x)`
`y1 =`
`   -0.0000  -1.0000   0   1.0000   0.0000`
	assign to `y1` the 5-element array $[\mathtt{sin(x(1)),sin(x(2)),\ldots,sin(x(5))}]=$ $[\sin(-3.1416), \sin(-1.5708), ..., \sin(3.1416)]$

`>> y2   = x.^2`
`y2 =`
`   9.8696   2.4674   0   2.4674   9.8696`
	assign to `y2` the 5-element array $[\mathtt{x(1)\char`\^2,x(2)\char`\^2,x(3)\char`\^2,x(4)\char`\^2,x(5)\char`\^2}]=$ $[(-3.1416)^2, (-1.5708)^2, (0)^2, (1.5708)^2, (3.1416)^2]$

`>> y3   = sin(4*x)`
`y3 =`
`   1.0e-015 *`
`    0.4899   0.2449   0  -0.2449  -0.4899`
	assign to `y3` the 5-element array $[\mathtt{sin(4*x(1)),\ldots,sin(4*x(5))}]=$ $[\sin(4(-3.1416)), \ldots, \sin(4(3.1416))]$

`>> y4   = sin(x.*x)`
`y4 =`
`   -0.4303   0.6243   0   0.6243  -0.4303`
	assign to `y4` the 5-element array $[\mathtt{sin(x(1)*x(1)),\ldots,sin(x(5)*x(5))}]=$ $[\sin((-3.1416)^2), \ldots, \sin((3.1416)^2)]$

plot command `>> plot(x,y1,'-o',x,y2,'-o',...` `          x,y3,'-o',x,y4,'-o')`	generate a plot simultaneously showing the four *pairs* of 5-element arrays: for each function, put a circle at each of its 5 data points and connect them with line segments
`>> x    = linspace(-pi,pi,100);`	represent the interval $[-\pi, \pi]$ with the 100-element array `x` (and suppress output)

`>> plot(x,y1,x,y2,x,y3,x,y4)`
`??? Error using ==> plot`
`Vectors must be the same lengths.`
	plot command results in error since `x` has length 100, whereas `y1,y2,y3,y4` have 5 elements each

`>> y1   = sin(x);`
`>> y2   = x.^2;`
`>> y3   = sin(4*x);`
`>> y4   = sin(x.*x);`
	repeat earlier assignments to generate 100 y-values corresponding to the 100 x-values

`>> plot(x,y1,x,y2,x,y3,x,y4)`	generate a plot simultaneously showing the four *pairs* of 100-element arrays

The results of the above tutorial are displayed in the following figures:

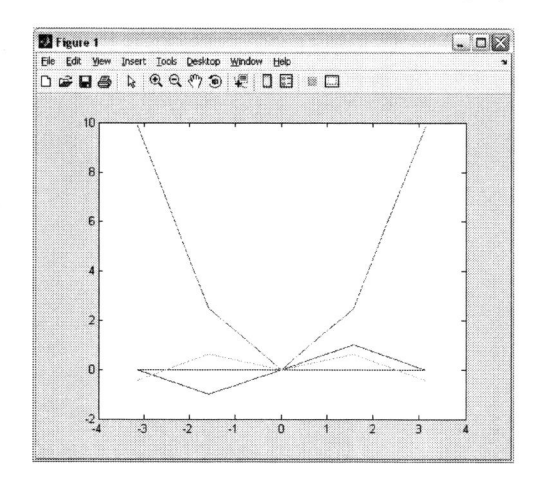

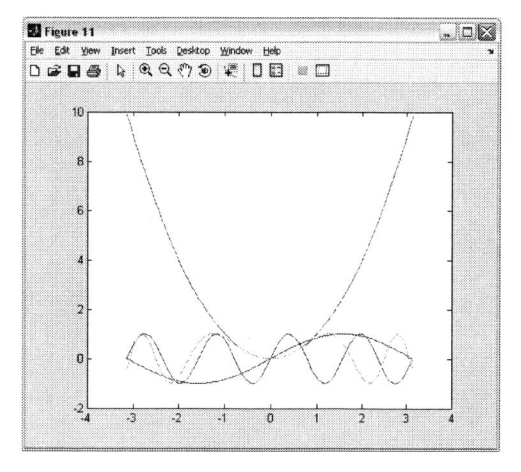

Just as a scalar function of a single variable on an interval domain is represented by a pair of arrays, MATLAB represents a scalar function of two variables on a rectangular domain as a *triple of two-dimensional arrays*. We will return to this topic after discussing multi-dimensional arrays in Chapter 15.

9.3 Topics covered in this chapter

In this chapter we continued our five-part journey into the extraordinarily rich subject of arrays. After explaining how arrays can be used to represent mathematical functions, we gave a taste of MATLAB's graphical capabilities by introducing some elementary plotting. The following MATLAB functions and constructs have been described:

1. Array access: `x(3)`, `x([1 2 3 2 1])`, `x(3:end)`

2. Array functions: `diff()`, `fliplr()`

3. Graphical output: `plot()`

Chapter 10

Plotting I

When we discussed arrays in the previous chapters we also introduced, in an ad-hoc manner, the `plot` command. This was appropriate since one of the essential uses of arrays is the graphical representation of mathematical functions. In this chapter we proceed to give a more comprehensive presentation of `plot`.

10.1 Plotting a collection of data points in the plane

Since our perceptions are so strongly influenced, if not dominated, by the faculty of vision, the value of plotting data hardly needs any explanation. It is sometimes true that plots are deceptive, and without zooming in on regions of interest, pathological behavior can go unnoticed. On the other hand, plots should be the first line of attack in exploring the behavior of functions, and when certain behaviors can be provably established, they are usually the best means available to an author for communicating these results.

We first recall our last version of NewtonAlg.m.

```
1  %%%%%%%%%%%%%%%%%%%%%%%%%%%%%%%
2  %%%%%%%%%%% NewtonAlg8.m %%%%%%%
3  %%%% initialization section %%%%%
4  %initialization (hardwired variables)
5  x0      = 2;
6  nIter   = 5;
7  %initialization (not hardwired)
8  xvals   = zeros(1,nIter);
9
10 %%%%%%%%%%%%%%%%%%%%%%%%%%%%%%%
11 %%%% algorithm section %%%%%%%%%%
12 xvals(1)   = x0;
13 for i=2:nIter
14     x          = xvals(i-1);
```

Chapter 10. Plotting I

```
15    xvals(i) = x - (x^2 - 5)/(2*x);
16 end
17
18 %%%%%%%%%%%%%%%%%%%%%%%%%%%%%%
19 %%%%%%% output section %%%%%%%%%%
20 fprintf('\niteration \t Xn \t\t |Xn - Xn-1| \t |Xn^2-5|');
21 fprintf('\n--------------------------------------------------');
22 fprintf('\n%d \t\t %f \t\t%f \t\t%f',...
23     [1:nIter; xvals; [0, abs(xvals(2:end) - xvals(1:end-1))];,...
24     abs(xvals.^2 - 5)]);
```

Executing the above code produces the following tabular output:

```
1 iteration      Xn           |Xn - Xn-1|     |Xn^2-5|
2 --------------------------------------------------
3 1            2.000000       0.000000        1.000000
4 2            2.250000       0.250000        0.062500
5 3            2.236111       0.013889        0.000193
6 4            2.236068       0.000043        0.000000
7 5            2.236068       0.000000        0.000000
```

Inspecting the above table, it is easy to observe that $|X_n - X_{n-1}| \longrightarrow 0$, and $|X_n^2 - 5| \longrightarrow 0$. On the other hand, by plotting X_n, $|X_n - X_{n-1}|$, and $|X_n^2 - 5|$ as n takes on the values $2, 3, 4, 5$ we can get visual feedback on the convergence of these quantities.

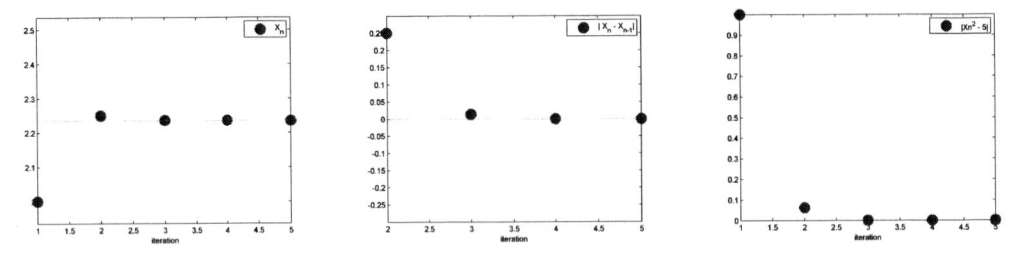

The above figures are produced by substituting the following plot code for the fprintf code in the output section of NewtonAlg8.m.

```
1 sqrt5       = sqrt(5);
2 allSqrtFive = sqrt5 * ones(1,nIter);
3 figure(100)
4 plot(1:nIter, xvalues,'o',1:nIter, allSqrtFive,':',...
5     'MarkerFaceColor','r','MarkerSize',14);
6 axis([1,nIter,sqrt5-0.3,sqrt5+0.3])
7 legend('X_n')
8 xlabel('iteration')
9
```

10.1. Plotting a collection of data points in the plane

```
10 allZeros    = zeros(1,nIter-1);
11 figure(200)
12 plot(2:nIter, abs(xvalues(2:end) - xvalues(1:end-1)),'o',...
13      2:nIter, allZeros,':','MarkerFaceColor','r','MarkerSize',14);
14 axis([2,nIter,-0.3,0.3])
15 legend('| X_n - X_{n-1}|')
16 xlabel('iteration')
17 figure(300)
18 plot(1:nIter, abs(xvalues.^2 - 5), 'o',...
19      'MarkerFaceColor','r','MarkerSize',14);
20 legend('|Xn^2 - 5|')
21 xlabel('iteration')
```

This example is especially simplistic in two respects. First, the information it conveys is easily discernible from the table of six-digit decimal numbers. Second, the plot represents a function with *integer arguments*, i.e. the domain is the set of whole numbers $\{2, 3, 4, 5\}$. More substantive applications of plotting involve functions whose arguments take values in an interval $[a, b] \subset \mathbb{R}$, and which display relationships difficult or impossible to discern from inspecting tables containing thousands of floating-point numbers.

The next tutorial session introduces the basics of plotting some continuous functions on an interval by displaying their (x, y)-pairs. We also show how to display multiple plots in one figure, and how to manipulate line-drawing attributes such as width and color.

```
1 %%%%%%%%%%%%%%%%%%%%%%%%%%%%%%%%
2 %%%%%%%%% PlottingTutorial.m %%%%
3 %create 1x100 array x discretizing interval [-pi,pi]
4 x   = linspace(-pi,pi,100);
5
6 %create a figure, arbitrarily assigned the figure number 100
7 figure(100)
8
9 %plot the data points (1,x(1)),...,(100,x(100))
10 plot(x)
11
12 %plot the data points (1,x(1)),...,(100,x(100))
13 plot(1:100,x)
14
15 %plot the data points (100,x(100)),...,(1,x(1))
16 plot(100:-1:1,x)
17
18 %assign to y1 the array [sin(x(1)),...,sin(x(100))]
19 y1  = sin(x);
20
```

```
21 %plot the data points (1,y1(1)),...,(100,y1(100))
22 plot(y1)
23
24 %plot the data points (x(1),y1(1)),...,(x(100),y1(100))
25 plot(x,y1)
26
27 %re-plot the (x,y1) data points using red instead of blue
28 plot(x,y1,'r')
29
30 %assign to y2 the array [(x(1))^2,...,(x(100))^2]
31 y2 = x.^2;
32
33 %plot the data points (x(1),y2(1)),...,(x(100),y2(100)) in green
34 plot(x,y2,'g')
35
36 %assign to y3 the array [sin(x(1)^2),...,sin(x(100)^2)]
37 y3 = sin(x.^2);
38
39 %plot the data points (x(1),y3(1)),...,(x(100),y3(100)) in yellow
40 % using a line thickness of 4
41 plot(x,y3,'y','LineWidth',4)
42
43 %tell subsequent plot commands not to clobber what's currently plotted
44 hold on
45
46 %assign to y4 the array [sin(x(1))*sin(x(1)),...,sin(x(100))*sin(x(100))]
47 y4 = sin(x.*x);
48
49 %plot the data points (x(1),y4(1)),...,(x(100),y4(100)) in black
50 plot(x,y4,'k')
51
52 %add a legend indicating which functions are graphed in yellow and black
53 legend('sin(x^2)','sin(x*x)')
```

> **Exercise 57**
>
> Suppose the array x is specified by the function $e^{sinh(t^3)}$, and assume the values of t are given by linspace(-10,10). Describe the *shape* of the graph which results from the command plot(x,x).

After creating the file PlottingTutorial.m and entering the above code, set a breakpoint at the first instruction and single-step the entire program. After stepping through each plot-related command, observe how the figure changes. The final image is reproduced below.

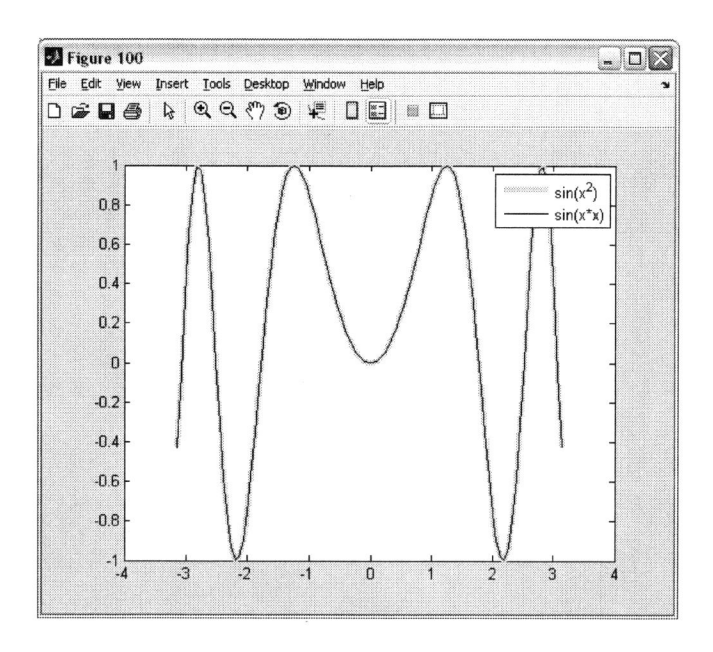

[Figure: Figure 100 window showing plot of $\sin(x^2)$ and $\sin(x*x)$ over $x \in [-4, 4]$.]

10.2 Controlling the appearance of plots

Adding supplementary textual information to your figures is not simply a matter of "cosmetics". First, it enables one to create figures that are more or less "self-documenting", which is to say, the results of a computer simulation can be meaningfully communicated even without collateral documentation. For example, an assignment in numerical analysis which consists solely of a well-documented figure and no accompanying essay can be more effective than one which consists of many pages of floating-point output in which clusters of data have been identified with comments like "notice how these numbers are getting smaller", or "notice how these numbers appear to be quadratically related to those other numbers". Second, one finds in their own research that certain simulations produce output worth examining in more complete detail, for example evidence of a new experimental relationship or a counter-example to a mathematical conjecture, and naturally one will want to snapshot these "smoking gun" plots by saving them to a file. In these cases, especially if specific parameter values and initial data are presumed, you will find that self-explanatory text embedded into the plots themselves is invaluable; when dealing with scores of figures, it is simply not practical to rely on encoding this information into a clever filename.

We continue our discussion of plotting by explaining how to add text for titles, legends, axis labels, and even explanatory comments targeted to specific parts of a figure. In the following Command Window session we assume the arrays x,y1,y2,y3,y4 are intact from the previous section. Also, note the many instances of the line continuation character '...' in the code.

figure function
```
1 >> figure(200)
2
3 >> plot(x,y1,x,y2,x,y3,x,y4)
4
```
make a new figure, assigned number 200

plot all four functions in one `plot` instruction (using `hold` is preferable)

legend function
```
 5
 6 >> legend('sin(x)','x^2',...
 7    'sin(x^2)','sin(x*x)')
 8
 9 >> str1    = 'sin(x)';
10 >> str2    = 'x^2';
11 >> str3    = 'sin(x^2)';
12
13 >> legend(str1, str2, str3, str3)
14
```
add legend by associating a string to each of the four plots (default position is upper-right corner)

create string variables utilizing LaTeX character for exponentiation ^

use `legend` command with string variables which contain LaTeX symbols

text function
```
15
16 >> text(-1.8, 4.2,...
17    '\leftarrow y = x^2','FontSize',18)
18
19
20 >> cr    = sprintf('\n');
21
22
23 >> text(-1, -1.3,...
24    ['\uparrow', cr, str1])
25
26
27
28 >> str4 = sprintf('%s\n%s',...
29    str3, '\downarrow');
30 >> text(-1.9, 1.15, str4)
```
add text positioned at $(-1.8, 4.2)$ in 18 point where text string is given explicitly (note use of LaTeX character `\leftarrow`)

trick for getting the "newline character" into a variable

add text positioned at $(-1, -1.3)$ in default Font size where text string is created by combining three strings into one array (note use of LaTeX character `\uparrow`)

third and best method to add text using string variable created with `sprintf` (note use of `\n` and LaTeX character `\downarrow`)

xlabel function
```
31
32 >> xlabel('-\pi \leq x \leq \pi')
33
```
label the x-axis $-\pi \leq x < \pi$
note use of LaTeX characters `\leq` and `\pi`

ylabel function
```
34
35 >> ylabel(['y = ',str3])
36
```
label the y-axis $y = \sin(x^2)$

title function
```
37 >> title(['illustrate the plot ',...
38    'command with four functions',cr,...
39    'using legend, text, xlabel ,',...
40    'ylabel, and title.'])
```
add a title (note how awkward compared with formatted `sprintf` technique)

10.2. Controlling the appearance of plots

hold on function
```
41 >> hold on
42
43
44 >> plot([x(1),x(end)],[0,0],'k-')
45
46
47 >> plot([0,0],[min([y1,y2,y3,y4]),...
48        max([y1,y2,y3,y4])],'k-')
49
50 >> xmin    = -2;
51 >> xmax    = 2;
52 >> ymin    = -1;
53 >> ymax    = 2;
```
axis function
```
54 >> axis([xmin,xmax,ymin,ymax])
55
56 >> plot([xmin,xmax],[0,0],'k-',...
57        'LineWidth',3)
58 >> plot([0,0],[ymin,ymax],'k-',...
59        'LineWidth',3)
60
61 >> xlabel([num2str(xmin),...
62        ' \leq x \leq ', num2str(xmax)])
63
64 >> s = sprintf('%d\\leq y\\leq %d',...
65        ymin, ymax);
66 >> ylabel(s)
```

use `hold on` to tell subsequent `plot` commands not to clobber existing plots	
add x-axis by plotting the line which connects $(x_1,0)$ and $(x_n,0)$	
add y-axis to accommodate each of the four functions (note data points can have same x-values)	
create variables to specify new axis limits	
use `axis` command to impose limits on display	
redraw the x-axis using extra thick lines	
redraw the y-axis using extra thick lines	
relabel the x-axis using second technique	
relabel the y-axis using preferred technique	

Exercise 58

Can you explain why a double backslash is required in line 64 of the code from above: `str = sprintf('%d \\leq y \\leq %d', ymin, ymax);` Can you suggest a method which avoids the double backslash?

Solution 58

This is called "escaping-the-escape", since we need to suppress (or escape) MATLAB's interpretation of the backslash character when composing the string `str`. In other words, we want the `\leq` deposited into `str` as-is, so that it will be intact as a recognizable LaTeX character by the subsequent `text()` command. An alternative method avoiding the double backslash is:
`str = sprintf('%d %s y %s %d', ymin, '\leq', '\leq', ymax);`

Chapter 10. Plotting I

The figure which results from executing the above plotting commands *up until the axis command* (line 54) is reproduced below.

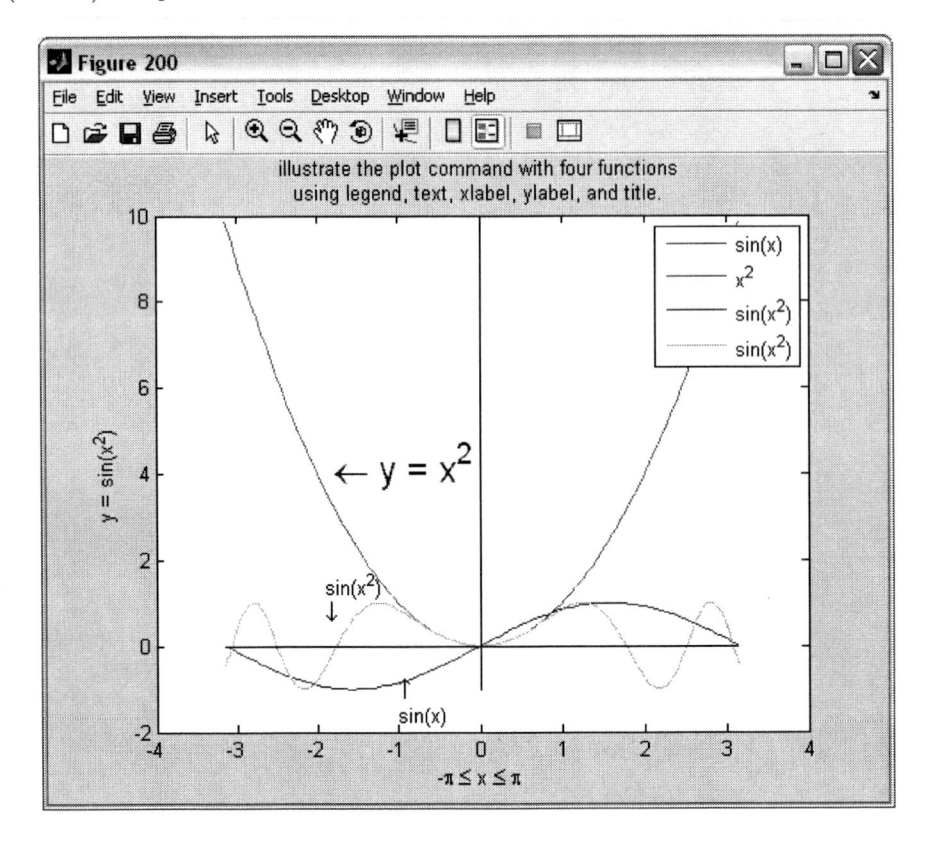

[Figure 200: illustrate the plot command with four functions using legend, text, xlabel, ylabel, and title. Legend: sin(x), x^2, sin(x^2), sin(x^2). Annotations: ← $y = x^2$, sin(x^2), sin(x). Axes: $y = \sin(x^2)$ vs $-\pi \leq x \leq \pi$.]

Exercise 59

Observe how the `axis` command distorts the location of the `text` commands. Lookup how the "Units" property works, and try to correct this.

Exercise 60

Lookup the `legend` command and determine how to reposition it in the lower-left corner of the figure. Manually reposition the legend anywhere on the figure using the mouse, and then determine the new coordinates using the Figure Properties dialog from the Edit menu.

10.2. Controlling the appearance of plots

> **Exercise 61**
>
> Using the Help Browser, investigate the use of other LaTeX symbols which can be used with the `text` function.

An important aspect of generating figures is the ability to directly print them, or to export them to an image file which can be included in a larger document. For example, this book was created as a .pdf-formatted document using the typesetting language LaTeX, and the figures included in this document were imported by LaTeX as .png-formatted image files. How were these .png-formatted image files originally created? Figures generated in MATLAB can be *exported* as image files of many types, the most common of which are the .png, .eps, .gif, and .jpg file types. Understanding how a particular document processing program such as LaTeX or PDFLaTeX interacts with each of these file types is best learned through experimentation. For example, saving our figures as .png-formatted image files has the nice benefit that the details of the image remain present in the document, even if some details of the text are marginally readable at normal resolution. Indeed, if you are viewing this book electronically as a .pdf-formatted file, you can view the above figure by zooming in to 200% magnification. A snapshot of the legend in the upper right, magnified two-fold, appears below on the left.

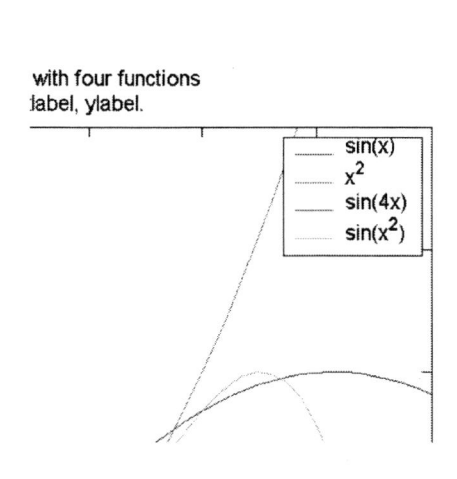

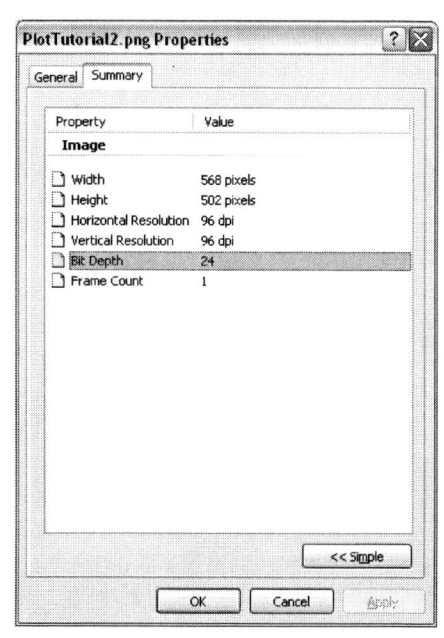

Some applications require that you specify a *bounding box* for an image, which should be faithful to the dimensions stored in the saved file. One way to determine these dimensions is to inspect the file properties; right-clicking on the file's icon and selecting Properties will display a dialog containing this information, similar to the dialog shown above on the right.

> **Exercise 62**
>
> Depending on your document creation tools, you may decide to use image files of a specific filetype such as .eps, .jpg, or .png. Using the "Save As" dialog from the Figure Window, save an image of your plot in each of these three formats. Also, save the figure file itself as a MATLAB .fig-file.

> **Exercise 63**
>
> Images displayed on computer monitors are adequately rendered at 72 dpi (dots per inch) using the RGB color model (for light), and this is MATLAB's default setting. On the other hand, it is preferable to render printed images at 300 dpi using the CMYK color model (for ink). Using the "Export Setup" dialog from the Figure Window, save an image of your plot as a .jpg-file, and also as a .png-file, rendered using these specific settings. Compare the sizes of each of the files generated in this and the previous exercise.

After doing Exercises 62 and 63 above, it is natural to inquire about the advantages and disadvantages of saving the .fig-file versus the .png-file. The first observation is that the saved figure file is faithful to the figure generated by your program. For example, if you created a three dimensional plot and saved the figure as a .fig-file, then at a later time you can open this file and perform operations like rotating the view-angle and magnifying a small section of the plot. The image file, on the other hand, cannot be used to recover the original figure. Moreover, if you export your figures to a specific format such as .eps, and then later decide to use another format such as .png, you will need to recreate the figure and save it again. Note that there exist third-party tools for converting between various image formats, such as eps2png.exe[1].

In spite of the apparent advantages described above of saving the figure file, only the image files are used when ultimately creating a document, and considerations of disk space and file clutter may compel one to save the image file only. Furthermore, since (at least in principle) all figures should be reproducible by running your program, the advantages of keeping the figure file around are somewhat superficial. Note that, because figures should be reproducible, one should not depend on the Figure Editor to add explanatory text to a figure, as this work would have to be repeated each time your program generates a figure worth saving. Indeed, this is one of the reasons we emphasize programmatically incorporating text into figures, especially when displaying runtime variables.

---

[1] Though down-sampling a 300 dpi image to 72 dpi is straightforward, up-sampling can be problematic.

10.3 Plotting parametric curves in the plane

Our emphasis in the previous section has been plotting functions on an interval domain such as $[-\pi, \pi]$, appropriately discretized using the array variable x = linspace(-pi,pi,50). Nonetheless, we still encounter some examples where the domain of the plot was a small set of whole numbers, for example [2:5] indicating "which iteration" of the Newton algorithm computing X_n is being plotted. We also encountered the example of drawing the y-axis using the command plot([0,0],[ymin,ymax]) to draw the line connecting the points $(0, \text{ymin})$ and $(0, \text{ymax})$. In this section we discuss plotting these more general data sets, and parametric curves in particular.

In our first example of a data set we imagine that the result of a test produces the following array of scores:
$$\{85, 70, 92, 85, 75, 90, 75, 92, 70, 85\}$$

If we wish to display the frequency distribution of test scores with a plot, we may proceed by first collecting this data into an array:

```
scores = [85, 70, 92, 85, 75, 90, 75, 92, 70, 85];
```

A grossly inefficient, yet accurate, method of extracting the frequencies from scores is by utilizing the find function in the following loop:

```
1 n       = length(scores);
2 freq    = zeros(1,n)
3 for k=1:n
4     val     = scores(k);           %inspect each score (for each k)
5     indices = find(scores == val); %find all occurrences
6     freq(k) = length(indices);     %and record the number of these occurrence
7 end
```

The array freq which has been constructed at this point contains, for its k'th element, the number of instances of the score scores(k).

Exercise 64

Lookup the find function and explain how the above code fragment works. Can you identify the inefficiency inherent in the above implementation?

To create a plot showing the frequency of each score, we may now execute the following instructions:

```
figure(100)
plot(scores,freq,'*r')
```

Chapter 10. Plotting I

The readability of the figure can be improved by adding some labels and using the following plot command which replaces the red asterisks with large solid red circles:

```
plot(scores,freq,'o','MarkerSize',10,'MarkerFaceColor','r')
xlabel('score');
ylabel('frequency');
ylim([0,4]);    %add some space above and below
```

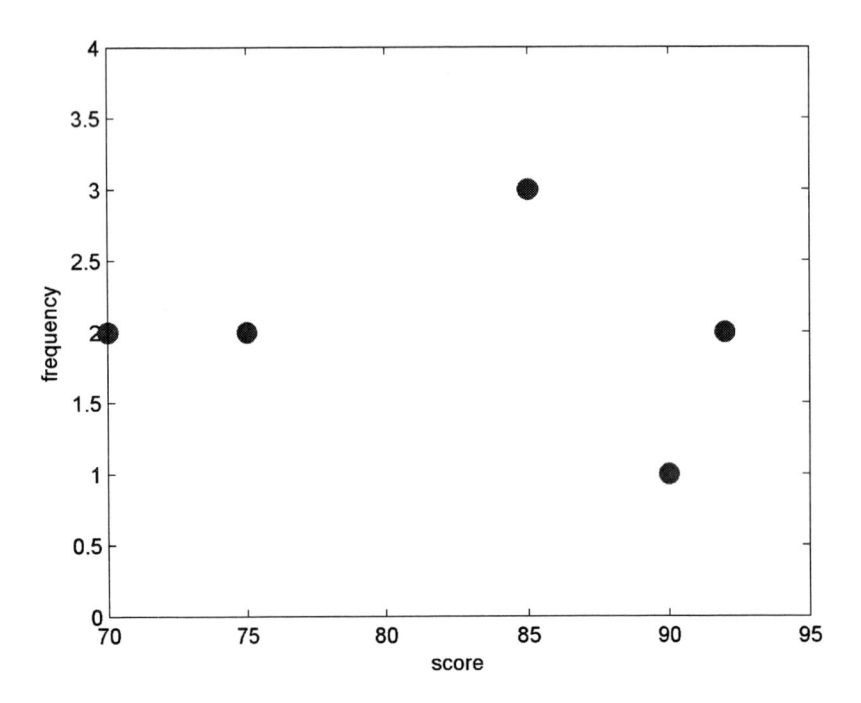

It is important to emphasize that `plot` does not require a unique y-value for each x-value. Consider this example which generates a random y-value in $[0,1]$ and assigns it to a randomly selected integer (the x-value) between 0 and 9 - and does this 50 times:

```
1 figure(200)
2 n = 50;
3 x = floor(10*rand(1,n));
4 y = rand(1,n);
5 plot(x,y,'r*')
```

More theoretically interesting examples arise among the so-called "parametric functions". These are curves given by a pair of functions $x = x(t), y = y(t)$ where t is the independent variable, whose domain is referred to as the "parameter space". The standard example is the circle with $t \in [-\pi, \pi]$:

10.3. Plotting parametric curves in the plane

```
1 figure(300)
2 n    = 40;
3 t    = linspace(-pi,pi,n);
4 x    = cos(t);
5 y    = sin(t);
6 plot(x,y)
7
8 %add explanatory text
9 textstr = sprintf('Plot of function \\gamma:[-\\pi,\\pi] \\rightarrow R^2\n');
10 textstr = sprintf('%swhere \\gamma(t) = [cos(t), sin(t)]\n',textstr);
11 textstr = sprintf('%susing %d vertices', textstr, n-1);
12 text(0.2, 0.4, textstr, 'FontSize', 16, 'Units', 'normalized');
13 %ensure that the curve looks like a circle rather than an ellipse
14 axis equal
```

Exercise 65

Modify the above code fragment to generate a regular octagon.

We show plots of "circles" using the parametric equations $[\cos(t), \sin(t)]$ implemented above, and using two choices of n.

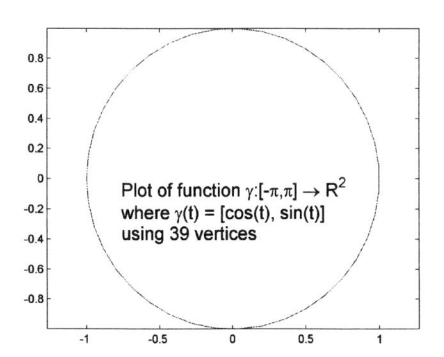

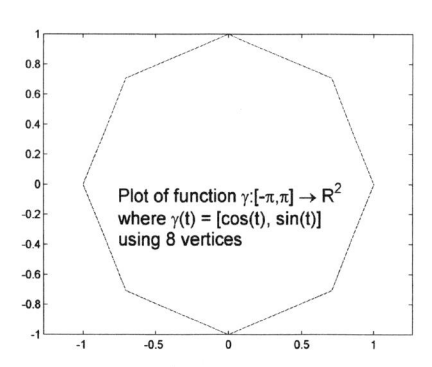

Note that the parameter space does not explicitly appear in the plot of a parametric function. For example, the identical "circle" will be plotted by changing the parameter space for t to be any interval of the form `linspace(n*pi,(n+2)*pi,n)` (where n is an odd integer). A less instructive example is provided by adding the following two lines, which will produce the same plot for *any* choice of parameter space:

```
r    = sqrt(x.^2 + y.^2);
plot(r,r.^2,'*')
```

> **Exercise 66**
>
> Does using an arbitrary parameter space of size 2π produce the identical "circle" plotted in the examples above? How does the size of **n** affect your answer?

10.4 Topics covered in this chapter

In this chapter we learned how to create figures, and to plot within these figures single-valued functions (e.g. $y = f(x)$) as well as data sets (e.g. [scores, frequencies]) and parametric functions (e.g. $[x(t), y(t)]$). We also described how to embellish plots with explanatory text including special LaTeX symbols, and how to save the resulting figures to image files. The specific MATLAB commands covered are summarized below:

1. Plotting functions and data sets: `figure()`, `plot()`

2. Plotting attributes: `LineWidth`, `FontSize`, `MarkerSize`, `MarkerFaceColor`, `Units`

3. Plotting control: `hold on`, `axis()`

4. Plotting appearance: `title()`, `text()`, `legend()`, `xlabel()`, `ylabel()`

5. LaTeX symbols: `\alpha`, `\pi`, `\leq`, `\uparraow`, `\leftarrow`, `\downarrow`

6. Miscellaneous functions: `find()`

Chapter 11

Computing $\sqrt{5}$: NewtonAlg.m

In this chapter we will consolidate techniques described in previous chapters to produce our first masterpiece - a well-designed MATLAB implementation of Newton's algorithm for computing the square root of five. Granted, this is not an especially ambitious programming project for numerical applications, but we will incorporate some important principles from numerical analysis to make it instructive. To be sure, our NewtonAlg.m will be used as a basis for much more sophisticated programs, namely a general root-finder for scalar nonlinear equations in Section 14.2, and for systems of nonlinear equations in Section 21.2. In fact, it is quite impressive how close we are to creating such programs; the missing pieces will fall into place when we cover the topics of function handles and matrix algebra in Part III. On the other hand, the material we have covered up to this point is more than sufficient to explore some important ideas in numerical analysis.

11.1 The order of convergence of iterative numerical algorithms

In this section we discuss the concept of "order of convergence". When an iterative algorithm is used to approximate a solution $\hat{x}$ to the equation $f(x) = 0$, so that $|x_{n+1} - \hat{x}| \to 0$, it is natural to ask "how fast" the iterates converge. For example, if

$$|x_{n+1} - \hat{x}| = \lambda \cdot |x_n - \hat{x}|, \qquad \lambda \in (0, \infty),$$

or even asymptotically, so

$$|x_{n+1} - \hat{x}| = \lambda_n \cdot |x_n - \hat{x}|, \qquad \lambda_n \to \lambda \in (0, \infty),$$

then we say that the convergence is "linear". Similarly, "quadratic" convergence is characterized by the existence of a constant λ for which

$$|x_{n+1} - \hat{x}| = \lambda_n \cdot |x_n - \hat{x}|^2, \qquad \lambda_n \to \lambda \in (0, \infty).$$

In general, we make the definition that $x_n \to \hat{x}$ with order of convergence α if:

$$\frac{|x_{n+1} - \hat{x}|}{|x_n - \hat{x}|^\alpha} \to \lambda, \qquad \text{for some } \lambda \text{ as } n \to \infty.$$

The value of the constant λ in the above definition is called the "rate of convergence".

The crudest approach to determining the order of convergence is to inspect a table displaying the quantities $|x_n - \hat{x}|$. Since $\hat{x}$ refers to the theoretically exact solution, in our examples we will substitute our *final* computed iterate x(end). How does one discern the order of convergence from a column of numbers? Roughly speaking, if each successive entry has the same number of zeros after the decimal point, then the convergence is linear; if twice as many zeros after the decimal point, then the convergence is quadratic; if thrice as many zeros then cubic, and so on.

We modify our last version NewtonAlg8.m to produce the desired table:

```
%%%%%%%%%%%%%%%%%%%%%%%%%%%%%%%%
% NewtonAlg9.m
%%%%% initialization section %%%%%
%initialization (hardwired variables)
x0       = 2;
nIter    = 6;
%initialization (not hardwired)
xvals    = zeros(1,nIter);

%%%%%%%%%%%%%%%%%%%%%%%%%%%%%%%%
%%%%% algorithm section %%%%%%%%%%
xvals(1)    = x0;
for i=2:nIter
    x        = xvals(i-1);
    xvals(i) = x - (x^2 - 5)/(2*x);
end

%%%%%%%%%%%%%%%%%%%%%%%%%%%%%%%%
%%%%%%% output section %%%%%%%%%%
xhat     = xvals(end);
diffs    = abs(xvals - xhat);
fprintf('\niteration \t Xn \t\t |Xn - Xo| \t\t |Xn^2 - 5|');
fprintf('\n-----------------------------\n');
fprintf('%d \t\t %12.10f \t\t%e \t\t%e\n',...
    [1:nIter; xvals; diffs; abs(xvals.^2 - 5)]);
```

Executing NewtonAlg9.m produces the following output, from which we crudely guess that the convergence is quadratic. Notice that by using the exponential formatting notation (%e), we can more easily discern the quadratic behavior of $|x_n - \hat{x}|$ by the doubling of the exponent at each iteration (i.e. $-1, -2, -5, -10$).

```
1 iteration     Xn              |Xn - Xo|         |Xn^2 - 5|
2 ----------------------------------------------------------
3 1             2.0000000000    2.360680e-001     1.000000e+000
4 2             2.2500000000    1.393202e-002     6.250000e-002
5 3             2.2361111111    4.313361e-005     1.929012e-004
6 4             2.2360679779    4.160143e-010     1.860474e-009
7 5             2.2360679775    0.000000e+000     8.881784e-016
8 6             2.2360679775    0.000000e+000     8.881784e-016
```

Exercise 67

Modify the above implementation by adding a fifth column to its tabular output which "verifies" the quadratic convergence. Can you estimate the value of λ? For a lucid explanation of why the exact value of λ is given by $\lambda = \frac{1}{2}[x - (x^2 - 5)/(2x)]''(\hat{x}) = \sqrt{5}/10$, see the article "On the Order of Convergence of Iterative Methods" by Chuck Allison: http://uvsc.freshsources.com/Order_of_Convergence.pdf.

11.2 Applying plotting techniques to numerical investigations

A more accurate approach to determining the order of convergence is to graph the logarithms $\log|x_{n+1} - \hat{x}|$ versus $\log|x_n - \hat{x}|$. The mathematical basis for this approach derives from taking the logarithm of the equation $\dfrac{|x_{n+1} - \hat{x}|}{|x_n - \hat{x}|^\alpha} = \lambda$:

$$\log|x_{n+1} - \hat{x}| = \alpha \log|x_n - \hat{x}| + \log(\lambda).$$

Thus, the order of convergence should be visible as the slope of a line through the data points constructed from the $(\log|x_n - \hat{x}|, \log|x_{n+1} - \hat{x}|)$-pairs. We can implement this idea by adding the following code to NewtonAlg9.m.

```
1 %perform log-log plot of diffs array entries versus previous entry
2 loglog(diffs(2:end),diffs(1:end-1),'-*')
3
4 %improves readability of log-log plot
5 grid on
6
7 %display the formula we are using directly on figure
8 str = sprintf('log|X_{n+1}-\\surd{5}| =');
9 str = sprintf('%s \\alpha log|X_n-\\surd{5}|+log(\\lambda)',str);
10 text(0.05,0.5,str,'Units','normalized','FontSize',14)
11
```

Chapter 11. Computing $\sqrt{5}$: NewtonAlg.m

```
12 %compute slope and y-intercept from first three entries
13 ind      = 3;
14 slopeNum = log(diffs(ind+1)) - log(diffs(ind));
15 slopeDen = log(diffs(ind))   - log(diffs(ind-1));
16 slope    = slopeNum/slopeDen;
17
18 %for purposes of computing rate-of-convergence,
19 % use exact order-of-convergence by rounding
20 roundSlope = round(slope);
21 logRate    = log(diffs(ind+1)) - roundSlope*log(diffs(ind));
22 rate       = exp(logRate);
23
24 %display estimated values of alpha (slope) and lambda (y-intercept)
25 str1     = sprintf('\\alpha = %3.2f',slope);
26 str2     = sprintf(' %s \n \\lambda = %6.4f',str1, rate);
27 text(0.2,0.2,str2,'Units','normalized','FontSize',16)
28
29 %give title to figure
30 title('Order of Convergence using loglog plot')
```

The output from the above loglog plot is reproduced below:

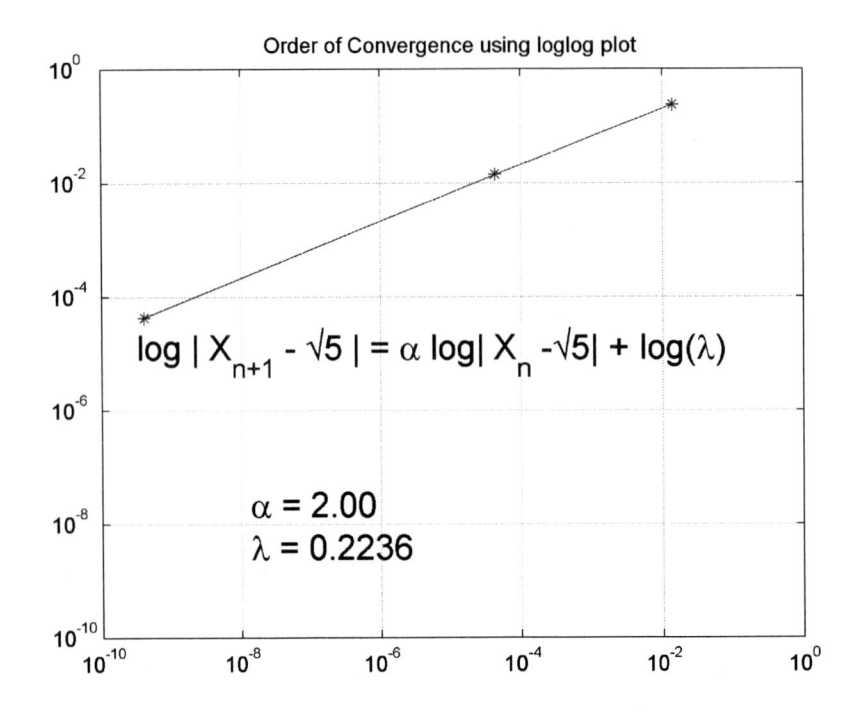

Order of Convergence using loglog plot

$\log |X_{n+1} - \sqrt{5}| = \alpha \log|X_n - \sqrt{5}| + \log(\lambda)$

$\alpha = 2.00$
$\lambda = 0.2236$

11.2. Applying plotting techniques to numerical investigations

Finally, we will generate some elementary plots to get more insight into the notion of order of convergence. Let us assume that the true order of convergence of our algorithm is $\alpha = 2$, so that
$$\frac{|x_{n+1} - \hat{x}|}{|x_n - \hat{x}|^2} \to \lambda \in (0, \infty).$$
Then we notice that evaluating the expressions $\frac{|x_{n+1}-\hat{x}|}{|x_n-\hat{x}|^\alpha}$ with $\alpha > 2$ would create denominators too small (numbers close to zero raised to a power greater than one[1] become still smaller), and therefore the expression would diverge to infinity. Similarly, if we plugged into our expression a value of $\alpha < 2$, then the denominators become too large and the expression converges to zero. In other words, to say that the true order of convergence is $\alpha = 2$ is a very delicate matter, since *any other value of* α would send the ratio $\frac{|x_{n+1}-\hat{x}|}{|x_n-\hat{x}|^\alpha}$ to 0 or ∞! From this point of view, we can experiment with our data by plotting
$$\frac{|x_{n+1} - \hat{x}|}{|x_n - \hat{x}|^\alpha}$$
for several values of α, and observe which plots tend to zero and which tend to infinity; the unique value of α for which the plot tends to a finite positive constant in $(0, \infty)$ will be the order of convergence. An implementation of NewtonAlg9.m along these lines is accomplished with the addition of the following code:

```
%guess order of convergence by graphing different exponents
figure(500)
hold on
colors = ['c','r','g','b','k','m','y'];
for j=2:7
    expon    = j/2;
    ratio    = diffs(2:end)./diffs(1:end-1).^expon;
    plot(ratio,colors(j))
end
legend('\alpha=1.0','\alpha=1.5','\alpha=2.0',...
            '\alpha=2.5','\alpha=3.0','\alpha=3.5')
axis([1,3,0,3])
title('Illustrating order of convergence')
str = sprintf('|X_{n+1} - \\surd{5}| / |X_{n} - \\surd{5}|^\\alpha');
str = sprintf('%s remains finite \n and positive only when', str);
str = sprintf('%s \\alpha = 2.0 \n \\downarrow', str);
text(0.15,0.2,str,'FontSize',14,'Units','normalized')
text(0.8,0.1,'\lambda \sim 0.22 \rightarrow',...
            'FontSize',14,'Units','normalized')
```

The figure generated by the above code appears below. We could make some additional comments here concerning the interpretation of the plotted output, but in the spirit of the previous chapter we will let the figure speak for itself.

---
[1]Values of α less than one are inconsistent with convergence.

114　　Chapter 11. Computing $\sqrt{5}$: NewtonAlg.m

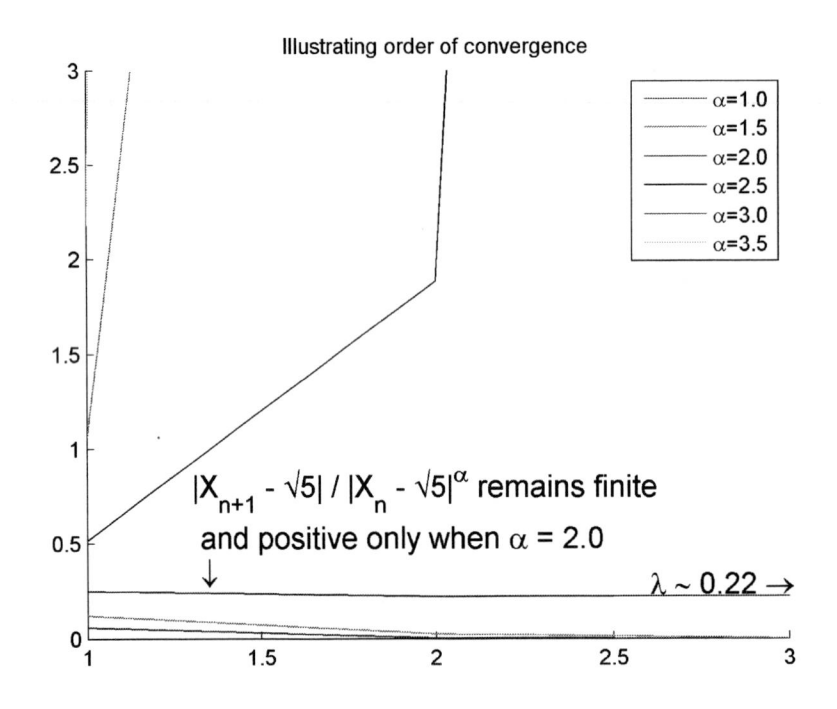

Illustrating order of convergence

[Figure: plot with legend $\alpha=1.0$, $\alpha=1.5$, $\alpha=2.0$, $\alpha=2.5$, $\alpha=3.0$, $\alpha=3.5$; annotation: $|X_{n+1} - \sqrt{5}| / |X_n - \sqrt{5}|^\alpha$ remains finite and positive only when $\alpha = 2.0$; $\lambda \sim 0.22 \rightarrow$]

Exercise 68

Using the Help Browser lookup the `input` command. Rewrite NewtonAlg.m so that the user is queried to guess the value of α, after which a fourth column of the table is displayed showing the corresponding λ_n, as well as a plot of $\dfrac{|x_{n+1} - \hat{x}|}{|x_n - \hat{x}|^\alpha}$.

11.3　Topics covered in this chapter

We have described three approaches to determining the order of convergence of an iterative numerical algorithm, and incorporated an implementation of each into NewtonAlg.m. The specific MATLAB commands we have covered are summarized below:

1. Plotting commands: `loglog()`

2. Plotting control: `grid on`

3. Miscellaneous: `input`

4. LaTeX symbols: `\surd, \sim`

Part III

Writing a complex MATLAB program

Chapter 12

Functions I

Functions are critically fundamental to all programming languages. In fact, without the capability of packaging specific program functionality into independently testable and useable code modules, an artificial limit is imposed on the complexity of any program. Put simply, if we need to compute the square root of five at one point in a larger calculation, and the square root of seven at another point, is our only option to reuse NewtonAlg.m, but modified by changing:

```
xvals(i) = x - (x^2 - 5)/(2*x);
```

to:

```
xvals(i) = x - (x^2 - 7)/(2*x);
```

There must be a better way!

Recall from Chapter 3 that we motivated the utility of loops by raising the following issue:

> The technique of implementing Newton's algorithm with the code
> $$x6 = x5 + (x5^2 - 5)/(2*x5)$$
> $$\ldots$$
> $$x96 = x95 + (x95^2 - 5)/(2*x95)$$
> is not practical when more than a few iterations are required.

Similarly, we now raise the issue:

> Re-implementing each instance of computing $\sqrt{M}$ by reproducing
> ```
> xvals(i) = x - (x^2 - M)/(2*x)
> ```
> from NewtonAlg.m, is not practical when many instances occur.

Just as MATLAB solves the first issue by building into the language the for-loop, it solves the second issue by building into the language "call-able" script files, called "functions". The ability to isolate a block of code which implements a specific functionality, and then package it in a form that can be reused by other programs, is the fundamental mechanism which makes complex programs possible. Even programs of modest complexity will call scores of functions, many of which will themselves call secondary functions. We are already familiar with some of MATLAB's built-in functions like `abs`; in a sense, user-definable functions can be thought of as a programmer's ability to extend the language.

12.1 A simple example of a user-defined function

We consider the simple one-line program which displays to the screen the text "HELP!":

```
1 %%%%%% DisplayHelp.m %%%%%%
2 %one-line program to display 'HELP!'
3 disp('HELP!')
```

Enter the above code into a script file with the filename DisplayHelp.m. Verify its behavior by running it from the Edit Window, and also by entering `DisplayHelp` from the command line in the Command Window. Next, create a second script file Main.m, whose code reads as follows:

```
1 %%%%%% Main.m %%%%%%
2 %one-line program which 'calls' function to display 'HELP~'
3 DisplayHelp
```

With both DisplayHelp.m and Main.m opened in the Edit Window, use the ArrangeDocuments icon to split the screen (horizontaly or vertically) so both files are displayed concurrently. Put breakpoints at each of the executable lines of code: at `disp('HELP')` (line 3) in DisplayHelp.m, and at `DisplayHelp` (line 3) in Main.m. Single-step the program Main.m from the debugger and notice the order in which the program execution proceeds. One says that the "function" DisplayHelp has been "called" or "invoked" by the program Main.m.

> **Exercise 69**
>
> Remove the breakpoint in DisplayHelp.m, but keep the breakpoint in Main.m. Run Main.m and single-step using the "Step" icon. How does single-stepping a function call behave? Next, run Main.m and single-step using the "Step in" icon which is found next to the Step icon among the Debugger Tools. When the Debugger stops in the file DisplayHelp.m, verify the "calling sequence" either by inspecting the Stack icon in the Debugger toolbar, or entering `dbstack` at the command-line. If you now look at the file Main.m, is there still a green arrow displayed at the line "currently being executed"? Finally, return to Main.m by using the "Step out" icon, or entering `dbstep out` at the command-line. See the figure below.

12.1. A simple example of a user-defined function

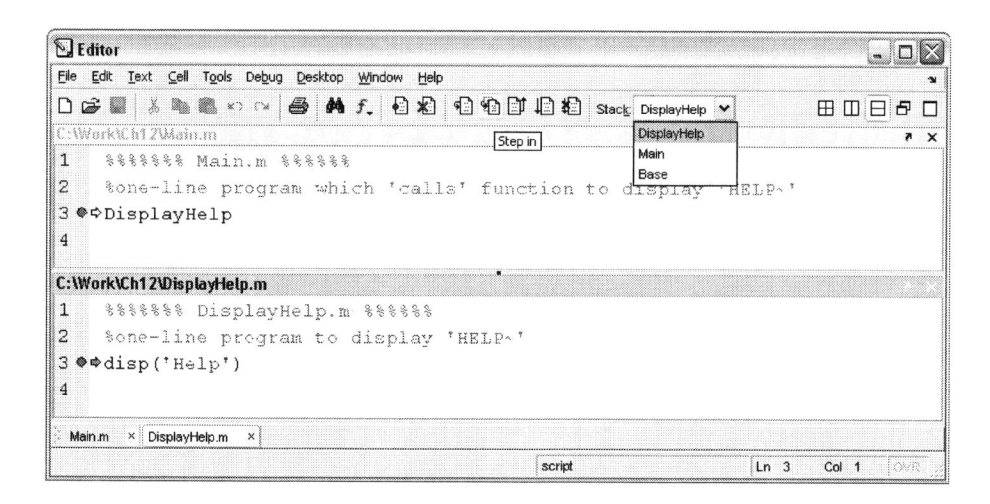

Strictly speaking, although MATLAB lets us get away with treating DisplayHelp.m as a function, it does not conform to the expected structure of a function. DisplayHelp is missing a first and last line which should appear in every function. The first line which needs to be added contains the keyword `function`, and the last line which needs to be added contains the instruction `return`. DisplayHelp now looks like:

```
1 function    DisplayHelp()
2 %one-line program to display 'HELP!'
3 disp('HELP!')
4 return
```

Notice that we removed the comment giving the name of the file. This is to illustrate that we will strictly enforce the convention that function names agree with the name of the file in which they are implemented, and so the initial comment, though desirable, is superfluous. In fact, create a *new* file, re-enter the above text (with or without an initial comment), and click the Save icon. Notice that when presented with the Save dialog the default filename is DisplayHelp.m, as MATLAB has done us the favor of presuming the filename and function name should agree.

Another convention we follow is using upper-case names for our functions, so that our user-defined functions are never confused, either by ourselves or third parties reading our code, with MATLAB's built-in functions. Notice that the comment appearing in the second line will also be displayed in the CurrentDirectory Window in the column labelled Description[1].

Since it is no more difficult to directly enter the line `disp('HELP!')` into your code than it is to enter the line `DisplayHelp`, the DisplayHelp function is of questionable value. On the other

---

[1] If the Description column is absent from your window, check the Browser Display Options in the Preferences:CurrentDirectory dialog.

hand, if DisplayHelp.m displayed a paragraph instead of one line of text, and if this paragraph of text needed to be displayed at several points in Main.m, then it becomes an extremely useful function. Even without the more sophisticated capabilities that functions provide and which we describe later in this chapter, we have already determined a compelling need for functions. We emphasize this point by formulating the following programming principle:

> Whenever the same block of code appears multiple times in a program, one should consider re-implementing this code by creating a function.

What are the trade-offs? On the positive side there is the organizational benefit of reducing clutter in Main.m by packaging repeated blocks of code into single reusable function files. Moreover, good decisions about how much functionality should be packaged into individual functions will determine how easily you can add complexity to your program. On the negative side, one should avoid creating a proliferation of files whose functionality is of limited generality - in many cases one will want to implement functions locally within the file from which it is called. When we learn about parameter passing in the next section, we will see that there are more subtle considerations when evaluating these trade-offs. In a larger sense, creating the complex programs which we study in Part III amounts to organizing one's code into functions; likewise, the topics already covered in Part II amount to the elements required to implement the code of a single function.

12.2 Passing arguments and returning values

We recall that in an earlier chapter we described, among the shortcomings of NewtonAlg.m, the hardwired nature of the initial guess x0, and the number of iterations nIter. The ability to pass parameters to functions as input arguments enables us to liberate NewtonAlg.m from this limitation. We now discuss the topic of passing initial data to a function, as well as returning to a function's caller the results of its calculations. We have already referred to user-defined functions as playing a role similar to MATLAB's built-in functions, and in this spirit we implement our own version of abs.

```
1 function y = AbsValue(x)
2 if x < 0
3     y = -x;
4 else
5     y = x;
6 end
7
8 return
```

Enter the above code into a new file and save it as AbsValue.m. Execute from the command-line the instruction AbsValue(-5) and observe that its behavior is identical to abs(-5).

To understand better how functions behave, enter the following code in a new file called Main.m.

```
1 %%% Main.m %%%
2 AbsValue(-5)
3 x = AbsValue(-5)
4 y = -3;
5 z = AbsValue(y)
6 w = AbsValue(AbsValue(randn));
```

As above, use the vertical split-screen feature to display the two files Main.m and AbsValue.m concurrently in the Edit Window. Set a breakpoint at the first instruction in AbsValue.m, and execute Main.m. When you get debug control in AbsValue.m, single-step and inspect the values of all the variables as the function executes. You can execute the `who` command in the Command Window to see the variables in one shot[2]. Observe that AbsValue.m is blind to the variables z and w, and, paying particular attention to x and y, observe how x initially reflects only *the value which is passed when it is called*, and is independent of any variable labelled x anywhere else in your code. This behavior should be no surprise, as one expects MATLAB's built-in functions to utilize their own variable names without danger of altering identically named variables employed in your program. This principle is referred to as "program scope", namely that all variables utilized in a function are local in nature and are considered private to the function: A function cannot alter, or even access, variables in other code modules (including its caller), other functions invoked by its caller, functions called from within the function, and of course MATLAB's built-in functions.

Exercise 70

Comment on the following implementation of AbsValue.m which omits the `else` block:
```
function x = AbsValue(x)
if x < 0
    x = -x;
end
return
```

Next, we explore passing non-numeric variables to a function. Using either copy & paste from the Command Window, or the `diary` command, perform command-line Help on `length`, `abs` and `loglog`, and capture the following text into a new file named OurHelp.m:

```
1 >> help length
2 LENGTH   Length of vector.
```

---
[2]Note that if you use the Workspace Window, which we discourage, then you may need to perform a Refresh when you ping-pong between Main.m and AbsValue.m.

122   Chapter 12. Functions I

```
 3      LENGTH(X) returns the length of vector X.  It is equivalent
 4      to MAX(SIZE(X)) for non-empty arrays and 0 for empty ones.
 5  >> help abs
 6  ABS    Absolute value.
 7      ABS(X) is the absolute value of the elements of X. When
 8      X is complex, ABS(X) is the complex modulus (magnitude) of
 9      the elements of X.
10  >> help loglog
11  LOGLOG Log-log scale plot.
12      LOGLOG(...) is the same as PLOT(...), except logarithmic
13      scales are used for both the X- and Y- axes.
```

A first attempt at implementing our homegrown version of help, at least for these three specific topics, is to pass an integer 1, 2, or 3 which will serve as a "selector".

```
 1  %%%%%%%% OurHelp.m %%%%%%%%%%%%%%%
 2  function OurHelp(selector)
 3  %on entry, selector = 1 if request help on 'length'
 4  %on entry, selector = 2 if request help on 'abs'
 5  %on entry, selector = 3 if request help on 'loglog'
 6  %on exit, no return value (help displayed during execution)
 7  if selector == 1
 8      str = sprintf('  LENGTH    Length of vector.\n');
 9      str = sprintf('%s \t LENGTH(X) returns the length of vector X. ',str);
10      str = sprintf('%s It is equivalent\n to MAX(SIZE(X))',str);
11      str = sprintf('%s \t for non-empty arrays and 0 for empty ones.\n',str);
12      fprintf(str)
13  elseif selector == 2
14      str = sprintf('  ABS    Absolute value of X.\n');
15      str = sprintf('%s \t ABS(X) is the absolute value of the elements',str);
16      str = sprintf('%s When \n X is complex, ABS(X) is the complex',str);
17      str = sprintf('%s \t modulus (magnitude) of \nthe elements of X.\n',str);
18      fprintf(str)
19  elseif selector == 3
20      str = sprintf('  LOGLOG Log-log scale plot.\n');
21      str = sprintf('%s \t LOGLOG(...) is the same as PLOT(...),',str);
22      str = sprintf('%s \t except logarithmic \n',str);
23      str = sprintf('%s \t scales are used for both the X- and Y- axes.\n',str);
24      fprintf(str)
25  else
26      fprintf('Unrecognized topic selector: \%d\n', selector)
27  end
28  return
```

12.2. Passing arguments and returning values

Test the behavior of OurHelp.m by entering `OurHelp(1+floor(3*rand))` from the command-line. In spite of our best efforts to document within the file OurHelp.m how this function is to be invoked, either at the command-line or by another function, this information is not transparent outside the file. Documenting the use of OurHelp really belongs in the caller's code, for example:

```
1 %%% Main.m %%%
2 ...
3 %we now display documentation on loglog by calling the function OurHelp
4 % OurHelp uses the following selector to choose the help topic
5 %   length (selector=1), abs (selector-2), loglog (selector=3)
6 OurHelp(3);
7 ...
```

Needless to say, there are better ways to implement OurHelp.m. Our second version makes use of passing a string variable to OurHelp. An obvious choice is to pass the strings 'length', 'abs', and 'loglog' themselves when seeking documentation. On the other hand, the following code is invalid:

```
1 if selector == 'length'
```

since one cannot use the == construct to perform a comparison of string variables. This should not be surprising since strings are a type of array (recall the isequal() command). Fortunately, MATLAB provides the command strcmp which will perform string comparisons. Our second version of OurHelp represents an obvious improvement:

```
1 %%%%%%%% OurHelp.m %%%%%%%%%%%%%%%%%
2 function OurHelp(selectorStr)
3 %on entry, selectorStr = 'length', 'abs', 'loglog'
4 %on exit, no return value (help displayed during execution)
5 if strcmp(selectorStr, 'length')
6     ...
7 elseif strcmp(selectorStr, 'abs')
8     ...
9 elseif strcmp(selectorStr, 'loglog')
10    ...
11 else
12     fprintf('Unrecognized topic: \%s\n', selectorStr)
13 end
14 return
```

The strcmp function, as well as its variants strnmpn, strcmpi and strncmpi, can be very useful functions, and find many applications when working with string variables. On the other hand, they are also inefficient and somewhat awkward to use. We therefore use this opportunity to introduce the switch statement to give yet a third, and arguably preferable, implementation of OurHelp.m.

```
1 %%%%%%% OurHelp.m %%%%%%%%%%%%%%
2 function OurHelp(selStr)
3 %on entry, selStr = 'length', 'abs', 'loglog'
4 %on exit, no return value (help displayed during execution)
5 switch selStr
6     case 'length'
7         str = sprintf('  LENGTH   Length of vector.\n');
8         ...
9         fprintf(str)
10    case 'abs'
11        str = sprintf('  ABS    Absolute value.n');
12        ...
13        fprintf(str)
14    case 'loglog'
15        str = sprintf('  LOGLOG Log-log scale plot.\n');
16        ...
17        fprintf(str)
18    otherwise
19        fprintf('Unrecognized topic: \%s\n', selStr)
20 end
21 return
```

As you can see from the above code, the keyword `switch` followed by the variable `selStr` indicates the variable (whether or not a string variable) whose value is to be compared. Notice the use of the keyword `otherwise` to capture the "fall-through" cases not covered by the cases explicitly identified above. The `switch-case-otherwise-end` construct has strong similarites with the `if-elseif-else-end` construct, and it would have been natural to introduce it in Chapter 6 on flow-control. The main difference is that, while it is especially well adapted to applications involving string comparisons, it can be used only when comparing a single variable for equality, and has no counterpart for complex Boolean conditionals like

```
if (x < 0 | y ~= 0);
```

Exercise 71

Suppose we want to enable a user to get help on loglog by typing either `OurHelp('loglog')`, `OurHelp('log-log')` or `OurHelp('LogLog')`. Modify both the second and third implementations of OurHelp.m to support this functionality.

12.2. Passing arguments and returning values

> **Solution 71**
>
> The `strcmp` version would be modified as follows:
>   `elseif strcmpi(selStr,'loglog') | strcmp(selStr,'log-log')`
> The `switch` version would be modified as follows:
>   `case {'loglog', 'log-log', 'LogLog'}`

We have demonstrated the use of functions with three simple examples: DispHelp.m (no input, no output), AbsValue.m (numeric input, numeric output), and OurHelp.m (string input, no output). There is a general structure to a function which accepts multiple input arguments and returns multiple output values, and to illustrate this general format we propose the following (contrived) example with three input parameters and two output parameters[3]:

```
function [y1, y2]  = FunctionExample(x1, x2, x3)
%example illustrating general format of function
% using three input arguments and two return values
%on entry:
%x1 = first passed parameter (scalar)
%x2 = second passed parameter (row vector)
%x3 = third passed parameter (boolean flag=1 if display sign of x1)
%on exit
%y1 = absolute value of x1
%y2 = number of non-zero elements in x2

y1 = abs(x1);
y2 = sum(x2 ~= 0);

if x3
    if x1 > 0
        fprintf('x1=%f is positive', x1);
    elseif x1 < 0
        fprintf('x1=%f is negative', x1);
    else
        fprintf('x1=%f is zero, hence no sign', x1);
    end
end

return
```

Enter the above code into a file named FunctionExample.m, and set a breakpoint at the first instruction. By executing the following commands from the Command Window and single-

---

[3]The `size()` function, introduced in Chapter 15, will be our first encounter with a built-in MATLAB function which returns multiple values.

stepping FunctionExample.m in the Debugger, you should be able to fully appreciate the structure and operation of the most general functions.

```
FunctionExample(-3, [4 5 6 7 8], 0)
a       = FunctionExample(-3, rand(1,17), 1)
[a,b]   = FunctionExample(-3, rand(1,17), 1)
```

> **Exercise 72**
>
> When single-stepping to line 13, type (x2 ~= 0) at the command-line. In particular, explain the construct
> y2 = sum(x2 ~= 0);

12.3 Implementing NewtonAlg as a function (NewtonAlg10.m)

In this final section we revisit our old friend NewtonAlg.m, and use what we have learned about functions to address the issue of hardwired variables. Recall that the input section contained initialization code which set the initial guess x0 to two, and the number of iterations nIter to six. We identified this fact as a shortcoming, since it required one to *edit the file* in order to use different values. By implementing NewtonAlg as a function which is passed x0 and nIter as parameters, we can free the code from this limitation.

```
%%%%%%%% NewtonAlg9.m %%%%%%%%%%%%%%%%
function    sqrtFive = NewtonAlg9(x0, nIter)
%on entry, x0 = initial guess to start Newton algorithm
%on entry, nIter = number of iterations to execute
%on exit, sqrtFive = result of nIter iterations

%%%%%%%%%%%%%%%%%%%%%%%%%%%%%%%%%%
%%%%% initialization section %%%%%
xvals   = zeros(1,nIter);

%%%%%%%%%%%%%%%%%%%%%%%%%%%%%%%%%%
%%%%% algorithm section %%%%%%%%%%
xvals(1)    = x0;
for i=2:nIter
    x       = xvals(i-1);
    xvals(i) = x - (x^2 - 5)/(2*x);
end

%%%%%%%%%%%%%%%%%%%%%%%%%%%%%%%%%%
%%% output (to screen) section %%%
```

12.3. Implementing NewtonAlg as a function (NewtonAlg10.m)

```
21 fprintf('\niteration \t Xn \t\t |Xn - Xn-1| \t |Xn^2-5|');
22 fprintf('\n------------------------------------------------');
23 fprintf('\n%d \t\t %f \t\t%f \t\t%f',...
24   [1:nIter; xvals; [0, abs(xvals(2:end)-xvals(1:end-1))]; abs(xvals.^2 -5)]);
25
26 %%%%%%%%%%%%%%%%%%%%%%%%%%%%%%%%%%%
27 %%% output (to caller) section %%%
28 %assign to return variable the result of last iteration
29 sqrtFive   = xvals(end);
30
31 return
```

When we compare the above implementation of NewtonAlg9.m to earlier versions, we see that it is strictly superior in the sense that we can recover the functionality of NewtonAlg8.m by invoking `NewtonAlg9(2,6)`. What if we consider the need to pass these parameters as a liability, as the user of this function may not have a clue as to a reasonable value to provide for either x0 or nIter? Using the built-in function `nargin`, which returns the number of arguments passed into a function, MATLAB provides an elegant way around this objection!

```
1 %%%%%%%% NewtonAlg10.m %%%%%%%%%%%%%%%%
2 function    sqrtFive = NewtonAlg10(x0, nIter)
3 %on entry, x0 = initial guess to start Newton algorithm
4 %on entry, nIter = number of iterations to execute
5 %on exit, sqrtFive  = result of nIter iterations
6
7 %%%%%%%%%%%%%%%%%%%%%%%%%%%%%%%%%%%
8 %provide default values if NewtonAlg10 called with no arguments
9 if nargin < 1
10     x0    = 2;
11     nIter = 6;
12 end
13
14 %%%%%%%%%%%%%%%%%%%%%%%%%%%%%%%%%%%
15 %%%% initialization section %%%%
16     ...
17 sqrtFive   = xvals(end);
18
19 return
```

> **Exercise 73**
>
> Describe the error which results from running NewtonAlg9.m directly from the Debugger. Observe that you can run NewtonAlg10.m from the Debugger, and justify the assertion that NewtonAlg10.m is superior to previous versions.

12.4 Topics covered in this chapter

In this chapter we introduced the fundamentals of creating a MATLAB function, including a description of input arguments, return values, and scope of local variables. We also discussed debugging methods of stepping-in and stepping-out of functions, and checking the calling hierarchy (stack). Finally, we explained the switch-case-otherwise-end construct, and compared it to the if-elseif-else-end construct. The following MATLAB commands, functions and keywords have been described:

1. Function keyword: `function(...)`, `[...]=function(...)`

2. Argument list function: `nargin`

3. Debug commands: `dbsetep in, dbstep out, dbstack`

4. String comparison function: `strcmp(), strcmpi()`

5. Flow control keywords: `return, switch, case, otherwise`

Chapter 13

Functions II

In the last chapter we introduced the topic of functions, and described some examples illustrating their structure and how they can be used to modularize your code. In particular, the ability to pass input arguments and return output values makes them adaptable to many uses. Although we demonstrated in NewtonAlg10.m how this feature could be used to remove variables with hardwired values, we have only begun to exploit the full potential of functions. In this chapter we will explore several more contexts in which functions can be used, and consequently our programming will achieve a sophistication previously unattainable.

13.1 Tolerance as a terminating condition (NewtonAlg12.m)

When changing the hardwired variable `nIter` in NewtonAlg8.m to a passed parameter in NewtonAlg9.m, we commented on the fact that the caller might have no basis for guessing an appropriate number to pass. Indeed, our own experience with x0=2 showed that iterating 6 times and greater yielded the same value as 5 iterations. Though this may have come to our attention by manually inspecting the tabular output from running NewtonAlg8.m with `nIter=6`, there is no reason that this conclusion could not be deduced programmatically.

In numerical analysis one introduces the concept of "tolerance". The idea is simply that, rather than *guessing* how many iterations to perform on an iterative algorithm, one iterates the algorithm until the successive approximations x_n are sufficiently close to each other, and hence presumably close to the true limit. Specifically, one specifies a small constant τ indicating the desired tolerance, and terminates the iterative algorithm when

$$|x_{n+1} - x_n| < \tau \text{ (absolute error)}, \quad \text{or} \quad \frac{|x_{n+1} - x_n|}{|x_n|} < \tau \text{ (relative error)}.$$

Since we need to compute the difference between successive iterations (see Exercise 11), we utilize two variables `xnew` and `xold`, and move `xnew` to `xold` before returning for the next loop iteration.

130   Chapter 13. Functions II

Consider, for example, the following variant of NewtonAlg10.m:

```
1 %%%%%%%%%%%% NewtonAlg11.m %%%%%%%%%%%%%%%%
2 function    sqrtFive = NewtonAlg11(x0, nIter, tol)
3 %on entry, x0 = initial guess to start Newton algorithm
4 %on entry, nIter = number of iterations to execute (actually maximum)
5 %on exit, sqrtFive = result of nIter iterations
6
7 %%%%%%%%%%%%%%%%%%%%%%%%%%%%%%%%%%
8 %provide default values if NewtonAlg11 called with no arguments
9 if nargin < 1
10     x0      = 2;         %initial guess
11     nIter   = 20;        %no more than 20 iterations
12     tol     = 1e-6;      %specify a tolerance of 0.000001
13 end
14
15 %%%%%%%%%%%%%%%%%%%%%%%%%%%%%%%%%%
16 %%%% initialization section %%%%%
17 xvals    = zeros(1,nIter);
18 xvals(1)= x0;
19
20 %%%%%%%%%%%%%%%%%%%%%%%%%%%%%%%%%%
21 %%%% algorithm section %%%%%%%%%%
22 xold     = x0;
23 for k=2:nIter
24     xnew        = xold - (xold^2 - 5)/(2*xold);
25     xvals(k)    = xnew;
26
27     %compute absolute error |xnew - xold|
28     abserr = abs(xnew - xold);
29     if abserr < tol
30         break   %jump outside for-loop to instruction following 'end'
31     end         %this 'end' is matched with the 'if', not the 'for'
32     xold    = xnew;
33 end             %this 'end' is matched with the 'for'
34
35 %reach this point if EITHER
36 % abserr = |xnew - xold| < tol (good-in this case k=actual number iterations),
37 % OR
38 % k reached nIter without achieving convergence within tolerance (bad)
39 if abserr < tol
40     %reset number iterations to k for use below in fprintf
41     %undesirable since nIter means different things at beginning
```

13.1. Tolerance as a terminating condition (NewtonAlg12.m)

```
42      % of file vs. end of file
43      nIter    = k;
44 else
45      fprintf('%d iterations executed without falling within tolerance %e',...
46          nIter, tol);
47 %    errordlg(errText,'Warning');    %cheap method of sending message to user
48 end
49
50 %%%%%%%%%%%%%%%%%%%%%%%%%%%%%%%%%%%%
51 %%% output (to caller) section %%%
52 %assign to return variable the result of last iteration
53 %note that early termination (see 'break') makes xvals(end) WRONG
54 sqrtfive   = xnew;
55
56 %%%%%%%%%%%%%%%%%%%%%%%%%%%%%%%%%%%%
57 %%% output (to screen) section %%%
58 diffs    = xvals(1:nIter) - sqrtFive;
59 fprintf('\niteration \t Xn \t\t |Xn - Xo| \t\t |Xn^2-5|');
60 fprintf('\n----------------------------------------------');
61 fprintf('\n%d \t\t %12.10f \t\t%e \t\t%e',...
62      [1:nIter; xvals; abs(diffs); abs(xvals.^2 - 5)]);
63
64 return
```

In NewtonAlg11.m we have implemented the use of tolerance as a criterian for terminating the iterative looping. The mechanism we use is the **break** statement, which causes the program to jump out of the for-loop and to continue execution at the line following the **end** statement which pairs with the **for**. Since the **break** instruction abruptly transfers control to another part of the program, it is an example of a "goto" construct. In keeping with the principle of *goto-less* code, we discourage the use of **break**, and it is for this reason that we did not introduce it in Chapter 6 where it arguably belongs.

On the subject of goto-less code, the previous chapter introduced yet another example of goto, namely the **return** instruction. Contrary to the documentation for **return** and the examples therein, we strongly abide by the programming principle that there should be a single exit point to any code module, and therefore we use **return** *only* as the final statement of a function.

Exercise 74

Lookup how the `continue` statement works. Use the `continue` statement in a for-loop to implement `xarray = abs(xarray)`.

The programming principle articulated here should not be viewed as a limitation. Indeed, forcing oneself to avoid the use of `break` normally results in superior coding. In NewtonAlg11.m, we logically have two terminating conditions:

```
if k > nIter    and    if abserr <= tol.
```

In other words, we loop *as long as* (`k < nIter`) *and* (`abserr > tol`), and we already have a perfectly good construct for implementing this logic:

```
while (abserr > tol) & (k <= nIter)
```

On the flip-side, we forfeit the automatic incrementing provided by the for-loop, and so we must manually initialize `k` to 1 (or 2), and manually bump `k` to `k+1` somewhere within the loop (either beginning or end); but this is a small price to pay for a while-statement which so naturally mirrors the English phrase:

> "while the absolute error is greater than the tolerance,
> and the maximum number of iterations is not exceeded, ..."

Two new issues arise from the implementation described above. First, the fact that `abserr` is undefined for the first iteration of the loop presents a problem. Since `tol` is typically of an order less that 10^{-5}, one might try initializing `abserr` to some arbitrarily large value which is sure to pass the `while (abserr > tol)` test (subsequent iterations *will* use meaningfully calculated values of `abserr`). MATLAB provides a better solution with the built-in constant `inf`, which by definition is greater than any numeric value. By initializing `abserr` to `inf`, we eliminate any arbitrariness and have a guarantee that the first iteration of the while-loop will execute.

The second issue we address is the need for the caller to know if the tolerance was ever achieved, and if it was, the caller might also like to know how many iterations executed to achieve this tolerance. Displaying a message to the screen that the algorithm terminated before achieving tolerance, as done in NewtonAlg11.m, falls short of either of these goals. In fact, we will see in the next section that NewtonAlg.m is not the appropriate place for *any* print statements. We partially address this issue by returning a second value, a Boolean variable which we call `success`, and which we define as (`abserr < tol`). In this next version we also return the *actual* number of iterations as a third return variable, though this too will be revisited in the next section.

```
1 %%%%%%%%%%%%%% NewtonAlg12 %%%%%%%%%%%%%%%%%%
2 function    [sqrtFive, success, actualIter] = NewtonAlg12(x0, nIter, tol)
3 %on entry, x0 = initial guess to start Newton algorithm
4 %on entry, nIter = number of iterations to execute (actually maximum)
5 %on entry, tol = small number which, if abs(Xn-Xn-1) < tol,
6 %           will terminate iteration
```

13.1. Tolerance as a terminating condition (NewtonAlg12.m)

```
7  %on exit, sqrtFive = result of nIter iterations until tolerance achieved
8  %on exit, success  = 1 if tolerance achieved within nIter iterations
9  %          success  = 0 otherwise
10 %on exit, actualIter = actual number of iterations
11
12 %%%%%%%%%%%%%%%%%%%%%%%%%%%%%%%%%%%
13 %provide default values if NewtonAlg12 called with no arguments
14 if nargin < 1
15     x0      = 2;         %initial guess
16     nIter   = 20;        %no more than 20 iterations
17     tol     = 1e-6;      %specify a tolerance of 0.000001
18 end
19
20 %%%%%%%%%%%%%%%%%%%%%%%%%%%%%%%%%%%
21 %%%%% initialization section %%%%%
22 xvals    = zeros(1,nIter);
23 xvals(1) = x0;
24 abserr   = inf;       %guarantees at least one iteration of while-loop
25
26 %%%%%%%%%%%%%%%%%%%%%%%%%%%%%%%%%%%
27 %%%%% algorithm section %%%%%%%%%%
28 xold    = x0;
29 k       = 1;
30 while (abserr > tol) & (k < nIter)
31     k          = k+1;
32     xnew       = xold - (xold^2 - 5)/(2*xold);
33     xvals(k)   = xnew;
34
35     %compute absolute error |xnew - xold|
36     abserr     = abs(xnew - xold);
37     xold       = xnew;
38 end
39
40 %%%%%%%%%%%%%%%%%%%%%%%%%%%%%%%%%%%
41 %%% output (to caller) section %%%
42 %assign to return variable the result of last iteration (NOT xvals(end))
43 actualIter = k;
44 sqrtFive   = xvals(actualIter);
45 success    = abserr < tol;
46
47 %%%%%%%%%%%%%%%%%%%%%%%%%%%%%%%%%%%
48 %%% output (to screen) section %%%
49 %% no longer belongs here, see next section!
```

```
50 %% use of 'nIter' and 'end' have been replaced with 'actualIter'
51 diffs    = xvals(1:actualIter) - sqrtFive;
52 fprintf('\niteration \t Xn \t\t |Xn - Xo| \t\t |Xn^2-5|');
53 fprintf('\n-----------------------------------------------');
54 fprintf('\n%d \t\t %f \t\t%e \t\t%e',...
55    [1:actualIter;xvals(1:actualIter);abs(diffs);abs(xvals(1:actualIter).^2-5)]);
56
57 return
```

> **Exercise 75**
>
> Test NewtonAlg12.m using each of the following five invocations (in which the trailing semicolons are intentionally omitted):
> ```
> NewtonAlg12
> NewtonAlg12(2, 4, 1e-10)
> x0 = 2; nIter=40; NewtonAlg12(x0, nIter, 1e-10)
> [sqrtFive, success, actualIter] = NewtonAlg12(2, 4, 1e-10)
> [x, withinTolerance, nIter] = NewtonAlg12(5, 40, 1e-10)
> ```

13.2 A complex program (Main.m, Tabulate.m, NewtonAlg13.m)

In Chapter 7, by using arrays for storage, we achieved a certain modularity to NewtonAlg which isolated the initialization, algorithmic, and output sections of the program. With the introduction of functions in Chapter 12, we were able to eliminate much of the initialization section by replacing hardwired variables with input arguments. In this section we will introduce a much greater modularity to NewtonAlg12.m by moving the output section to an altogether independent function.

Naturally, when we create a separate function which prints a table of the successive approximations x_n, and possibly successive differences $|x_{n+1} - x_n|$, rates of convergence $\frac{|x_{n+1}-x_n|}{|x_n-x_{n-1}|^\alpha}$, and resultants $|x_n^2 - 5|$, we require a mechanism for communicating to this function the entire collection of approximations x_n[1]. To accomplish this, we will pass to a new function Tabulate the array xvals, which until now has been internal to the code for NewtonAlg. Consequently, we need to modify NewtonAlg12.m to *return* as an output argument the entire array xvals.

This raises the question of the role, if any, to be played by returning the argument actualIter. On the one hand, if we do not communicate to the caller of NewtonAlg12 the actual number of iterations, then how is the caller to know that the final answer can be found in xvals(actualIter)? On the other hand, since all the entries

---
[1] In this regard, one may wish to revisit Exercise 38.

13.2. A complex program (Main.m, Tabulate.m, NewtonAlg13.m)

```
                    xvals(actualIter+1),..., xvals(nIter)
```

are garbage left over from initializing `xvals` to size `nIter`, it would be conceptually better (not to mention memory efficient) to avoid returning the over-allocated array, and instead return an array of precisely the meaningful values `xvals(1:actualIter)`. A side benefit of this approach is that it obviates the need to return either `actualIter` or `sqrtFive`, as these numbers can be retrieved using the constructs `length(xvals)`, and `xvals(end)`.

Our next version of NewtonAlg which accomplishes the goals described above is presented in the following implementation NewtonAlg13.m:

```
1  %%%%%%%%%%% NewtonAlg13 %%%%%%%%%%%%%%%%%%%
2  function    [xvals, success] = NewtonAlg13(x0, nIter, tol)
3  %on entry, x0 = initial guess to start Newton algorithm
4  %on entry, nIter = number of iterations to execute (actually maximum)
5  %on entry, tol = small number which, if abs(Xn-Xn-1) < tol,
6  %           will terminate iteration
7  %on exit, success  = 1 if tolerance achieved
8  %           within nIter iterations (0 otherwise)
9  %on exit, xvals  = array (row vector) of approximations Xn
10 %           until tolerance achieved
11 %% caller can extract actual iterations from length(xvals)
12 %% caller can extract final Xn from xvals(end)
13
14 %%%%%%%%%%%%%%%%%%%%%%%%%%%%%%%%%%%%
15 %provide default values if NewtonAlg13 called with no arguments
16 if nargin < 1
17     x0     = 2;          %initial guess
18     nIter  = 20;         %no more than 20 iterations
19     tol    = 1e-6;       %specify a tolerance of 0.000001
20 end
21
22 %%%%%%%%%%%%%%%%%%%%%%%%%%%%%%%%%%%%
23 %%%%% initialization section %%%%%
24 xvals    = zeros(1,nIter);
25 xvals(1)= x0;
26 abserr   = inf;      %guarantees at least one iteration of while-loop
27
28 %%%%%%%%%%%%%%%%%%%%%%%%%%%%%%%%%%%%
29 %%%%% algorithm section %%%%%%%%%%
30 xold    = x0;
31 k       = 1;
32 while (abserr > tol) & (k < nIter)
33     k       = k+1;
```

Chapter 13. Functions II

```
34      xnew      = xold - (xold^2 - 5)/(2*xold);
35      xvals(k)= xnew;
36
37      %compute absolute error |xnew - xold|
38      abserr    = abs(xnew - xold);
39      xold      = xnew;
40 end
41
42 % loop variable k contains the last valid index into xvals
43 actualIter  = k;
44
45 %%%%%%%%%%%%%%%%%%%%%%%%%%%%%%%
46 %%% output section %%%
47 % return to caller array xvals
48 %   since only xvals(1:actualIter) is valid
49 %   whereas xvals(actualIter+1:nIter) is garbage
50 %   we delete the invalid entries using the empty-array
51 xvals(actualIter+1:end) = [ ];
52 success       = abserr < tol;
53
54 return
```

The one construct used in the above code which requires further explanation is the assignment which appears in line 51:

```
xvals(actualIter+1:end) = [ ];
```

The bracketed array symbols [ ] used without containing any data are referred to as the *empty array*, and will be discussed in greater detail in Chapter 16. Simply put, the statement z = [ ] assigns to z an array which contains *no entries*. Our use of the empty array in NewtonAlg13.m effectively trims down the array xvals from an over-allocated array of size nIter to an optimally allocated array of size actualIter.

Exercise 76

If we make the assignment z = [ ], what is length(z)? If z = 1:20, and then we make the assignment z(20) = [ ], what does length(z) become? What is accomplished by the assignment z(2:2:end) = [ ]?

Now that NewtonAlg13.m has been modified to return the (correctly sized) array xvals, we proceed to create the other components of our program. Note that, whereas in previous sections our use of the term *program* has referred to blocks of code residing in a single M-file, our subsequent use of the term will refer to a collection of M-files, each responsible for a particular element of a larger task. The two additional files we require are Main.m and Tabulate.m. Main.m will play the role of a "conductor", orchestrating how the other modules are invoked, and how their return values are manipulated. For our present purposes, Main will call NewtonAlg13, and if `success` is returned with the Boolean value of True (indicated by the logical value 1), then Main will call Tabulate with the passed parameter `xvals`, which is the first variable returned by NewtonAlg. If one wants to use some of the plotting techniques described in Chapter 11, then Main.m is the appropriate place to include code to decide which plotting techniques to use, and to invoke these techniques by calling appropriately implemented functions. In some programming contexts the file Main.m is referred to as a "shell" for executing NewtonAlg13 and Tabulate.

We remark that, in the following code, Main gives the name `withinTolerance` to the second parameter returned by NewtonAlg13. The freedom of Main to choose its own variable names is completely consistent with the rules regarding the "local scope" of a function's variables; that NewtonAlg13 internally uses the name `success` for the same variable is invisible to Main, where the language `if withinTolerance` is more self-documenting than `if success`.

```
%%%%%%%%%% Main.m %%%%%%%%
%%%%%%%% initialization section %%%%%
x0        = 2;
maxIter   = 10;
tolerance = 1e-10;

%%%%%%%%%%%%%%%%%%%%%%%%%%%%%%
%%%%%%%% algorithm section %%%%
[xvals, withinTolerance]    = NewtonAlg13(x0, maxIter, tolerance)

%%%%%%%%%%%%%%%%%%%%%%%%%%%%%%
%%%%%%%% output section %%%%%%
if withinTolerance
    Tabulate(xvals);
    fprintf('Square root of five: \t \%f\n', xvals(end));
else
    fprintf('Failed to converge within tolerance of \%e in \%d iterations\n',..
        tolerance,nIter);
end

return
```

Notice how we choose not to hardwire the input arguments when we call NewtonAlg13. Indeed, we could have used the statement (see Exercise 75)

```
NewtonAlg13(2, 10, 1e-10);
```

but the same programming principles we developed in earlier versions like NewtonAlg7 apply no less to Main.m, which has also been given an input, algorithm, and output sections. Although we approached the task of modularizing our program into functions from the point of view of exporting the output section of NewtonAlg, we could equally well have renamed NewtonAlg as the Main module, and then created functions implementing the algorithm section (to be renamed NewtonAlg and called from Main) and also the output section (to be renamed Tabulate and called from Main). In practice, it is quite typical to identify blocks of code of evolving complexity that should be re-implemented as functions, and then replace these code blocks with function calls.

Our remaining task is to create the file Tabulate.m which implements the function Tabulate according to the output code previously written into NewtonAlg12.

```
1 %%%%%%%%% Tabulate.m %%%%%%%%
2 function Tabulate(x)
3 %separate function for printing
4 %on entry, x = array (row vector) of approximations Xn
5 %on exit, no return value
6 n     = length(x);
7
8 xend  = x(end);
9 fprintf('\niteration \t Xn \t\t |Xn - Xo| \t\t |Xn^2 - 5|');
10 fprintf('\n--------------------------------------------');
11 fprintf('\n%d \t\t %12.10f \t\t%e \t\t%e',...
12      [1:n; x; abs(x-xend); abs(x.^2 - 5)]);
13
14 return
```

Note that, since the array passed to Tabulate is correctly sized, we have been able to simplify some code from NewtonAlg12, like replacing xvals(1:actualIter) with xvals.

At this point we should be quite pleased with our program, which is to say the threesome of functions NewtonAlg13, Tabulate, and Main.m. If judged by the standards of Part II, our current implementation suffers from only one shortcoming, and it is a significant one: All our program is good for is computing the square root of five. This is not an altogether fair criticism, since our program has also been designed to enable us to explore concepts from numerical analysis like rates and order of convergence. In fact, we have yet to fully incorporate into our current program the ideas from Section 11.2 which relate to convergence. Our next version will do just this, and we will address in the next chapter the "only good for computing the square root of five" criticism.

We would like to enhance the tabular output of Tabulate.m so that the user can gain insight into the meanings of order and rate of convergence. For this purpose, we will display the table of successive differences $|x_{n+1} - x_n|$, and then prompt the user to guess the order of convergence. MATLAB provides an instruction enabling a program to prompt the user for input[2], and naturally enough, it is called input() and returns the numeric value typed by the user. Of course, the program is in a position to make its own determination of the order of convergence, and so the user's guess can be verified. Moreover, we will design Tabulate to output a table of the quantities $\lambda_n = \frac{|x_{n+1} - \hat{x}|}{|x_n - \hat{x}|^\alpha}$, which, if the value of α has been correctly chosen, should demonstrate convergence to the correct value of λ.

```
%%%%%%%%% Tabulate.m %%%%%%%%%%%
function Tabulate(x)
%separate function for printing
%on entry, x = array (row vector) of approximations Xn
%on exit, no return value
n       = length(x);    %number of iterations
xend    = x(end);       %Xo=final convergent

fprintf('\niteration \t Xn \t\t |Xn - Xo| \t\t |Xn^2 - 5|');
fprintf('\n--------------------------------------------');
fprintf('\n%d \t\t %12.10f \t\t%e \t\t%e',...
    [1:n; x; abs(x - xend); abs(x.^2 - 5)]);

%query user to make a guess at the order of convergence
orderConv   = input('\n\nMake guess at order of convergence: ');

%display table of lambda's using user's guess at alpha
fprintf('\n\n\niteration \t X_n \t\t Lambda_n (alpha=%d)',orderConv)
fprintf('\n--------------------------------------------')
for k=2:n
    x1  = x(k-1);
    x2  = x(k);
    %discontinue calculating ratios if 0/0
    if (x2 == xend)
        %subsequent code should use lastInd as last
        % index to compute |Xn - Xo|/|Xn-1 - Xo|^alpha
        lastInd = k-1;
        break
    end
    rateConv    = abs(x2-xend)/abs(x1-xend)^orderConv;
    %print Xn and Lambda_n and guess at order
    fprintf('\n%d \t\t %12.10f \t\t %e',k, x2, rateConv);
end
```

---

[2]See Exercise 68.

Chapter 13. Functions II

```
35 %at this point, lastInd = index to use in computing lambda
36 %compute |Xn - Xo|
37 diffs    = x - xend;
38 %if program's guess for orderConv differs from user's, print program's
39 %programmatic calculation of order and rate of convergence
40 %compute slope and y-intercept from last three entries
41 slopeNum = log(diffs(lastInd))   - log(diffs(lastInd-1));
42 slopeDen = log(diffs(lastInd-1)) - log(diffs(lastInd-2));
43 slope    = slopeNum/slopeDen;
44
45 %for purposes of computing rate-of-convergence,
46 % use exact order-of-convergence by rounding
47 alpha    = round(slope);
48
49 if (orderConv ~= alpha)
50     %display table of lambda's with program's guess at alpha
51     fprintf('\n\n\niteration \t X_n \t\t Lambda_n (alpha=%d)',alpha)
52     fprintf('\n-------------------------------------------')
53     for k=2:lastInd
54         x1 = x(k-1);
55         x2 = x(k);
56         rateConv   = abs(x2-xend)/abs(x1-xend)^alpha;
57         % print Xn and Lambda_n and program's guess at order
58         fprintf('\n%d \t\t %12.10f \t\t %e',k, x2, rateConv);
59     end
60 end
61
62 fprintf('\n\n');
63
64 return
```

Exercise 77

Suppose we want the Tabulate function to support two behaviors; one in which the user is prompted to guess the order of convergence, and a second in which the program uses its own internal calculation of the order of convergence. Modify Tabulate.m accordingly by adding a second input argument whose value can be the string `'PromptUser'`. You should also use the `nargin` construct to give this version of Tabulate a default behavior.

13.3 Topics covered in this chapter

In this second of three chapters on MATLAB functions, we showed how functions are used in practice by writing our first *complex program*. The input, algorithm, and output sections of NewtonAlg10.m have been replaced with three functions: a function implementing the Newton algorithm (NewtonAlg.m), a function dedicated to generating formatted output (Tabulate.m), and a shell (Main.m) which orchestrates how the pieces work together. We also introduced the empty array, which will be described in detail in Chapter 16. The MATLAB constructs covered in this chapter are summarized below:

1. Flow control: `break, continue`

2. Built-in constants: `inf`

3. User-input: `input()`

4. Empty array: `[ ]`

Chapter 14

Functions III

At this point we have accumulated a substantial amount of expertise in MATLAB programming, and yet our current version still suffers from the serious criticism that it is only useful for computing the square root of five. In this chapter we will explain an extremely powerful mechanism in MATLAB, known in programming theory as function indirection, which enables us to elegantly overcome this limitation. First, however, we demonstrate that with a minimum of effort we can adapt our program to compute the square root of any (positive) number. The change to the NewtonAlg function is summarized in the following fragment of NewtonAlg14.m:

```
1 %%%%%%%%%% NewtonAlg14.m %%%%%%%%%%%%%%%%%%
2 function    [xvals, success] = NewtonAlg14(x0, nIter, tol, M)
3 %on entry, x0 = initial guess to start Newton algorithm
4 %on entry, nIter = number of iterations to execute (actually maximum)
5 %on entry, tol = small number: if abs(Xn-Xn-1) < tol then terminate
6 %on entry, M = number to evaluate the square root of
7 %on exit, success  = 1 if tolerance achieved within nIter iterations (else 0)
8 %on exit, xvals  = row vector of approximations Xn until tolerance achieved
9 %% caller can extract actual iterations from length(xvals),
10 %% caller can extract final Xn from xvals(end)
11 ...
12 ...
13 %%%%%%%%%%%%%%%%%%%%%%%%%%%%%%%%%%%%
14 %%%% algorithm section %%%%%%%%%%%
15 xold    = x0;
16 k       = 1;
17 while (abserr > tol) & (k < nIter)
18     k      = k+1;
19     %formula for Newton iteration modified to solve F(X) = X^2 - M = 0
20     xnew    = xold - (xold^2 - M)/(2*xold);
21     xvals(k)= xnew;
22
```

Chapter 14. Functions III

```
23       %compute absolute error |xnew - xold|
24       abserr   = abs(xnew - xold);
25       xold     = xnew;
26 end
27 ...
28 ...
29 return
```

Note that only two lines of code have been changed - we have added a fourth input parameter M to the argument list, and we have replaced

    xold^2 - 5   with   xold^2 - M.

Of course, Main.m needs to change the line which calls NewtonAlg14 by passing a value for M.

> **Exercise 78**
>
> Our implementation of NewtonAlg14 ignores a problem with the `nargin` code. Identify the problem, and fix it by making M the first passed argument.

Now, what if we wanted to compute the cube root of 5, or any other number? We could pass an additional parameter r to NewtonAlg14 indicating the root we wish to extract, but then the formula for the Newton iteration must change in the following way:

  `xnew = xold - (xold^r - M)/(r*xold^(r-1));   %solve X^r - M = 0`

This discussion shows that we have always been one line of code away from computing the r'th-root of any positive number M, but if we want to compute a root of

$$f(x) = x^8 - 5x^6 + x^3 - 2x^2 + 7x - 13, \quad \text{or} \quad f(x) = \tan^{-1}(x^3 + e^{\cos 2x}),$$

then we clearly need a more extensible mechanism. In a sense, we need to pass to NewtonAlg14 not simply the M or the r, but rather the actual line of code which needs to be modified for each choice of $f(x)$. Though such a heavy-handed approach is possible using the techniques of this chapter, it is unthinkable to maintain a line of NewtonAlg's code, which references private variables xold and xnew, outside of the NewtownAlg.m file. Moreover, we do not want to make the caller of NewtonAlg responsible for a line of code which is so inextricably bound to the specifics of the Newton algorithm, namely

$$x_{n+1} = x_n - \frac{f(x_n)}{f'(x_n)}.$$

What is not specific to the Newton algorithm are the functions $f(x)$ and $f'(x)$, and so we seek a solution along the lines of calling NewtonAlg in the form:

  `[xvals, withinTolerance] = NewtonAlg(x0, nIter, tol, f(x), f'(x));`

In the following sections we will learn how to pass the *functions* $f(x)$ and $f'(x)$ as parameters.

14.1 Calling functions indirectly using function handles

Philosophically, there are two ideas which are truly fundamental concepts in Computer Science: self-reference and indirection. Self-reference is manifest in the flip-flop circuit, which is the building block of all computer logic, and in software it is the basis for recursive programming. Indirection is the idea, known to anyone familiar with following links on the web, that instead of specifying "the data *itself*", one specifies "*where to find* the data". Indirection appears in hardware design in any application that involves table-lookups, most notably memory management. In this section we describe one of the most important applications of indirection in software, namely the use of "function handles". If the introduction of functions transported us from the Stone Age to the Renaissance, then using function handles will transport us to the Twentieth Century.

Exercise 79

What potential problem is associated with announcing one's office hours to a class of 200 students, and how is this problem solved by announcing instead the web-address of a homepage (on which office hours are posted)?

In Chapter 13 we described the direct method of calling a function, such as DisplayHelp or Tabulate, from within a program. Since the original version of DisplayHelp.m was used only to motivate the discussion of functions, we never returned to cast it into the final form required of a valid function. We do this now by including in DisplayHelp.m the necessary two additional lines of code.

```
1 %%%%%%%%%%% DisplayHelp.m %%%%%%%%
2 function DisplayHelp()
3 %on entry, no arguments
4 %on exit, no return values
5 disp('Help')
6 return
```

There are four methods of *indirectly* calling a function, which we illustrate in the following tutorial session.

```
1 >> %Direct method
2 >> DisplayHelp
3 Help
```

just a reminder of how we called DisplayHelp in Chapter 13

Chapter 14. Functions III

```
 1  >> %Indirect method using strings
```
eval
```
 2  >> eval('DisplayHelp')
 3  Help
```
tell MATLAB to take the string 'DisplayHelp' and behave *as if* we had typed the string directly as a MATLAB statement

feval
```
 5  >> feval('DisplayHelp')
 6  Help
```
tell MATLAB to take the string 'DisplayHelp' and behave *as if* we had directly called the function whose name is 'DisplayHelp'

```
 8  >> funcStr = 'DisplayHelp';

10  >> eval(funcStr)
11  Help
```
use `eval` with the string variable `funcStr` instead of the hardwired string 'DisplayHelp'

```
13  >> feval(funcStr)
14  Help
```
use `feval` with the string variable `funcStr` instead of the hardwired string 'DisplayHelp'

```
16  >> %Indirect method
17  >> % using function handles
```
str2func
```
18  >> hFunc1 = str2func(funcStr);
```
create a "function handle", which is an internal MATLAB data-type, which can be used to call the function whose name is `funcStr`.

```
20  >> hFunc1()
21  Help
```
use the function handle `hFunc1` just as if you were typing the name of the function used to create the function handle ('DisplayHelp')

@ function handle
```
23  >> hFunc2 = @DisplayHelp;

25  >> hFunc2()
26  Help
```
use the `@` construct as equivalent way to create a handle to the function DisplayHelp

inline
```
28  >> %using inline function handles
29  >> hFunc3 = inline('x^2 - 5');
```
when the implementation of the function amounts to a short line of code, *and* if the function is not re-used elsewhere, then `inline()` may be used in place of creating the function in an M-file

```
31  >> hFunc3(7)
32  ans = 44
```
compute $f(7)$ where $f(x) = x^2 - 5$

```
34  >> feval(hFunc3,7)
35  ans = 44
```
arguments to a function called indirectly are passed as additional parameters to `feval`

anonymous @ function handle
```
37  >> %using anonymous function handles
38  >> hFunc4 = @(x,y) x^2 - 5*y;
```
essentially equivalent to `inline()`, the `@()`... constructs an "anonymous" function handle whose input arguments are specified in parenthesis, followed by the code implementing the function

```
40  >> hFunc4(7,2)
41  ans = 39
```
compute $f(7,2)$ where $f(x,y) = x^2 - 5y$

```
43  >> feval(hFunc4,7,2)
44  ans = 39
```

> **Exercise 80**
>
> Lookup `inline` and `function_handle` in the Help documentation. Explain the behavior of each of these function invocations:
> ```
> f = inline('x^2 - 5*y'); f(7,2)
> f = inline('x^2 - 5*y','y','x'); f(7,2)
> g = @(x,y) x^2 - 5*y; g(7,2)
> g = @(y,x) x^2 - 5*y; g(7,2)
> f(g(7,2),feval(f,7,2))
> h = @(x) f(x,x); h(3)   %h's dependence on f is not dynamic
> f = inline('10*x*y'); h(3)
> ```

14.2 Adapting NewtonAlg to any equation (ScalarNewton.m)

Using the powerful methods of *indirect function invocation* described in the previous section, we can easily adapt our "square root of five finder" to a general purpose root-finder, i.e a solver for nonlinear scalar equations $f(x) = 0$. Since this will be our final version, we simply name it ScalarNewton.m instead of NewtonAlg15.m.

We still use Main.m as a shell, but in this version it will also be responsible for defining the function whose roots are sought, as well as its derivative function. The `inline()` method is used to create the function handles which will be passed as two additional parameters to ScalarNewton.

```matlab
%%%%%%%%% Main.m %%%%%%%%%
%%%%%%% initialization section %%%%
x0        = 2;
maxIter   = 10;
tolerance = 1e-10;

funcStr    = 'x^2 - 5';
funcDerStr = '2*x';

f  = inline(funcStr);
df = inline(funcDerStr);

fprintf('\nComputing roots of (%s) using Newton algorithm:',funcStr);
fprintf('\n\t x0=%f, tolerance=%e, and max iterations = %d\n',...
        x0, tolerance, maxIter, F, DF);
%%%%%%%%%%%%%%%%%%%%%%%%%%%%%%%
%%%%%%% algorithm section %%%%
[xvals, withinTolerance]    = ScalarNewton(x0, maxIter, tolerance, f, df)
```

Chapter 14. Functions III

```matlab
19 %%%%%%%%%%%%%%%%%%%%%%%%%%%%%
20 %%%%%%% output section %%%%%%
21 if withinTolerance
22    fprintf('Found root: \t %f\n', xvals(end));
23    Tabulate(xvals);
24 else
25    fprintf('Failed to converge within tolerance of %e after %d iterations\n',...
26            tolerance, maxIter);
27 end
28
29 return
```

```matlab
1  %%%%%%%%%%%% ScalarNewton.m, primary function ScalarNewton %%%%%%%%%%
2  function [xvals, success] = ScalarNewton(x0, maxIter, tol, F, DF)
3  %on entry, x0 = initial guess to start Newton algorithm
4  %on entry, nIter = number of iterations to execute (actually maximum)
5  %on entry, tol = small number: if abs(Xn-Xn-1) < tol then terminate
6  %F  = handle to function whose roots we seek
7  %DF = handle to derivative function
8  %call with F = inline('x^2-5'), DF = inline('2*x')
9  % or call with F = @MyFunc, DF = @MyFuncDer
10 %on exit, xvals  = row vector of approximations Xn until tolerance achieved
11 %on exit, success = 1 if tolerance achieved within nIter iterations (else 0)
12 abserr = inf;
13 xvals  = zeros(1,maxIter);
14 xvals(1)= x0;
15 k      = 1;
16 while (abserr > tol) & (k < maxIter)
17     xold   = xvals(k);
18     xnew   = xold - feval(F,xold)/feval(DF,xold);
19     abserr = abs(xnew - xold);
20     k      = k + 1;
21     xvals(k)= xnew;
22 end
23
24 %trim down xvals (over-allocated!)
25 %caller can use length(xvals) to get actual iterations
26 xvals(k+1:end) = [ ];
27 success = abserr < tol;
28
29 return
```

14.3 Subfunctions (RootFinder.m)

We conclude this chapter by extending our program to one more level of generality. Imagine that we are asked to solve not one, but several nonlinear scalar equations. After all, in a numerical analysis course one is not simply interested in how Newton's algorithm performs for a particular equation like $x^2 - 5$, but also in contrasting its performance for different categories of equations and different choices of initial value x_0.

Naively, one could take the code in Main.m, use copy & paste, and in the pasted block of code modify the hardwired assignments to `funcStr` and `funcDerStr`. But we already know that whenever we perform copy & paste, it's likely that there's a function, or a loop, or both, screaming to be implemented. Conceptually, just as Main.m was created as a shell for NewtonAlg13 and Tabulate, we now wish to create a shell for Main. One option is to rename Main.m to RootFinder.m, and restructure its code to be a function which is passed all of its hardwired variables like `x0, funcStr, funcDerStr`. Of course, a new Main.m will need to be created which calls RootFinder multiple times, preferably in a loop. Our approach will be a variation of this theme, in that we will create a function RootFinder, but we will refrain from implementing it in a separate file RootFinder.m. In this way we will introduce the useful MATLAB construct of a "subfunction".

The urge to recognize a block of code that can (and therefore probably should) be packaged as a distinct function, is a healthy instinct. On the other hand, there is a legitimate reluctance to creating a proliferation of small files which contain functions of limited applicability, for example those performing specific *helper functionalities* on behalf of another function which has grown too unwieldy. MATLAB recognizes the value of including functions in a file which are subordinate to the "primary" function appearing at the top of the file. These secondary functions, called *subfunctions*, appear *below* the code of the primary function. Moreover, the primary function must be implemented as a valid function using the `function` keyword. Thus, the code of our earlier Main.m from Section 14.2 must be recast into the following form:

```
1 %%%%%%%%%%%% Main.m, primary function Main %%%%%%%%%%%%%%%%%%%
2 function Main()
3 ...
4 return
```

As emphasized earlier, we will always terminate our functions with a `return` statement, though this can be substituted with an `end` statement, or omitted altogether. The subfunctions in a file behave in all respects as if they were a primary function in an external file (like the ones we have written so far) with the one exception that they *cannot* be invoked *from* other files. This limitation should not be surprising, since one cannot expect MATLAB to search through all M-files to locate a function with a given name every time a function call is made. This fact also explains why, if the name of an M-file differs from the name given to the primary function in an M-file, the function is nonetheless invoked by using the filename. Another consequence of this rule is that one is free to choose names for functions in within an M-file without fear

Chapter 14. Functions III

that the function name has been, or will be, used in another M-file. In this sense they have similar properties to passed arguments with regard to their "local scope".

Below is a new version which allows our previous implementation to be applied to a collection of different functions and initial values. The structure of this program is as follows:

File	Functions	Functions called
Main.m	Main	RootFinder
	RootFinder	ScalarNewton, Tabulate
ScalarNewton.m	ScalarNewton	-
Tabulate.m	Tabulate	-

In the function Main, the collection of different functions is specified by the variable `funcStrs`, which is an array of strings giving the formula for each function, and also a variable `funcDerStrs` giving the formula for the derivative of each function. Additionally, we have the numeric array `x0s` specifying the initial values to use when applying the Newton algorithm to each of the functions. The only new construct we must be alerted to is the appearance of the braces {...} used to specify the array of strings, instead of the usual brackets [...] with which we are familiar from using numeric arrays. These "cell arrays" are fully explained in Chapter 16.

```
%%%%%%%%%%% Main.m, primary function Main %%%%%%%%%%%%%%%%%
function Main()

%%%%%%% initialization section %%%%%
funcStrs    = {'x.^2 - 5'; 'x.^3 - 4*x + 2'; '4*x - cos(x).^2'};
funcDerStrs = {'2*x'; '3*x^2 - 4'; '4 + 2*sin(x)*cos(x)'};
x0s         = {2, 2, 5};
maxIter     = 100;
tol         = 1e-10;

%%%%%%%%%%%%%%%%%%%%%%%%%%%%%
for k=1:length(funcStrs)
    x0         = x0s{k};          %note the braces when accessing k'th entry
    funcStr    = funcStrs{k};     %next f(x) in string array
    funcDerStr = funcDerStrs{k};  %next f'(x) in string array
    RootFinder(x0, tol, maxIter, funcStr, funcDerStr);
end

return

%%%%%%%%%%% Main.m, subfunction RootFinder %%%%%%%%%%%%%%%%%
function    RootFinder(x0, tol, maxIter, funcStr, funcDerStr)

```

14.3. Subfunctions (RootFinder.m)

```
24 f    = inline(funcStr);
25 df   = inline(funcDerStr);
26
27 fprintf('\n------------------------------------------')
28 fprintf('\nComputing roots of (%s) using Newton algorithm:',funcStr);
29 fprintf('\n\t x0=%f, tolerance=%e, and max iterations = %d\n',...
30         x0, tol, maxIter);
31 fprintf('\n------------------------------------------')
32
33 [x, withinTol] = ScalarNewton(x0, maxIter, tol, f, df);
34 if withinTol
35     root    = x(end);
36     fprintf('\nFound root: \t %f\n', root);
37     Tabulate(x,f,funcStr);
38 else
39     fprintf('Failed to converge within tolerance of %e after %d iterations',...
40           tol,maxIter)
41 end
42 return
```

```
1 %%%%%%%%%%% Tablulate.m, primary function Tabulate %%%%%%%%%%%%%%%%
2 function Tabulate(x, F, funcStr)
3 %on entry, x = array (row vector) of approximations Xn
4 %on entry, F = function handle
5 %on entry, funcStr = formula for function as text
6 %on exit, no return value
7 n     = length(x);      %number of iterations
8 xend  = x(end);         %Xo=final convergent
9
10 fprintf('\niteration \t Xn \t\t |Xn - Xo| \t\t |%s|', funcStr);
11 fprintf('\n------------------------------------------');
12 fprintf('\n%d \t\t %12.10f \t\t%e \t\t%e',...
13     [1:n; x; abs(x - xend); abs(F(x))]);
14
15 %%%%%%%%%%%%%%%%%%%%%%%%%%%%%%%%%%%%%%%%%%%%
16 %compute order of convergence
17 for k=2:n
18     x1 = x(k-1);
19     x2 = x(k);
20     %discontinue calculating ratios if 0/0
21     if (x2 == xend)
22         %subsequent code should use lastInd as last index
23         % to compute |Xn - Xo|/|Xn-1 - Xo|^alpha
```

Chapter 14. Functions III

```matlab
24              lastInd = k-1;
25              break
26         end
27  end
28
29  %at this point, lastInd = index to use in computing lambda
30  %compute |Xn - Xo|
31  diffs    = x - xend;
32  %if program's guess for orderConv differs from user's, print program's
33  %programmatic calculation of order and rate of convergence
34  %compute slope and y-intercept from last three entries
35  slopeNum = log(diffs(lastInd)) - log(diffs(lastInd-1));
36  slopeDen = log(diffs(lastInd-1)) - log(diffs(lastInd-2));
37  slope    = slopeNum/slopeDen;
38
39  %for purposes of computing rate-of-convergence,
40  % use exact order-of-convergence by rounding
41  alpha    = round(slope);
42
43  %%%%%%%%%%%%%%%%%%%%%%%%%%%%%%%%%%%%%%%%%%%
44  %query user to make a guess at the order of convergence
45  userAlpha  = input('\n\nMake guess at order of convergence: ');
46
47  if (userAlpha == alpha)
48         %display table of lambda's with program's guess at alpha
49         fprintf('\n\niteration \t X_n \t\t Lambda_n (alpha=%d)',alpha)
50         fprintf('\n-------------------------------------------')
51         for k=2:lastInd
52              x1 = x(k-1);
53              x2 = x(k);
54              rateConv  = abs(x2-xend)/abs(x1-xend)^alpha;
55              % print Xn and Lambda_n using program's guess at order
56              fprintf('\n%d \t\t %12.10f \t\t %e',k, x2, rateConv);
57         end
58  else
59         %display table of lambda's using user's guess at alpha
60         str = sprintf(\n\niteration \t X_n \t\t Lambda_n (alpha=%d)');
61         fprintf('%s\t\t Lambda_n (alpha=%d)', str, alpha, userAlpha)
62         fprintf('\n-------------------------------------------')
63         for k=2:n
64              x1 = x(k-1);
65              x2 = x(k);
66              rateConv         = abs(x2-xend)/abs(x1-xend)^alpha;
```

```
67          userRateConv   = abs(x2-xend)/abs(x1-xend)^userAlpha;
68          %print Xn and Lambda_n using user's guess at order
69          fprintf('\n%d \t\t %12.10f \t\t %e \t\t %e',...
70              k, x2, rateConv, userRateConv);
71      end
72  end
73
74  fprintf('\n\n');
75
76  return
```

> **Exercise 81**
>
> Re-implement Tabulate.m using subfunctions so the primary function reads:
> ```
> function Tabulate(x, F, funcStr)
> %on entry, x = array (row vector) of approximations Xn
> %on entry, F = function handle
> %on entry, funcStr = formula for function as text
> %on exit, no return value
> DisplaySuccessiveDifferences(x, F, funcStr)
> alpha = ComputeAlpha(x)
> userAlpha = GetUserAlpha()
> if (alpha == userAlpha)
>     DisplayAlpha()
> else
>     DisplayAlphaAndUserAlpha()
> end
> return
> ```
> Revisit Exercise 68 using subfunctions.

14.4 Topics covered in this chapter

In this final chapter on functions we have described the method of invoking functions indirectly through the use of function handles. This important mechanism makes it possible to transform Newton13.m from a root-finder for $x^2 - 5$ to a root finder for general scalar functions $f(x)$. We also explained subfunctions, and introduced cell arrays (described in detail in Chapter 16). The specific MATLAB commands which have been covered are summarized below:

1. Creating function handles: `@, str2func(), inline()`

2. Invoking function handles: `eval(), feval()`

3. Cell arrays: `{...}`

Chapter 15

Arrays IV

In the previous sections we have introduced arrays and described many of their properties, as well as the array operations which can be performed on them. It turns out that the arrays we have discussed have been exclusively $(1 \times n)$-arrays, or *row-vectors*. Arrays of other dimensions can be created, initialized, and operated on by more general array operations. In general, by virtue of MATLAB's comprehensive support for the manipulation of two-dimensional arrays (also called *matrices*), the whole subject of Linear Algebra (also called *Matrix Algebra*), can be explored and utilized in our future MATLAB programming.

15.1 Multi-dimensional arrays and Matrix Algebra

For starters, the operations we have used to create row-vectors, namely

```
zeros(1,n), ones(1,n), rand(1,n)
```

are also available for two dimensional arrays in the form

```
zeros(m,n), ones(m,n), rand(m,n).
```

It is important to observe that m designates the number of rows, and n designates the number of columns. Thus, `rand(m,1)` creates an $(m \times 1)$-array, also called a *column-vector of length m*.

Additionally, MATLAB provides the `eye(n,n)` command to create the $(n \times n)$ identity matrix

$$I = \begin{pmatrix} 1 & 0 & \cdots & 0 \\ 0 & 1 & \cdots & 0 \\ \vdots & \vdots & \ddots & 0 \\ 0 & \cdots & 0 & 1 \end{pmatrix}.$$

Also, the .* operation can be employed to perform a component-wise product of two matrices of the same size. Note that if x is a $(1 \times n)$ row vector, and y is an $(m \times 1)$ column vector, then x.* y does not make sense, since the (1,2)-component of x has no counterpart among the components of y. This may be confusing at first, since in our treatment of one dimensional arrays as row vectors, we accessed the "second" component of x as x(2) rather than x(1,2); actually, this was a shortcut afforded to us by MATLAB, and in fact we were accessing the (1,2)-component of x! In general, the construct x(i,j) is used to access the (i,j)-th component of the $(m \times n)$-array x, assuming $1 \leq i \leq m$ and $1 \leq j \leq n$.

Finally, if we have two matrices A and B in which the number of columns of A matches the number of rows of B, then the "multiplication" operator * can be applied to effect a matrix product: When A is $(p \times q)$-array and B is a $(q \times r)$-array then A * B will produce a $(p \times r)$-array.

With these preparations, we proceed to illustrate in a tutorial fashion the basics of MATLAB's exceptional Linear Algebra capabilities. We first discuss some methods of extracting the most basic attributes of a multi-dimensional array, namely its length in each dimension.

```
 1 >> x    = rand(3,4)
 2     0.9218    0.4057    0.4103    0.3529
 3     0.7382    0.9355    0.8936    0.8132
 4     0.1763    0.9169    0.0579    0.0099
 5
 6 >> [m,n] = size(x)
 7 m =    3
 8 n =    4
 9
10 >> m = size(x,1)
11 m =    3
12
13 >> n = size(x,2)
14 n =    4
15
16 >> N = length(x)
17 N =    4
```

size function (lines 6–8): apply size function to two dimensional array x to retrieve the number of rows and the number of columns into the variables m and n

(lines 10–11): another way to extract from x the number of rows

(lines 13–14): another way to extract from x the number of columns

length function (lines 16–17): the length of a two dimensional array is the *larger* of its column length and its row length (for a square matrix there is no distinction)

create the (3×4)-array of 3 row-vectors of 4 entries each (or 4 column-vectors of 3 entries each), whose 12 entries are random numbers in the interval $[0,1]$

Exercise 82

Does size(x) return a row vector or a column vector? Under what circumstances will length(x) agree with size(x)? If x is a one-dimensional array, does length(x) agree with size(x,1)? What is size(size(x))?

In the following Command Window session we cover initializing arrays and some operations which create new arrays from old arrays, including extracting individual entries and sub-arrays.

15.1. Multi-dimensional arrays and Matrix Algebra

zeros function
```
1 >> z   = zeros(2,2)
2 z =  0    0
3      0    0
4
```
initialize (2×2)-array z to zero matrix

eye function
```
5 >> z   = eye(2,2)
6 z =  1    0
7      0    1
8
```
initialize (2×2)-array z to identity matrix

rand function
```
9  >> z   = rand(2,2)
10 z = 0.6813    0.8318
11     0.3795    0.5028
12
```
initialize (2×2)-array z to random entries in the interval $[0, 1]$

```
13 >> x   = rand(1,3)
14 x = 0.8462    0.5252    0.2026
15
```
initialize (1×3) row vector x to random entries

```
16 >> y   = rand(3,1)
17 y = 0.6721
18     0.8381
19     0.0196
20
```
initialize (3×1) row vector y to random entries

componentwise product operator .*
```
21 >> w   = x.*y
22 ??? Error using ==> .*
23 Matrix dimensions must agree.
24
```
componentwise multiplication of arrays can only be performed on arrays of the same size

matrix product operator *
```
25 >> w   = x*y
26 w = 1.0129
27
28 >> size(w)
29 ans =  1    1
30
```
assign to w the result of matrix multiplication of (1×3)-array with (3×1)-array

multiplying (1×3)-array with (3×1)-array (sometimes called the inner-product, or scalar product) produces a (1×1)-array (i.e. scalar)

```
31 >> w   = y*x
32 w = 0.5688    0.3530    0.1362
33     0.7092    0.4401    0.1698
34     0.0166    0.0103    0.0040
35
36 >> size(w)
37 ans =  3    3
```
assign to w the result of matrix multiplication of (3×1)-array with (1×3)-array

multiplying (3×1)-array with (1×3)-array (sometimes called the outer-product, or Kronecker-product) produces a (3×3)-array

158   Chapter 15. Arrays IV

> **Exercise 83**
>
> If x = zeros(3,1) and y = rand(3,1), what can you say about each of the following arrays:
>   x'* y,   x* y',   x.* y?
> If instead x = ones(3,1), explain how x'* y produces a matrix whose rows agree with y. How about y'* x?

---

end-of-row   1 >> w = [1, 2; 3, 4; 5, 6]
  symbol   2 w = 1   2
    ;   3   3   4
       4   5   6
       5
       6 >> x   = 1:3
       7 x = 1   2   3
       8
  matrix   9 >> y   = x'
transpose 10 y = 1
operator ' 11   2
      12   3
      13
      14 >> w   = y * x
      15 w = 1   2   3
      16   2   4   6
      17   3   6   9
      18
  isequal 19 >> isequal(w, w')
  function 20 ans = 1
      21
  w(i, j) 22 >> z = w(1,3)
      23 z = 3
      24
      25 >> z = w(3,2)
      26 z = 6
      27
w(i:j, k:l) 28 >> z = w(2:3,1:3)
      29 z = 2   4   6
      30   3   6   9

assign to w an explicitly given (3×2)-matrix, where the semicolon symbol (;) is used to indicate "end of row"

assign to x the (1×3) row vector; note that this is the same as $[1, 2, 3]$

assign to y the *transpose* of x, a (1×3) column vector (in general, x is $m \times n$, then x' is $n \times m$); note that this is the same as $[1; 2; 3]$

assign to w the matrix product of y and x, a (3×3)-array

verify w agrees with its transpose w', indicating w is a symmetric matrix

assign to z the (1,3)-entry of w

assign to z the (3,2)-entry of w

assign to z the (2×3)-array formed by extracting all entries of w with row-index equal to 2 or 3, and column-index equal to 1, 2, or 3: [w(2,1),w(2,2),w(2,3); w(3,1),w(3,2),w(3,3)] which is to say the 2nd and 3rd rows of w

15.1. Multi-dimensional arrays and Matrix Algebra

31	`>> z = w(2,1:end)`	assign to `z` the 2nd row of `w`, for any size matrix
32	`z = 2   4   6`	
33		

symbol :
34	`>> z = w(3,:)`	assign to `z` the 3rd row of `w`, using the colon symbol (:) as shorthand for `1:end`
35	`z = 3   6   9`	
36		

37	`>> z = w(:,[3,1])`	assign to `z` the (3×2)-array $[w(1,3),w(1,1);w(2,3),w(2,1);w(3,3),w(3,1)]$
38	`z = 3   1`	
39	`    6   2`	
40	`    9   3`	
41		

diag function
42	`>> d = diag(w)`	assign to `d` the diagonal of `w` - a (3×1) column vector
43	`d = 1`	
44	`    4`	
45	`    9`	
46		

diag function
47	`>> dw = diag(d)`	assign to `dw` the (3×3) diagonal matrix whose diagonal entries are the components of the column vector `d`
48	`dw = 1   0   0`	
49	`     0   4   0`	
50	`     0   0   9`	

Exercise 84

Revisit Exercise 39.

Exercise 85

Suppose you need to test an algorithm you have implemented which requires a symmetric matrix as input. Suggest a way to (non-deterministically) create a symmetric matrix of size `dim`. How about a skew-symmetric matrix? How about a symmetric positive semi-definite matrix?

Solution 85

```
A = randn(dim,dim); Asym = A + A';
A = randn(dim,dim); Askew = A - A';
A = randn(dim,dim); Apos = A * A';
```

Exercise 86

Lookup the function eig in Help. Explain the following:
```
A = rand(3,3); A = A + A'; [eVec, eVal] = eig(A)
isequal(eVal, diag(diag(eVal)))
isequal(eVec * eVec', eye(3,3)), norm(eVec * eVec' - eye(3,3))
isequal(A, eVec * eVal * eVec'), norm(A - eVec * eVal * eVec')
```

Exercise 87

Lookup the function qr in Help. Explain the following:
```
[Q, R] = qr(rand(3,3))    %Q is 'random' orthogonal matrix
isequal(R .* R', R .* diag(diag(R)))
isequal(Q * Q', eye(3,3)), norm(Q * Q' - eye(3,3))
```

Exercise 88

Using qr, suggest another way to non-deterministically create a symmetric matrix. How about a symmetric positive semi-definite matrix of norm less than or equal to one?

Solution 88

```
A = randn(dim,dim);
[Q, R] = qr(A);
Asym = Q * diag(randn(dim,1)) * Q';
Anonneg = Q * diag(rand(dim,1)) * Q';
```

Exercise 89

Let the variable th denote an angle $\theta \in [-\pi, \pi]$. Construct the matrix Rot2 which represents a counter-clockwise rotation in $\mathbb{R}^2$ by θ. How about a rotation in $\mathbb{R}^n$ by angle θ in the $\{x_i, x_j\}$-plane? Finally, verify that your answers satisfy the orthogonality condition $R^t = R^{-1}$.

15.1. Multi-dimensional arrays and Matrix Algebra

Solution 89

```
Rot2 = [cos(th) -sin(th);sin(th) cos(th)];
Rotn = eye(n,n); Rotn([i,j],[i,j]) = Rot2;
isequal(Rotn*Rotn',eye(n,n)).
```

The above examples of producing new arrays from old arrays all arose from either matrix multiplication or the extraction of subarrays (even the `diag` function). In the following paragraphs we discuss a fundamental operation which does not belong to either category, namely matrix inversion.

In courses in Linear Algebra one encounters the concepts of null-space and range-space, column and row rank, under- and over-determined systems, left- and right-inverses, existence and uniqueness of solutions, etc. The short story is that n equations in n unknowns will *generally* have a unique solution, but not always. Supposing $n = 2$, the system in the two unknowns given by $\begin{Bmatrix} x_2 = 0 \\ x_2 = 1 \end{Bmatrix}$ is an example of an over-determined system, while $\begin{Bmatrix} x_2 = 0 \\ x_2 = 0 \end{Bmatrix}$ is an example of an under-determined system. If the linear system is expressed by the $n \times n$ matrix equation

$$A\mathbf{x} = \mathbf{y},$$

where $\mathbf{y} \in \mathbb{R}^n$ is given and $\mathbf{x} \in \mathbb{R}^n$ is to be determined, then the following are equivalent:

1. A is invertible (i.e. A has a left-inverse, and also a right-inverse, and they agree)
2. For arbitrary $\mathbf{y} \in R^n$, there exists a unique $\mathbf{x} \in R^n$ solving the linear system $A\mathbf{x} = \mathbf{y}$
3. The column rank of A is n
4. The row rank of A is n
5. The range-space of A is $\mathbb{R}^n$
6. The nullity of A is 0

More generally, if A is a rectangular $m \times n$ matrix, considered as a linear mapping from $\mathbb{R}^n$ to $\mathbb{R}^m$, the following are equivalent:

1. A has a left-inverse ($m \times m$)
2. For arbitrary $\mathbf{y} \in R^m$, there exists some $\mathbf{x} \in R^n$ solving the linear system $A\mathbf{x} = \mathbf{y}$
3. The column rank of A is m
4. The range-space of A is $\mathbb{R}^m$

If $m > n$, then it is impossible for any of these equivalent properties to hold. In particular, only when $m \leq n$ can A have a left-inverse. Similarly, the following are equivalent:

1. A has a right-inverse ($n \times n$)

2. When (for some $\mathbf{y} \in \mathbb{R}^m$) there is an $\mathbf{x} \in \mathbb{R}^n$ solving $A\mathbf{x} = \mathbf{y}$, then $\mathbf{x}$ is necessarily unique

3. The row rank of A is n

4. The nullity of A is 0

If $m < n$, then it is impossible for any of these equivalent properties to hold. In particular, only when $m \geq n$ can A have a right-inverse. Note that the properties first enumerated for an invertible square matrix A are consequences of the above properties for right and left inverses holding simultaneously when $m = n$. This is a consequence of the following fact (when $m = n$):

$$A \text{ has a left-inverse} \iff A \text{ has a right-inverse.}$$

Needless to say, this superficial summary is not meant to serve as a proper review of the important subject of solving linear systems; it is merely a warmup to the following session in which we explore more deeply MATLAB's support for matrix algebra.

```
 1  >> A = rand(3,3)
 2  A =  0.9501    0.4860    0.4565
 3       0.2311    0.8913    0.0185
 4       0.6068    0.7621    0.8214
 5
 6  >> detA = det(A)
 7  detA = 0.4289
 8
 9  >> Ainv = inv(A)
10  Ainv =  1.6740   -0.1196   -0.9276
11         -0.4165    1.1738    0.2050
12         -0.8504   -1.0006    1.7125
13
14  >> Ainv = A^-1
15  Ainv =  1.6740   -0.1196   -0.9276
16         -0.4165    1.1738    0.2050
17         -0.8504   -1.0006    1.7125
18
19  >> Aleftinv = eye(3)/A
20  Aleftinv =  1.6740   -0.1196   -0.9276
21             -0.4165    1.1738    0.2050
22             -0.8504   -1.0006    1.7125
```

det function (line 6–7): create a random (3×3) matrix w - hope that it's invertible

confirm that w is indeed invertible by verifying its determinant is non-zero

inv function (line 9–12): use the `inv` function to compute the matrix inverse

power operator (line 14–17): raising the invertible matrix A to the power (-1) gives A^{-1}, which is defined by $AA^{-1} = A^{-1}A = I$

right division operator / (line 19–22): matrix right division gives left-inverse to A

MATLAB's definition of right division is "X=B/A solves the linear equation X*A=B", so Aleftinv = I/A solves Aleftinv*A = I

15.1. Multi-dimensional arrays and Matrix Algebra

left division operator `\`

```
23 >> Arightinv = A\eye(3)
24 Arightinv =  1.6740   -0.1196   -0.9276
25             -0.4165    1.1738    0.2050
26             -0.8504   -1.0006    1.7125
27
28 >> x = A\[3; 2; 1]
29 x = 3.8554
30     1.3032
31    -2.8398
32
33 >> x = Arightinv*[3; 2; 1]
34 x = 3.8554
35     1.3032
36    -2.8398
```

matrix left division gives right-inverse to A

MATLAB's definition of left division is "X=A\B solves the linear equation A*X=B", so Arightinv = A\I solves A*Arightinv = I

use matrix left division to solve linear system
$$\begin{pmatrix} 0.9501 & 0.4860 & 0.4565 \\ 0.2311 & 0.8913 & 0.0185 \\ 0.6068 & 0.7621 & 0.8214 \end{pmatrix} x = Ax = \begin{pmatrix} 3 \\ 2 \\ 1 \end{pmatrix}$$

reuse the right inverse `Arightinv` already computed to solve $Ax = \begin{pmatrix} 3 \\ 2 \\ 1 \end{pmatrix}$

Exercise 90

Let `w` be a square matrix. When is `w^(-1)` the same as `w.^(-1)`?

Exercise 91

Let `w` be a diagonal matrix, each of whose diagonal entries is positive. One way to generate such a matrix is to use `w = diag(1+rand(1,n))`. Give a performance comparison of the following techniques for inverting `w`:
`inv(w)`
`w^(-1)`
`diag(diag(w).^(-1))`
`diag(1./diag(w))`
`w\eye(size(w))`
`w/eye(size(w))`

Exercise 92

Show algebraically why x = Arightinv * b solves $A\mathbf{x} = \mathbf{b}$.

Solution 92

A*(Arightinv * b) = A*((A\I) * b) = (A*(A\I)) * b = I * b = b.
The first equality follows from the definition of Arightinv, the second equality follows from associativity of matrix multiplication, and the third equality follows from the definition of MATLAB's left division operator.

Exercise 93

When solving $A\mathbf{x} = \mathbf{b}$, what is the relationship between the statements x = Aleftinv * b and x = Arightinv * b?

Solution 93

x = Arightinv * b $\implies$ $A\mathbf{x} = \mathbf{b}$ (existence of a solution)
$A\mathbf{x} = \mathbf{b}$ $\implies$ x = Aleftinv * b (uniqueness of a solution)

Exercise 94

Let A be some invertible matrix, and b an arbitrarily selected column vector. Compare the performance of the following methods for solving Ax = b:
x = A^(-1)*b;
x = inv(A)*b;
x = A\b;
[Low, Upp] = lu(A); x = Upp\(Low\b);
[Q, R] = qr(A); x = R\(Q' * b);
We will compare the performance of these four methods in a later section, after we have discussed a mechanism to guarantee that the methods are applied to the same representative sample of invertible matrices.

15.1. Multi-dimensional arrays and Matrix Algebra

After discussing how scalar functions of a single variable on an interval domain are represented by pairs of arrays, we briefly mentioned that MATLAB represents a scalar function of two variables on a rectangular domain as a *triple of two-dimensional arrays*. We illustrate this natural extension with some examples. Once again, we indulge in utilizing some sophisticated plotting commands (`meshgrid, surf`) whose definitions are not fully described until we discuss three dimensional plotting in Chapter 20.

```
1 %represent the function (x,y) --> z = sin(x) * cos(y)
2 % on [1,4]x[1,6] as a triple of 2-dim arrays
3 x     = 1:4;
4 y     = 1:6;
5 z     = sin(x).*cos(y)        %error - arguments have mismatched sizes
6
7 [X,Y] = meshgrid(x,y);        %X is 4x6 array (i,j)->x(i)
8                               %Y is 4x6 array (i,j)->y(j)
9 Z     = sin(X).*cos(Y)        %each of the arguments (X & Y) are 4x6
10 surf(X,Y,Z)                  %Z is 4x6 array (i,j)->z(x(i),y(j))
11
12 %represent the function z = sin(x/20) * exp(-(x^2+y^2)/1000)
13 % on R^2 as a triple of 2-dim arrays
14 x     = 1:40;
15 y     = 1:60;
16 [X,Y] = meshgrid(x,y);
17 Z     = sin(X/20).*exp((-Y.^2-X.^2)/1000);
18 surf(X,Y,Z)
```

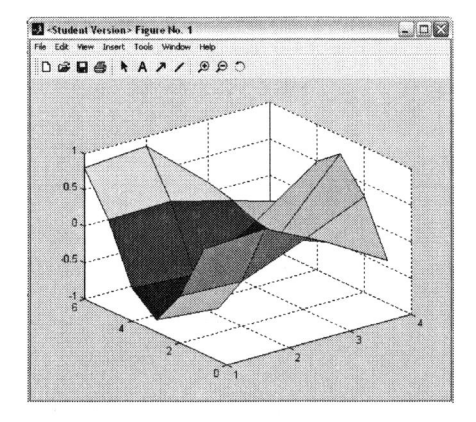

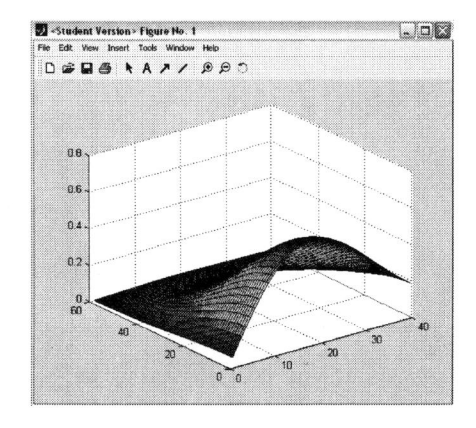

Chapter 15. Arrays IV

> **Exercise 95**
>
> Locate the Help documentation describing the array operations, a snapshot of which appears in the figures below. Verify the behavior of all the constructs illustrated in the Examples section. Familiarize yourself with the Algorithm section.

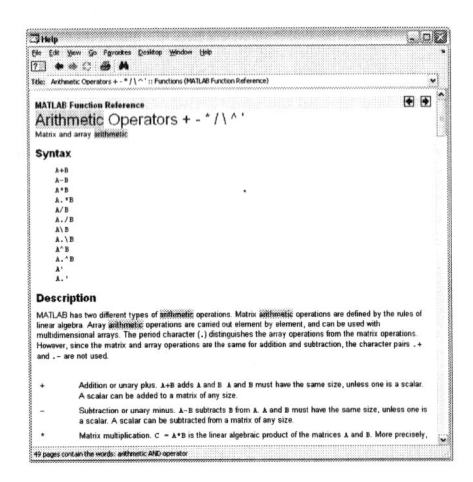

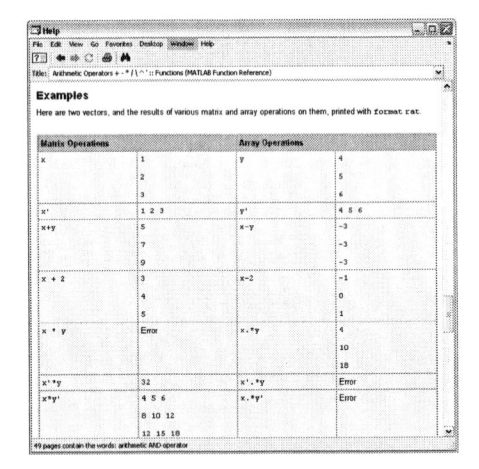

15.2 Topics covered in this chapter

In this chapter we explained the fundamental MATLAB constructs and operations pertaining to matrix algebra. Using two dimensional arrays, we gave a taste of MATLAB's three dimensional graphics capabilities by introducing elementary surface plotting. The specific MATLAB commands we have covered are summarized below:

1. Array initialization: `zeros()`, `ones()`, `rand()`, `randn()`, `eye()`

2. Array attributes: `size()`, `length()`

3. Special characters used with arrays: `end`, `;`, `:`

4. Array access: `x(3,4)`, `x([1 2 3 2 1],:)`, `x(3:end,2:end-1)`

5. Array operations: `*`, `^`, `/`, `\`, `diag()`, `transpose (')`, `inv()`

6. Graphical output: `meshgrid()`, `surf()`

Chapter 16

Arrays V

In previous chapters we have come across some ad-hoc techniques, like the use of the empty array when trimming an over-allocated array, or the use of a cell array when packing a collection of function strings into a new kind of array. In this chapter we develop some of these techniques using a more methodical approach, and also introduce some important new constructs critical to adding structure to complex programs.

16.1 The empty array and dynamic allocation

Recall from NewtonAlg13.m in Chapter 13 our use of the empty array to "trim" an array that had initially been over-allocated:

```
xvals    = zeros(1,nIter);
...
xvals(actualIter+1:end) = [ ];   %trim xvals to correct size
```

This technique works by assigning to a subarray (specified by the left hand side) the empty array (specified by the right hand side). In fact, the empty array is a perfectly legitimate array which can be assigned to any array variable. In particular,

```
xarray = [ ];
```

assigns to the variable `xarray` the empty array. This raises the question of what happens when the following statement is subsequently executed:

```
xarray(1) = pi;
```

After all, assigning a value to the first entry of `xarray` exceeds `xarray`'s capacity to hold data, being an array of length zero. This comment applies equally to any array that is "underallocated" with respect to subsequent assignments. Thus, we are led to explore what happens when we execute assignments such as

Chapter 16. Arrays V

```
xarray(3) = pi;
xarray = zeros(3,1);
xarray(5) = pi;
xarray(5,2) = sqrt(2)
```

The rule is that, when such assignments are encountered, MATLAB will "grow" the array to accommodate the assignment. The following exercise illustrates how this rule works.

> **Exercise 96**
>
> Determine the size and components of `xarray` after executing each of the following assignments:
> ```
> xarray = [ ]
> xarray(3) = pi
> xarray = zeros(3,1)
> xarray(5) = pi
> xarray(5,2) = sqrt(2)
> xarray(6) = sqrt(5)
> xarray = eye(4,2)
> xarray(4,4) = 1
> ```

This behavior of growing arrays during program execution is called "dynamic allocation." Another example is illustrated by the following exercise:

> **Exercise 97**
>
> Determine the size and components of `xarray` after executing each iteration of the for-loop:
> ```
> xarray = [ ]
> for k=1:5
>     xarray = [xarray k]
> end
> ```

Although this exercise gives a contrived method of generating the array `1:5`, it does suggest an interesting method of generating the array `1:n` *but which omits a particular index*:

```
1  xarray    = [ ];
2  n         = 5;
3  omitIndex = 3;
4  for k=1:n
5      if k==omitIndex
6          continue
7      end
8      xarray = [xarray k];
9  end
```

16.1. The empty array and dynamic allocation

> **Exercise 98**
>
> Compare the above method of generating [1,2,4,5] to the following:
> ```
> x = 1:n;
> xarray = x(find(x-omitIndex));
> ```

Some people are of the opinion that dynamic allocation is a cool, even distinguishing feature of MATLAB, since it frees the programmer from the burden of bothering about the sizes of arrays. In fact, it is no such thing - dynamic allocation is a convenience for those in need of a quick-and-dirty method of knocking out a table, or graph, or some other result. Outside these limited circumstances where one may be justified in not being troubled with issues of performance, readability, and program design, dynamic memory allocation should be avoided. As the goals of the current course are to prepare students to write code which functions as part of larger programming projects, we will always pre-allocate our array variables.

> **Exercise 99**
>
> Using the Search tab in the Help Browser, read up on the topic of "Array Preallocation" or "Techniques for Improving Performance and Memory Usage."

> **Solution 99**
>
> "... for and while loops that incrementally increase, or grow, the size of a data structure each time through the loop can adversely affect performance and memory use. Repeatedly resizing arrays often requires that MATLAB spend extra time looking for larger contiguous blocks of memory and then moving the array into those blocks. You can often improve on code execution time by preallocating the maximum amount of space that would be required for the array ahead of time."

We emphasize this important point by formulating the following programming principle:

> <u>Do not use</u> dynamic array allocation in serious programs; limit its use to small-scale experimentation in which debugging or validating code, rather than performance, is the goal. If the method of pre-allocating an array results in over-allocation, then use the efficient technique of "array trimming" to release the over-allocated memory.

16.2 Cell arrays

Recall our first encounter with cell arrays, namely in Chapter 14 where the primary function in Main.m created a new kind of array using curly braces instead of square brackets:

```
1 funcStrs    = {'x.^2 - 5'; 'x.^3 - 4*x + 2'; '4*x - cos(x).^2'};
2 funcDerStrs = {'2*x'; '3*x^2 - 4'; '4 + 2*sin(x)*cos(x)'};
```

It is an easy matter to see that the use of brackets for constructing the above "array of strings" results in an error.

```
1 >> funcStrs    = ['x.^2 - 5'; 'x.^3 - 4*x + 2'; '4*x - cos(x).^2']
2 ??? Error using ==> vertcat
3 CAT arguments dimensions are not consistent.
```

The explanation for the error is simply that we are trying to create an array whose first row consists of eight elements (the characters 'x', '.', '^', '2', ' ', '-', ' ', '5'), while the second row consists of fourteen elements, and the third row consists of fifteen elements. If we pad the strings of eight and fourteen characters by pre-pending [1] spaces, so that they contain fifteen characters each, then the error will be "fixed".

```
1 funcStrs3x15 = ['       x.^2 - 5'; '  x.^3 - 4*x + 2'; '4*x - cos(x).^2'];
2 >> size(funcStrs)
3 ans =
4     3    15
5 >> funcStrs3x15(1,:)
6 ans =
7        x.^2 - 5
8 >> funcStrs3x15(2,:)
9 ans =
10   x.^3 - 4*x + 2
11 >> funcStrs3x15(3,:)
12 ans =
13 4*x - cos(x).^2
```

Of course, this technique of "beefing up" all the rows to be the same length as the longest row is not a practical solution, and was suggested only to illustrate the source of the error message `"arguments dimensions are not consistent"`. Our basic problem is that our "array of strings" does not conform to the types of arrays to which we are accustomed, namely rectangular ($m \times n$)-arrays of numeric or character data. In other words, we need some accommodation, either for non-rectangular arrays of numeric/character data, or rectangular arrays of non-numeric/non-character data. MATLAB recognizes the second variant, and accordingly

---

[1] Appending spaces will work as well, except their presence will not be visible when displaying the strings. Some MATLAB functionality along these lines is explored in Exercise 100 below.

16.2. Cell arrays

provides the construct called a "cell array". Instead of padding the strings in `funcStrs` with spaces so that each row will be the same fifteen characters in length, one may simply change the surrounding brackets `[...]` to braces `{...}`:

```
1 funcStrs    = {'x.^2 - 5'; 'x.^3 - 4*x + 2'; '4*x - cos(x).^2'};
```

Cell arrays are not simply a mechanism for accommodating rows of variable-length, as each entry of the cell array is a data type unto itself. Indeed, `funcStrs` is a 3×1 rectangular array, each of whose one-element rows is a string (not simply an array of characters!)

```
1 >> size(funcStrs)
2 ans =
3      3     1
4 >> funcStrs(1)
5 ans =
6     'x.^2 - 5'
```

> **Exercise 100**
>
> Lookup the functions `char()` and `cellstr()`, and explain the difference between our array `funcStrs3x15` and the array `char(funcStrs)`, as well as the difference between our array `funcStrs` and the array `cellstr(funcStrs3x15)`. Write a code fragment to display the last character of each of the strings in `funcStrs3x15` and also in `funcStrs`.

> **Solution 100**
>
> ```
> funcStrs3x15(:,end)
> for k=1:length(funcStrs) a = char(funcStrs(k)), a(end), end
> ```

There must be a more direct way of getting our hands on the *text* of the string `funcStrs(k)` than using `char(funcStrs(k))`. Indeed, MATLAB allows you to directly access the data of any entry in a cell array using the `{..}` construct:

```
1 >> char(funcStrs(1))    %access the cell entry and convert to text
2 ans =
3 x.^2 - 5
4 >> funcStrs{1}    %access the data of cell entry directly using braces
5 ans =
6 x.^2 - 5
```

The above exercise should suggest that cell arrays are more subtle than we have let on. Indeed, from a certain point of view, cell arrays can *also* be considered to be non-rectangular arrays. We elucidate these subtleties in the following tutorial session:

`{.. ; ..}` symbol
 ```38 >> colStrs = {'first';'second';'third'}```
 ```39 colStrs =```
 ```40   'first'```
 ```41   'second'```
 ```42   'third'```
 ```43 ```
	create a (3×1) cell array of strings

`{.. , ..}` symbol
 ```44 >> rowStrs = {'first','second','third'}```
 ```45 rowStrs =```
 ```46   'first'   'second'   'third'```
 ```47 ```
	create a (1×3) cell array of strings

```48 >> rowStrs3 = rowStrs(3)```
 ```49 rowStrs3 =```
 ```50   'third'```
 ```51 ```
	rowStrs3 is the third cell entry - a string

```52 >> length(rowStrs3)```
 ```53 ans =   1```
 ```54 ```	

```55 >> rowText3 = rowStrs{3}```
 ```56 rowText3 =```
 ```57 third```
 ```58 ```
	don't confuse the cell array entry (the string) with its data (the *characters* of the string)

```59 >> length(rowText3)```
 ```60 ans =   5```
 ```61 ```	

```62 >> triangle = {[1]; [1, 1]; [1, 2, 1]}```
 ```63 triangle =```
 ```64   [1]```
 ```65   [1x2 double]```
 ```66   [1x3 double]```
 ```67 ```
	assign to `triangle` a (3×1) cell array of variable-length row vectors

```68 >> b3 = triangle(3)```
 ```69 b3 =   [1x3 double]```
 ```70 ```
	assign to `b3` the third entry in the cell array

```71 >> B3 = triangle{3}```
 ```72 B3 =   1   2   1```
 ```73 ```
	assign to `B3` the data of the third entry in the cell array

```74 >> triangle{4} = [1, 3, 3, 1];```	grow the cell array by adding a fourth entry: a (1×4) row vector (dynamic allocation)

```
            1 >> Triangle = cell(1,4)
            2 Triangle =     [ ]    [ ]    [ ]    [ ]
            3
            4 >> Triangle(1:3) = triangle(1:3)';
            5
            6 >> Triangle{4} = 'fourth';
            7
            8 >> Triangle =
            9  [1]  [1x2 double]  [1x3 double]  'fourth'
```

cell function — create a new (1×4) cell array with empty entries

transpose operator — use cell array transpose to copy cell entries

there need be no consistency among the data of each cell array entry - some are strings with character data, others are arrays with numeric data

The distinction between the *cell array entry* and its *data* should be reminiscent of our discussion from Section 14.1 on indirection:

> ...instead of specifying "the data *itself*", one specifies "*where to find* the data".

16.3 Topics covered in this chapter

In this chapter we discussed in detail empty arrays and cell arrays, as summarized below:

1. Empty array: `[ ]`, `x(N+1:end) = [ ]`, `isempty()`

2. Cell arrays: `{...}`, `cell()`, `char()`, `cellstr()`

Chapter 17

Sharing Data I

In this chapter we explain global variables and structures; two important constructs MATLAB provides to facilitate writing complex programs in which functionality is distributed among several files and multiple functions. To motivate our discussion of structures and global variables, we will write a program with a graphical user interface, also called a "GUI".

Thus far, our only mechanisms for receiving user input are explicitly passed parameters to Main(), and the rather limited input() command. The purpose of OdeMain.m, developed below in three incremental phases, is to plot the solution to the ODE

$$\dot{y} = Ay + B, \qquad y(0) = Y0, \qquad t \in [0, T1].$$

The four parameters A, B, Y0, T1 will be input by the user using the graphical interface. Our implementation of the GUI will reside in a distinct file called OdeGui.m, which will demonstrate one important use of global variables. We will also utilize one of MATLAB's built-in ODE solvers ode45(), giving us a second opportunity to motivate the use of global variables. Both of these examples will exploit the very important technique of using a "callback function". Finally, by streamlining the code in OdeGui.m, we will motivate the use of MATLAB structures.

17.1 Global variables and callbacks (OdeMain.m)

First, we describe how to use MATLAB's ode45() function. This built-in ODE solver for solving

$$\dot{y} = F(t, y), \qquad y(t_0) = y_0, \qquad t \in [t_0, t_1]$$

works by specifying the interval domain $[t_0, t_1]$ on which a solution is sought, and the initial value of the solution y_0 at the initial time t_0. Additionally, the programmer is required to specify the ODE $F(t, y)$; the method by which this specification is accomplished is by actually coding a function which implements $\dot{y} = F(t, y)$ according to the following format:

```
function ydot   = NameOfFunctionImplementingF(t, y)
    %supply code implementing F(t,y)
```

Chapter 17. Sharing Data I

```
3      % according to which ydot is determined by t and y(t)
4      ydot    = ....
5 return
```

For example, if our ODE was $\dot{y} = \sin(ty^2)$, then we could write

```
1 function ydot    = F(t, y)
2     ydot    = sin(t*y^2);
3 return
```

A handle to the function implementing $F(t, y)$ is supplied to ode45() as the first parameter:

```
[t,y]    = ode45(@F, [t0,t1], y0);
```

During the execution of ode45(), F(t,y) will be called many times, and upon its conclusion ode45() will return [t,y], an array of t-values in $[t_0, t_1]$, along with an array of the corresponding $y(t)$-values. Thus, plot(t,y) can be used to plot the solution. Of course, t(1) will agree with t_0, t(end) will agree with t_1, and y(1) will agree with y_0. The mechanism of supplying to ode45() a function handle is referred to as supplying a "callback", and is no different from the function handles we introduced in Chapter 14 where we described how to call functions indirectly. Indeed, the following code is also acceptable (though less adaptable):

```
[t,y]    = ode45(@(t,y) sin(t*y^2), [t0,t1], y0);
```

Exercise 101

What goes wrong if one uses @(y,t) in the first argument to ode45()?

Our present task of solving the ODE $\dot{y} = Ay + B$ where A and B are supplied by the user at runtime, means that known values of A and B cannot be coded into our implementation of $F(t, y)$. One might consider an approach where A and B are passed as parameters to F, but ode45() *requires* that the function implementing the ODE is passed t and y only. The solution is for A and B to be assigned values in OdeMain before ode45() is called, and for these values to be "shared" with the code implementing $F(t, y)$, effectively violating the rules controlling the "scope" of variables. This provision for overriding the local scope of a variable is supplied by the keyword global. Specifically, the implementation of $F(t, y)$ can be given as follows:

```
1 function ydot    = F(t, y)
2 %the global variables A & B are shared with code outside of this function
3 global A B
4     ydot    = A*y + B;
5 return
```

17.1. Global variables and callbacks (OdeMain.m)

Global variables are generally a bad idea, since they are at odds with all the principles we emphasized in breaking a complex program into self-contained modules. Indeed, this is why all variables are of local-scope by default! On the other hand, there is no other solution to the problem we are faced with, since ode45() cannot possibly accommodate all flavors of $F(t, y, A, B, ..)$ where additional parameters are passed, not to mention the problem of how MATLAB's built-in ode45() could get its hands on these values of $A, B, ..$ to pass to $F(t, y, A, B, ...)$.

If we allow the user to specify the parameters $A, B, t_1, y(t_0) = y_0$ using the input() statement, then we can give the following implementation of our program. Note that the keyword global must be used in all functions in which the parameters are given global scope.

```matlab
%%%%%%%%%%%%%%%%%%%%%%%%%%%%%%
%%%% OdeMain.m, primary function OdeMain() %%%%
%%%%%%%%%%%%%%%%%%%%%%%%%%%%%%
function OdeMain()
%solve ODE y' = A*y + B, t=[0,T1], y(0)=Y0
%specify global scope of variables A,B shared
% with subfunction ODEimplementation()
global   A B

%initialize global variables
A   = input('specify A:');
B   = input('specify B:');
%initialize local variables
Y0  = input('specify initial y-value Y0:');
T1  = input('specify final time T1:');

%solve ODE using MATLAB's built-in ode45
[t, y]  = ode45(@ODEimplementation, [0 T1], Y0);

%plot results
figure(100)
plot(t,y)
textstr = sprintf(...
  'solving ODE y'' = %g y + %g \non interval [0,%g] with y(0)=%g',A,B,T1,Y0);
text(0.15,0.75,textstr,'units','normalized');

return

%%%%%%%%%%%%%%%%%%%%%%%%%%%%%%
%%%% OdeMain.m, secondary function ODEimplementation() %%%%
function ydot    = ODEimplementation(t,y)
```

```
32 %specify global scope of variables A,B shared with OdeMain()
33 global   A B
34       ydot    = A*y + B;
35 return
```

17.2 GUI programming (OdeGui.m)

As promised, we will next replace the `input()` statements with code implementing a graphical interface, and in so doing we will see an even more elaborate application of global variables and callback functions. Though `ODEimplementation()` remains unchanged, the next version of `OdeMain()` introduces the global variable `gStartODE`, which is shared with the function `OdeGui()`. This variable will be set to True by `OdeGui()` when the user presses a push-button labelled "Start ODE".

At this point we also introduce the naming convention of prepending the letter "g" to variables with global scope, as well as prepending the letter "h" to variables which are GUI function handles. Naming conventions along these lines are easily abused and generally lead to ugly code (e.g. prepending a "b" to a self-evidently Boolean variable like `withinTolerance`), but clearly identifying global variables has particular benefits, and can often save the reader the trouble of hunting around in the wrong places for the description or initialization of an unfamiliar variable. The function `OdeMain()` takes the following final form:

```
1  %%%%%%%%%%%%%%%%%%%%%%%%%%%%%%
2  %%%% OdeMain.m, primary function OdeMain() %%%%
3  %%%%%%%%%%%%%%%%%%%%%%%%%%%%%%
4  function OdeMain()
5  %solve ODE y' = A*y + B, t=[0,T1], y(0)=Y0
6  global   gStartODE gA gB gY0 gT1
7
8  %initialize globals
9  %initialize to false flag indicating "Start ODE" button was pushed
10 gStartODE  = 0;
11 %initialize parameters to y' = y, y0=1, t=[0,1]
12 gA       = 1;
13 gB       = 0;
14 gY0      = 1;
15 gT1      = 1;
16 hFig     = OdeGui('init');
17
18 %use GUI to determine:
19 %  terminating time gT1,
20 %  initial value y(0)=gY0,
21 %  ODE parameters gA and gB
```

```
22 % Gui will set global gStartODE when button pushed
23 while ~gStartODE
24      %spin in do-nothing loop while waiting for button
25      pause(0.1);
26 end
27 %solve ODE using MATLAB's built-in ode45
28 [t, y] = ode45(@ODEimplementation, [0 gT1], gY0);
29
30 %plot results
31 figure(hFig)
32 plot(t,y)
33 textstr = sprintf(...
34     'solving ODE y'' = %g y + %g \non interval t=[0,%g] with y(0)=%g',A,B,T1,Y0);
35 text(0.15,0.75,textstr,'units','normalized');
36
37 return
```

We now create a second file named "OdeGui.m" implementing the graphical interface. The code `OdeGui()` is passed a parameter `cmd`, which can have one of the two values `'init'` or `'startODE'`. After initializing the global variables `gA`, `gB`, `gY0`, `gT1` to some default values, and setting `gStartODE` to False, `OdeMain()` will call `OdeGui()` once with `cmd` set to `'init'`, and then *waits* - perpetually looping until the global variable `gStartOde` changes value from 0 to 1. So who sets the variable `gStartOde` to 1? This will occur in `OdeGui()` when it is passed the parameter `cmd` set to `'startODE'` - but then who executes that function call? In other words, someone, somewhere, must execute the command

```
OdeGui('startODE')
```

or indirectly through the equivalent (using double-quotes to insert a single-quote into a string)

```
eval('OdeGui(''startODE'')')
```

This is accomplished using callbacks, i.e. creating a push-button control which is instructed to issue the command `eval('OdeGui(''startODE'')')` when the user has clicked on the graphical button of the user-interface-control (also called a "uicontrol").

A second point needs to be clarified before presenting the code of OdeGui.m. Our description of global variables followed the idea that a primary function may need to "share", or "make accessible" to secondary functions (or even primary functions in other files) variables which, by default, are visible only locally within the function. Actually, we should recall that there are two aspects of a variable having local scope:

i. Locally scoped variables are invisible to *all* other functions; their values are neither accessible nor modifiable by other functions, which likewise can freely use these same variable names without conflict.

ii. Locally scoped variables "disappear" when the function exits and control is returned to its caller; values assigned to local variables from prior invocations are lost.

Thus, our description motivating global variables notwithstanding, the following is a precise characterization of a variable having global scope:

i. Globally scoped variables are visible to, and modifiable by, *all* other functions which declare the same variable names with the keyword `global`; other functions which omit the global declaration of these variables can freely use the same variable names without conflict.

ii. Globally scoped variables "persist" when the function exits and control is returned to its caller; even if no other functions declare these variables to be global, subsequent invocations of the function will find values assigned to these variables intact.

Now let's say we have a need for variables retaining their values from one invocation to the next, but do *not* want to share these variables with other functions. Assuming we adhere to the convention of prepending the letter "g" to global variables shared by several functions, then one solution is to declare such variables with the keyword `global`, but to suppress the leading "g" in the variable name. On the other hand, conventions are never followed religiously, and MATLAB provides a more definitive solution by introducing the keyword `persistent`. Persistent variables behave like local variables with respect to property (i), and like global variables with respect to property (ii).

With these preparations concluded, we present the code for OdeGui.m. In reading the code one will notice several instances of "magic numbers"; unfortunately, magic numbers are typical of GUI programming, and are somewhat forgivable in this context.

```
%%%%%%%%%%%%%%%%%%%%%%%%%%%%
%%%% OdeGui.m, primary function OdeGui() %%%%
%%%%%%%%%%%%%%%%%%%%%%%%%%%%
function hFig   = OdeGui(cmd)
global      gStartODE gA gB gY0 gT1
persistent  hA hB hY0 hT1

switch cmd
    case 'init'
        hFig    = figure(100);
        [hA, hB, hY0, hT1]   = InitGui(gA,gB,gY0,gT1);
    case 'startODE'
        gA  = RetrieveTextValue(hA);
        gB  = RetrieveTextValue(hB);
        gY0 = RetrieveTextValue(hY0);
        gT1 = RetrieveTextValue(hT1);
        gStartODE   = 1;
```

17.2. GUI programming (OdeGui.m)

```
18 end
19
20 return
21
22 %%%%%%%%%%%%%%%%%%%%%%%%%%%%%
23 %%%% OdeGui.m, secondary function InitGui() %%%%
24 %%%%%%%%%%%%%%%%%%%%%%%%%%%%%
25 function    [hA, hB, hY0, hT1] = InitGui(A,B,Y0,T1)
26 %Note: A, B, Y0, T1 are passed local variables
27 %Note: hA, hB, hY0, hT1 are returned local variables
28 y   = 0.02;
29
30 cmdText = 'OdeGui(''startODE'');';
31 uicontrol('callback',cmdText,...
32     'units','normalized','position',[0.02, 0.01, .17, .08],...
33     'style','pushbutton','string','Solve ODE','FontWeight','bold');
34
35 hA  = CreateTextItem(.30, y, 'A:   ', A);
36 hB  = CreateTextItem(.50, y, 'B:   ', B);
37 hY0 = CreateTextItem(.70, y, 'Initial Y:   ', Y0);
38 hT1 = CreateTextItem(.90, y, 'Final T:   ', T1);
39
40 return
41
42 %%%%%%%%%%%%%%%%%%%%%%%%%%%%%
43 %%%% OdeGui.m, secondary function CreateTextItem() %%%%
44 %%%%%%%%%%%%%%%%%%%%%%%%%%%%%
45 function hEditText = CreateTextItem(x, y, textStr, initVal)
46 %return handle to edit-text item so its value can be retieved after editing
47 widthStatic = 0.11;
48 widthEdit   = 0.06;
49 height      = 0.04;
50
51 hEditText   = uicontrol('units','normalized',...
52     'position', [x,y,widthEdit,height],...
53     'style','edit','string',num2str(initVal));
54 %no need to keep around handle to static text item
55 uicontrol('units','normalized',...
56     'position', [x-widthStatic,y,widthStatic,height],...
57     'style','text','string',textStr,'FontWeight','bold','FontSize',10);
58
59 return
60
```

```
61 %%%%%%%%%%%%%%%%%%%%%%%%%%%%%%
62 %%%% OdeGui.m, secondary function RetrieveTextValue() %%%%
63 %%%%%%%%%%%%%%%%%%%%%%%%%%%%%%
64 function val     = RetrieveTextValue(hText)
65          str = get(hText,'string');
66          val = str2double(str);
67 return
```

A snapshot of the resulting figure, displaying both the GUI and ODE solution, is shown below:

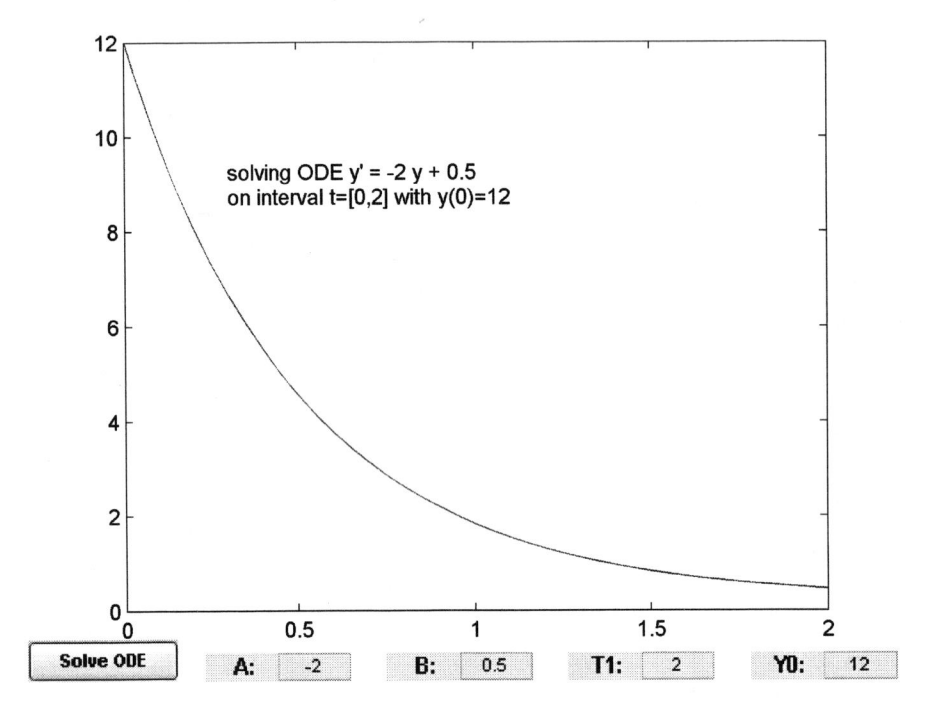

[Figure: Plot of ODE solution showing "solving ODE y' = -2 y + 0.5 on interval t=[0,2] with y(0)=12", with GUI controls: Solve ODE button, A: -2, B: 0.5, T1: 2, Y0: 12]

One may wonder why we wrote InitGui() to be passed the values gA,gB,gY0,gT1, when we could have so easily made these variables share-able with OdeGui() by simply adding the line:

```
1 global   gA gB gY0 gT1
```

In fact, why not go all the way and avoid returning the handles to the four interface controls by writing:

```
1 function    InitGui()
2 global   gA gB gY0 gT1
3 global   ghA ghB ghY0 ghT1
4 ...
5 return
```

Indeed, this is *precisely* the kind of unstructured programming we wish to avoid - carried to its conclusion this methodology will do away with all parameter passing by making all variables global, thereby obscuring the functionality achieved by modularizing complex tasks into self-contained functions. Note that it was in this spirit of modularity that we introduced the self-contained and independently useful function `RetrieveTextValue()`; the following lines of code are functionally equivalent, but burden the reader with the specifics of how data is retrieved from a uicontrol.

```
1    case 'startODE'
2        %retrieve text value from edit uicontrol
3        gA  =  str2double(get(hA,'string'));
4        ...
```

By invoking our user-defined function named `RetrieveTextValue(hA)` we have made the comment redundant, and the obscure `str2double(get(...))` code invisible.

We have ignored the issue, typical of user interface programming, of validating the user's input. This observation applies equally to our first version where we used the `input()` command. For example, if the text inserted into the edit-text field of the interface is not numeric, we should have some way of detecting this fact and rejecting the input. By passing a callback to the uicontrol for the edit-text control, we can arrange for program control to be passed to a function of our choosing, presumably `OdeGui()` with `cmd='editText'`. Functions which intercept a stream of data (in the present case we are dealing with keyboard input) and check that the data conform to a specific format (e.g. numeric data, possibly falling within a definite range of values), are called "filters". As this topic is peripheral to our main subject of structures and global variables, we address it in an exercise.

Exercise 102

Modify OdeGui.m to constrain the text entered by the user into the edit-text fields to be numeric. Make an additional modification to enforce the the requirement that t_1 be positive.

Solution 102

Lookup the use of the `tag` field of a uicontrol. When creating the edit-text control, specify a callback and a tag. You should also find the MATLAB function `isnan()` useful in validating the text input.

17.3 Structures

Naturally, we must address the question of handling a GUI which contains scores of user interface controls, and for which we would want to avoid passing parameter lists with scores of arguments:

```
function [hA, hB, hC, ...] = InitGui(A, B, C, ...)
```

MATLAB provides an important mechanism for dealing with this issue, by allowing the programmer to consolidate many variables, often consisting of different data types, into a single variable referred to as a "structure". Our next version of OdeGui.m will apply this method to consolidate the variables `A,B,Y0,T1` into a structure named `params`, which can be passed between functions as a single variable.

In most languages, the typical example motivating structures is the proverbial "employee record". When a program needs to manipulate data associated with an employee database, it is natural to organize the data for each employee into an employee record consisting of "fields". At a minimum, these fields would include:

{LastName, FirstName, SocialSecurityNum, DateOfHire, Position, Department}

By representing such a collection of data in a single variable for each employee, a program can create functions that are passed an employee record, and then work by accessing and manipulating the data of specific fields.

While the term "record" is standard among database applications, MATLAB and many other programming languages employ the equivalent terminology "structure". Formally, a MATLAB structure is a collection of "(name, value)-pairs"; the "name" refers to the field name, such as "SocialSecurityNum", and the "value" refers to the field's data, such a "123-45-6789". An example of an employee record is

{'Newton', 'Isaac', 123456789, 607403, 'Chief Scientist', 'Engineering'}

MATLAB provides the keyword `struct` to create a structure with this data:

```
exampleStruct  = struct('LastName','Newton','FirstName','Isaac',...
    'SocialSecurityNum',123456789,'DateOfHire',datenum('1-4-1663'),...
    'Position','Chief Scientist','Department','Engineering');
```

In this example, the SocialSecurityNum field is a 9-digit number, the DateOfHire field is a serialized date[1], and all other fields contain string values. Data from a specific field of the structure is retrieved using the "(name of structure).(name of field)" construct, as in

```
socSecNum   = exampleStruct.SocialSecurityNum;    %numeric value
hireDateStr = datestr(exampleStruct.DateOfHire);  %convert datenum to string
```

---
[1] Consult Help on `datenum()` and `datestr()` to learn about serialized dates.

At first glance, motivated by consolidating long lists of parameters into a single variable, one might think to apply the structure concept to OdeGui.m by creating the following structures and corresponding function calls:

```
1      ...
2      initValues  = struct('initAval',gA,'initBval',gB,...
3                           'initY0val',gY0,'initT1val',gT1);
4      editHandles = InitGui(initialValues);
5      ...
6 function editHandles    = InitGui(initValues)
7      ...
8      hT1 = CreateTextItem(.90, y, 'Final T:  ', initValues.initT1val);
9      editHandles = struct('handleA',hA,'handleB',hB,...
10                          'handleY0',hY0,'handleT1',hT1);
11 return
```

Though this may be a worthwhile warmup exercise, it is misguided program design, since it is rather like making a structure of *all employee names*, and another structure of *all employee positions*. The data which should be consolidated should relate to a single edit-text control, and indeed, this is how uicontrols are internally organized by MATLAB.

> **Exercise 103**
>
> Put a breakpoint at the `return` statement (line 40) in `InitGui()` and run OdeMain. When the program enters the Debugger, do a `get(hA)` and see if any of the *fields* of the uicontrol *structure* are familiar. While still in the Debugger, insert a breakpoint at the statement `gStartODE=1`. Upon breaking at line 17, explain the results of executing the following commands:
> ```
>   hPushButton = findobj('style','pushbutton')
>   pushButton = get(hPushButton)
>   isstruct(pushButton)
>   callbackStr = pushButton.Callback
>   eval(callbackStr)
>   dbstack
> ```

In this final version of OdeGui.m we utilize a structure to represent the data associated with each of the four edit-text controls. Analogous to our employee record which tracks the first and last names and social security number of an employee, our edit-text structure will track the (static) text displayed to the left of the edit-text control, the initial value displayed in the edit-text control, and the uicontrol handle returned by MATLAB after creating the edit-text control. Since there will be four instances of these structures, we should address an earlier issue of passing each of these in a long and cumbersome argument list of parameters. Our solution is to create a *persistent* (1×4)-array **params** to hold the four (and potentially many

186   Chapter 17. Sharing Data I

more than four) edit-text structures. The individual edit-text structures can be accessed from `params` from simple indexing, for example `params(4).handle` will be the handle to the edit-text control associated with the final time gT1.

```matlab
%%%%%%%%%%%%%%%%%%%%%%%%%%%
%%%% OdeGui.m, primary function OdeGui() %%%%
%%%%%%%%%%%%%%%%%%%%%%%%%%%
function hFig    = OdeGui(cmd)
global   gStartODE gA gB gY0 gT1
persistent  params

switch cmd
    case 'init'
        hFig    = figure(200);
        %create structures for each editable text field of GUI
        % initialize with value (from OdeMain) and static text label
        % NOT GOOD PRACTICE to assume values have been set by caller
        Astruct    = struct('val',gA,'handle',0,'text','A:');
        Bstruct    = struct('val',gB,'handle',0,'text','B:');
        Y0struct   = struct('val',gY0,'handle',0,'text','Y0:');
        T1struct   = struct('val',gT1,'handle',0,'text','T1:');
        %create persistent variable params to hold four structs
        params     = [Astruct, Bstruct, Y0struct, T1struct];
        %InitGui will return params with the handle fields initialized
        params     = InitGui(params);
    case 'startODE'
        %set the gStartODE flag to true,
        % and retrieve parameter values from edit-text of GUI
        gStartODE  = 1;
        %occurrence of 1,2,3,4 below qualify as "magic numbers"
        gA  = RetrieveTextValue(params(1).handle);
        gB  = RetrieveTextValue(params(2).handle);
        gY0 = RetrieveTextValue(params(3).handle);
        gT1 = RetrieveTextValue(params(4).handle);
end

return

%%%%%%%%%%%%%%%%%%%%%%%%%%%
%%%% OdeGui.m, secondary function InitGui() %%%%
%%%%%%%%%%%%%%%%%%%%%%%%%%%
function params = InitGui(params)
y    = 0.01;
```

17.3. Structures

```
40
41 cmdText = 'OdeGui(''startODE'');';
42 uicontrol('callback',cmdText,...
43     'units','normalized','position',[.02 y .17 .06],...
44     'style','pushbutton','string','Solve ODE','FontWeight','bold');
45
46 for k=1:length(params)
47     x    = .30 + (k-1)*0.2;
48     %create the text control in GUI,
49     % and set uicontrol handle field of params(k) structure
50     params(k).handle    = CreateTextItem(x,y,params(k).text,params(k).val);
51 end
52
53 return
```

Notice that *after* OdeMain completes execution the figure, and the graphical interface it contains, will persist. In fact, the code to OdeGui() persists as well, as can be verified by adding a breakpoint to OdeGui(), and then pressing the "Start ODE" push-button. Needless to say, this is an undesirable behavior. Furthermore, if OdeMain() simply deletes the figure before returning, then the user will have no chance to view the plot! The next exercise suggests modifying the present version so that the program can be run repeatedly, and will be well-behaved upon termination.

Exercise 104

Add a push-button labelled "Exit" to the user interface, and then wrap the relevant code in OdeMain() in a while-loop (e.g. `while gRunning ... end`) which breaks when the user presses the Exit button. After breaking, does it matter whether you use close(hFig) or delete(hFig)? Note that the program will be ill-behaved upon clicking in the figure's close box.

Exercise 105

Consult Help on the topic of "Function Handle Callbacks". Investigate the following alternatives to adding the Exit button (see also Section 19.3):
set(hFig, 'CloseRequestFcn', 'OdeGui(''Exit'');');
set(hFig, 'CloseRequestFcn', 'gRunning = 0;');
Debugging Tip: When debugging a graphical interface, you may need to get control in the Command Window by repeatedly pressing control-C, and then you can delete the figure with the delete(gcf) command.

Exercise 106

It is good practice to take pause and inspect your code for possible ways of eliminating global variables. Can you find a way to eliminate all the global variables shared between `OdeMain()` and `OdeGui()`? See the program HelixMain.m in Chapter 19 for one approach.

17.4 Topics covered in this chapter

In this chapter, the first of two on sharing data, we explored callbacks, structures and global variables as mechanisms for coping with the increasing complexity of large programs. We also learned how to use MATLAB's built-in ODE-solver, and wrote a graphical user interface (GUI) employing push-buttons and edit-text fields. The specific topics covered are summarized below:

1. Scope keywords: `global`, `persistent`

2. Structures: `struct()`, `isstruct()`

3. GUI functions: `uicontrol()`, `findobj()`, `get()`, `set()`

4. GUI (uicontrol) styles: `'pushbutton'`, `'edit'`, `'text'`

5. Built-in ODE-solver: `ode45()`

6. Miscellaneous: `isnan()`, `delete()`, `datenum()`, `datestr()`

Chapter 18

Sharing Data II

In this chapter we return to Exercise 94 in which one is asked to execute a performance comparison of five methods for solving the linear equation $Ax = b$. We recall that it is important to run each algorithm a large number of times in order to compute execution times which exceed the resolution of MATLAB's internal timer. Additionally, since performance will generally be dependent on the specific A, we should strive to determine each method's "average performance", in the sense of applying each method to a broad selection of A's, being careful to exclude any A which is non-invertible. Finally, in order to enforce a fair comparison, each method must be applied to an identical set of A's and b's. In summary, our "test data" should consist of a large set of invertible matrices to which each of the five methods can be applied in a reproducible manner. The requirement of reproducibility is not only important for the independent verification of our performance results, but also in case additional techniques for solving $Ax = b$ are to be compared.

18.1 MAT-files (CompareAXeqB.m)

Creating an array of invertible matrices is a task which, although new, is well within our grasp; in effect, we want a "row vector" of "$n \times n$ matrices", and MATLAB has no difficulty in creating such a beast (in mathematics this beast is called a "tensor"). The appropriate code, which constructs a 3-tensor[1] of size (dim) × (dim) × (numSamples), is as follows:

```
%each A is 12x12, and we want 10000 of them for testing
numSamples  = 10000;
dim         = 12;
%randomA will be our 3-tensor of size dim x dim x numSamples
randomA     = zeros(dim,dim,numSamples);
%b is a single column vector chosen with random entries
randomB     = randn(dim,1);
```

---

[1]Strictly speaking, this would be called a $(2,1)$-tensor, since each $n \times n$ matrix is a linear transformation in the context of solving $Ax = b$. For our purposes, it is enough to imagine a three dimensional array of numbers.

Chapter 18. Sharing Data II

```
 8 k       = 1;
 9 while k <= numSamples
10     A       = randn(dim,dim);
11     %if A non-invertible, reject it
12     if det(A) < 0.01
13         continue
14     end
15     %if A invertible, store it in our "array-of-arrays"
16     randomA(:,:,k) = A;
17     %bump k after invertible A has been added to randomA
18     k       = k + 1;
19 end
```

> **Exercise 107**
>
> Referring to the above code fragment, explain the meaning of each of the following constructs.
> randomA(1,2,3)
> randomA(3,2,1)
> randomA(:,:,3)
> randomA(end,end,:)

At this point, we could do a performance comparison of our five methods using the following code:

```
 1 %%%%%%%%%%%%%%%%%%%%%%%%%%%
 2 tic
 3 for k=1:numSamples
 4     A      = randomA(:,:,k);
 5     x      = A^(-1)*b;
 6 end
 7 timer     = toc;
 8
 9 fprintf('\naverage time using A^(-1)b: %g', timer/numSamples);
10
11 %%%%%%%%%%%%%%%%%%%%%%%%%%%
12 tic
13 for k=1:numSamples
14     A      = randomA(:,:,k);
15     x      = inv(A)*b;
16 end
17 timer     = toc;
```

```matlab
19 fprintf('\naverage time using inv(A): %g', timer/numSamples);

21 %%%%%%%%% inv(A) = A\eye(dim) %%%%%%%%%%%%
22 tic
23 for k=1:numSamples
24     A    = randomA(:,:,k);
25     x    = A\b;
26 end
27 timer = toc;

29 fprintf('\naverage time using A\\b: %g', timer/numSamples);

31 %%%%% A = LU (LU-decomp) => inv(A) = U\L\eye(dim) %%%%
32 tic
33 for k=1:numSamples
34     A         = randomA(:,:,k);
35     [Low,Upp] = lu(A);
36     x         = Upp\(Low\b);
37 end
38 timer = toc;

40 fprintf('\naverage time using Upp\\Low\\b: %g', timer/numSamples);

42 %%%%%% A = QR (QR-decomp) => inv(A) = R\Q' %%%%%%%%%
43 tic
44 for k=1:numSamples
45     A     = randomA(:,:,k);
46     [Q,R] = qr(A);
47     x     = R\(Q'*b);
48 end
49 timer = toc;

51 fprintf('\naverage time using R\\Q''*b: %g', timer/numSamples);
```

Though this code accomplishes what is asked in Exercise 94, it falls short of preserving the reproducibility of the test data (also called the "data set"). Specifically, once we exit our MATLAB session, the arrays **randomA** and **randomB** are lost, and consequently the performance comparison is not repeatable. We now introduce an important feature of MATLAB to address this limitation, namely MATLAB's ability to save and retrieve data (i.e. workspace variables) using a MAT-file. To illustrate this new functionality, we present the following tutorial session in the Command Window.

```
 1  >> clear
 2
 3  >> who
 4
 5  >> b=randn(3,1)
 6  b =
 7      1.1908
 8     -1.2025
 9     -0.0198
10
11  >> who
12  Your variables are:
13  b
14
15  >> save('SampleMatFile.mat','b');
16
17
18
19
20  >> dir S*
21  SampleMatFile.mat
22
23  >> clear
24
25  >> who
26
27
28  >> load('SampleMatFile.mat');
29
30  >> who
31  Your variables are:
32  b
33  >> b
34  b =
35      1.1908
36     -1.2025
37     -0.0198
```

Line 1: remove all variables in the workspace

Line 3: verify that no variables exist in the current workspace

Line 5: create the variable b by assigning to it a randomly generated (3×1) column vector

Line 11: b is now returned when displaying all variables currently in the workspace

save function — Line 15: executing the save() command with parameters SampleMatFile.mat and b creates a file in the current directory named "SampleMatFile.mat" which contains the variable b (both the variable's name and its data are stored)

dir function — Line 20: notice the file 'SampleMatFile.mat' appears in the Directory Window

Line 23: remove b from the workspace

Line 25: verify that b has been removed

load function — Line 28: executing the load() command with the filename SampleMatFile.mat retrieves all variables previously written to the file

Line 30: verify that the variable b has been restored

Line 33: verify that b's data is intact

We now consolidate these ideas to create the program "CompareAXeqB" which can be called once with the parameter 'create' to generate the MAT-file, and subsequently called (in different sessions, as long as the MAT-file resides in the current directory or default path) with the parameter 'compare' (or with any other parameter, or even no parameter) to perform the timing comparisons. If someone wanted to reproduce our results, it would suffice to provide them with the file "RandomArray.mat". Moreover, if someone wanted to perform a timing comparison with yet a sixth method, it is a simple matter to add the appropriate code.

```matlab
%%%%%%%%%%%%%%%%%%%%%%%%%%%%%%%%%%%%%%%%
function CompareAXeqB(selector,dim,numSamples)
%solving Ax=b for numSamples random (dim x dim) matrices
% using different techniques
%call once with selector='create' to create RandomArray.mat MAT-file
if nargin < 1
    selector   = 'compare';
elseif nargin < 3
    %default is 10000 random 12x12 matrices
    dim        = 12;
    numSamples = 10000;
end

switch selector
case 'create'
    %each A is (dim x dim), and we want numSamples of them for testing
    randomA    = zeros(dim,dim,numSamples);
    %b is a single column vector chosen with random entries
    b   = randn(dim,1);
    k   = 1;
    while k <= numSamples
        A   = randn(dim,dim);
        %if A non-invertible, reject it
        if det(A) < 0.01
            continue
        end
        %if A invertible, store it in our "array-of-arrays"
        randomA(:,:,k) = A;
        k   = k + 1;
    end
    %save the variables RandomA and b to a file RandomArray.mat
    save('RandomArray.mat','randomA','b');
    %give feedback on successful creation of MAT-file
    D   = dir('RandomArray.mat');
    fprintf('File %s created, size = %d bytes \n', D.name, D.bytes);
otherwise
    %retrieve variables RandomA and b as they were at time of save()
```

```
38      load('RandomArray.mat');
39      %assigns values to variables named 'randomA' and 'b'
40      %note that we do not save dim and numSamples,
41      % as these can be deduced as 'derived quantities'
42      [dim,dim,numSamples]   = size(randomA);
43
44      %%%%%%%%%%%%%%%%%%%%%%%%%%%
45      tic
46      for k=1:numSamples
47          A    = randomA(:,:,k);
48          c    = A^(-1)*b;
49      end
50      timer   = toc;
51
52      fprintf('\naverage time using A^(-1)b: %g', timer/numSamples);
53      %%%%%%%%%%%%%%%%%%%%%%%%%%%
54      ...
55      %%%%%%%%%%%%%%%%%%%%%%%%%%%
56 end
57
58 return
```

Exercise 108

Critique the following code fragment:
```
if det(A) < 0.01
    continue
end
```

Solution 108

In theory, the outer-loop might never terminate if **randn** struggles to produce a matrix with **det > 0.01**. Recall our discussion of "magic numbers" buried in code. The behavior of matrix solvers for ill-conditioned matrices is a challenging topic in Numerical Analysis, and the user of CompareAXeqB might want to know that all matrices being considered have **det > 0.01**. Finally, the **continue** construct violates our emphasis on "goto-less" code.

18.2 Lookup tables (Pascal.m)

In this next example, we use a MAT-file to store a table of pre-computed values of binomial coefficients. The advantage of using a table for this purpose is that the computational overhead is expended at the time the table is created rather than at "execution time" (or "runtime"). In particular, if the running program needs to evaluate the binomial coefficient $\binom{n}{k}$ hundreds of times during a calculation, the coefficient need not be computed over and over again hundreds of times; rather, it can be efficiently "looked up" in a table, having previously been computed at an earlier time and saved in a file. This example illustrates a very general technique, widely used in numerical and database applications, in which runtime calculations are facilitated by highly efficient table-lookups in memory. Note that, since the table is created "off-line" in a matter of speaking, the algorithm employed for creating the table can be chosen for simplicity of implementation rather than computational efficiency. The algorithm we use is based on the well-known mathematical fact

$$\binom{n}{k} = \binom{n-1}{k-1} + \binom{n-1}{k}.$$

In other words, if **a** is a row vector of length n representing the nth row of Pascal's triangle, namely the n binomial coefficients

$$\mathbf{a} = \left[\binom{n-1}{0}, \binom{n-1}{1}, \ldots, \binom{n-1}{n-2}, \binom{n-1}{n-1}\right],$$

then the $(n+1)^{th}$ row of length $(n+1)$ is given by

$$\mathbf{b} = \left[\binom{n}{0}, \binom{n}{1}, \ldots, \binom{n}{n-1}, \binom{n}{n}\right] = [\mathbf{a},\ 0] + [0,\ \mathbf{a}].$$

To use the following program Pascal.m for generating and accessing the binomial coefficients $\binom{n}{k}$, a one-time call is made by passing the parameter `'create'`, along with an optional second parameter for the maximum value of n (we choose a default value of $n = 40$). After the one-time call has executed, the file "Pascal.mat" will be created in the current directory. By copying the files Pascal.m and Pascal.mat to another directory, the functionality of the program can be made available to other applications. Another program wishing to use this method of accessing binomial coefficients would issue a one-time call to Pascal.m with the parameter `'init'`, which will load the data of all binomial coefficients $\binom{n}{k}$ ($1 \leq n \leq 40$) from Pascal.mat into memory, where it is stored in Pascal.m's locally-scoped, but *persistent* variable `BinomCell`. To retrieve the values $\binom{n}{k}$ for $k = 0, .., n$ into an array, without any computation, one need only call

```
b = Pascal(n)    %b=[nC0,nC1,..,nCn] row vector of binomial coefficients
```

from which $\binom{n}{k}$ can be extracted as `b(k+1)`. In other words, `Pascal(n)` for $n = 1, 2, \ldots$ returns the $(n+1)^{th}$ row of Pascal's triangle.

There is one additional point to be considered before writing Pascal.m, which arises from the fact that Pascal's triangle is in fact a "triangle", and not a rectangular array. We give two versions, the first of which illustrates the use of cell arrays, and the second of which illustrates some creative manipulations with the eval() function.

```
%%%%%%%%%%%% Pascal.m %%%%%%%%%%%%%%%%
% call once (ever) Pascal('create') to create Pascal.mat file on disk
% call once (each instance of running program) Pascal('init')
%   to load Pascal.mat into memory
% subsequent calls to Pascal(2), Pascal(3), etc.
% will return row vectors b=[1 2 1], b=[1 3 3 1], etc.

function b = Pascal(selector,nMax)
%on entry, selector = 'create' to generate Pascal.mat with BinomCell
%          selector = 'init' to load Pascal.mat, keep BinomCell around
%          selector = 1,2,... to return b=[nC0,nC1,..,nCn]
persistent BinomCell

if nargin < 2
    nMax    = 40;
end

b   = 0;    %must return 'b' even if ignored by caller
switch selector
case 'create'
    %BinomCell is cell array whose n'th entry is the array [nC0,..,nCn]
    BinomCell       = cell(nMax,1);
    %n=1 corresponds to the second row of Pascal's triangle [1C0 1C1]
    BinomCell{1}    = [1 1];
    for n=2:nMax
        %construct next row of Pascal's triangle (see formula above)
        a           = BinomCell{n-1};
        BinomCell{n} = [a 0] + [0 a];
    end
    %save the cell array BinomCell to file Pascal.mat
    save('Pascal.mat','BinomCell')
case 'init'
    %initialize persistent variable BinomCell in memory by loading MAT-file
    load('Pascal.mat','BinomCell');
otherwise
    %selector indicates the numeric row of our stored array
    % which is one less than the row of Pascal's triangle
    b = BinomCell{selector};
end
return
```

18.2. Lookup tables (Pascal.m)

Our next version, which we will call "Binomial.m", gets around the problem of storing a non-rectangular array by creating a distinct variable for each row of Pascal's triangle. Namely, we assign to variables

    B1, B2, B3, ..., B40

the arrays

    [1 1], [1 2 1], [1 3 3 1], ...

Two new problems arise when we try to implement this idea. The first problem is that we will have 40 variables to save to our MAT-file, and we'd like to avoid executing a command such as

    save('Binomial.mat','B1','B2',...);

MATLAB provides an easy solution to this by using `save('Binomial.mat')` without specifying individual variable names, resulting in *all* workspace variables (currently in scope) being saved. By executing the `clear` command we can guarantee that only the variables of interest will be written to Binomial.mat. In addition, since we wish to avoid specifying that each of the variables B1,B2,... be persistent with a command such as

    persistent B1,B2,...

we consolidate all of these variables into a persistent structure `BinCoef`, whose fields are the variables B1,B2,..., and which is created using the instruction

    BinCoef = load('Binomial.mat');

The second problem which arises is more serious; how can we avoid using the following forty lines of code (or even *variable* number of lines if we allow a passed parameter to specify the maximum number of rows):

```
1 B1  = [1];
2 B2  = [B1 0] + [0 B1];
3 ...
4 B40 = [B39 0] + [0 B39];
```

This is reminiscent of our original motivation for introducing the for-loop in NewtonAlg1. But we have a more subtle problem to address here, since variable names are *not* themselves the data of string variables belonging to our program. Is it possible to use MATLAB's string manipulation capability to mimic the effect of our writing a line of code with B1,B2,... being the name of a variable appearing on the left-hand-side of an assignment statement? The answer can be found in the `eval()` command, which can take a string argument and execute it *as if* it appeared as a line of executable code! With these preparations, we present an alternative approach to evaluating binomial coefficients using table-lookup.

```
1  %%%%%%%% Binomial.m %%%%%%%%%%
2  % call once Binomial('create') to create Binomial.mat M-file
3  % call once Binomial('init') to load Binomial.mat M-file
4  % subsequent calls to Binomial(2), Binomial(3), etc.
5  % will return b=B2=[1 2 1], b=B3=[1 3 3 1], etc.
6  function b = Binomial(selector, maxN)
7  persistent  BinCoef
8
9  b   = 0;     %must return 'b' even if ignored by caller
10 switch selector
11 case 'create'
12     %creates variables Bn=[nC0,...,nCn]
13     % and saves them to Binomial.mat MAT-file
14     %clear workspace since we'll be saving all variables to MAT-file
15     if nargin < 2
16         maxN    = 40;
17     end
18
19     %B1 = 2nd row of Pascal's triange
20     B1      = [1, 1];
21     r_h_s   = 'B1';
22
23     for n=2:maxN
24         %l_h_s is our string variable holding
25         % the name of MATLAB array variable B1,B2,...
26         %   which will be left-hand-side of assignment statement
27         %   and indicates the next row to be created
28         l_h_s   = ['B' num2str(n)];    %for example, l_h_s = 'B2'
29         %evalstr is our string variable holding
30         % the left_hand_side and computation with the right-hand-side
31         % of the assignment statement to be executed
32         %   for example, B2 = [0 B1] + [B1 0]
33         evalstr = [l_h_s '= [0,' r_h_s '] + [' r_h_s ',0]'];
34         %execute evalstr as if we had just issued it as MATLAB command
35         eval(evalstr);
36         %make the new row l_h_s become the old row r_h_s for next iteration
37         r_h_s   = l_h_s;
38     end
39
40     %save variables of interest currently in workspace
41     % (namely B1,B2,..Bk=k'th row of Pascal's triangle)to MAT-file
42     %   remove three variables from workspace we don't want saved
43     clear maxN, l_h_s, r_h_s
```

```
44     save('Binomial.mat') %effectively save('Binomial.mat',B1,B2,...B40);
45
46 case 'init'
47     %initialize by loading data file
48     %all variables from workspace at time of 'save' are packed into
49     % structure BinCoef, and retrievable using BinCoef.B1, etc.
50     % the structure BinCoef needn't be recreated since it is persistent
51     %if we did not consolidate variables into structure BinCoef,
52     % how could we make them persistent??
53     BinCoef = load('Binomial.mat');
54 otherwise
55     %retrieve variable from BinCoef data
56     %B1=[1 1], B2=[1 2 1]
57     %in general, "Bn"=[nC0,...,nCn]
58     b   = eval(['BinCoef.B' num2str(selector)]);
59 end
60
61 return
```

Exercise 109

Compare Pascal.m and Binomial.m with regard to the size of their respective MAT-files, time to create the MAT-files, and execution time in retrieving the row of binomial coefficients.

18.3 Topics covered in this chapter

In this chapter we introduced MAT-files, and explained how they can be used to share data with other programs, as well as subsequent instances of the same program. We also revisited the `eval()` command, applying it in a novel context. The following MATLAB commands have been explained:

1. MAT-files: `load()`, `save()`

2. Miscellaneous: `dir`

Chapter 19

Plotting II

19.1 Plotting parameterized curves in three dimensions

We have already seen that MATLAB can produce two dimensional plots of parametric equations given by $\alpha(t) = [x(t), y(t)] \in \mathbb{R}^2$, where each component is a real-valued function defined on a given interval $[a, b]$. A typical example is the motion of a particle whose position is given by $\alpha(t)$, a vector-valued function of time. Suppose we wish to view the independent variable t increasing as the motion evolves in time. In other words, we wish to *graph* the function $\alpha(t)$ in three dimensions, showing its dependence on t. Though one usually makes the independent variable the first axis when graphing functions in Calculus courses, it is more typical in Physics courses to imagine time evolving "upwards". For example, if our particle travelled in a circular motion according to

$$\alpha(t) = [x(t), y(t)] = [\cos t, \sin t] \in \mathbb{R}^2, \qquad t \in [-\pi, \pi],$$

then it is natural to plot the following vector-valued function when viewing the particle's position evolving in time:

$$\gamma(t) = [\cos t, \sin t, t] \in \mathbb{R}^3, \qquad t \in [-\pi, \pi].$$

The resulting curve in three dimensions is called a helix, and it can be generated by MATLAB with the `plot3` function applied to a *triple* of one-dimensional arrays:

```
numLoops   = 5;
t   = numLoops*linspace(-pi,pi,200);
x   = cos(t);
y   = sin(t);
z   = t;

figure(100)
plot3(x,y,z);           %plot3(cos(t),sin(t),t)) also works
str = 'plot of \\gamma(t) = [cos(t), sin(t), t]';
text(1.0, 2.2, str, 'FontSize', 12);
```

This code will produce the following three dimensional plot:

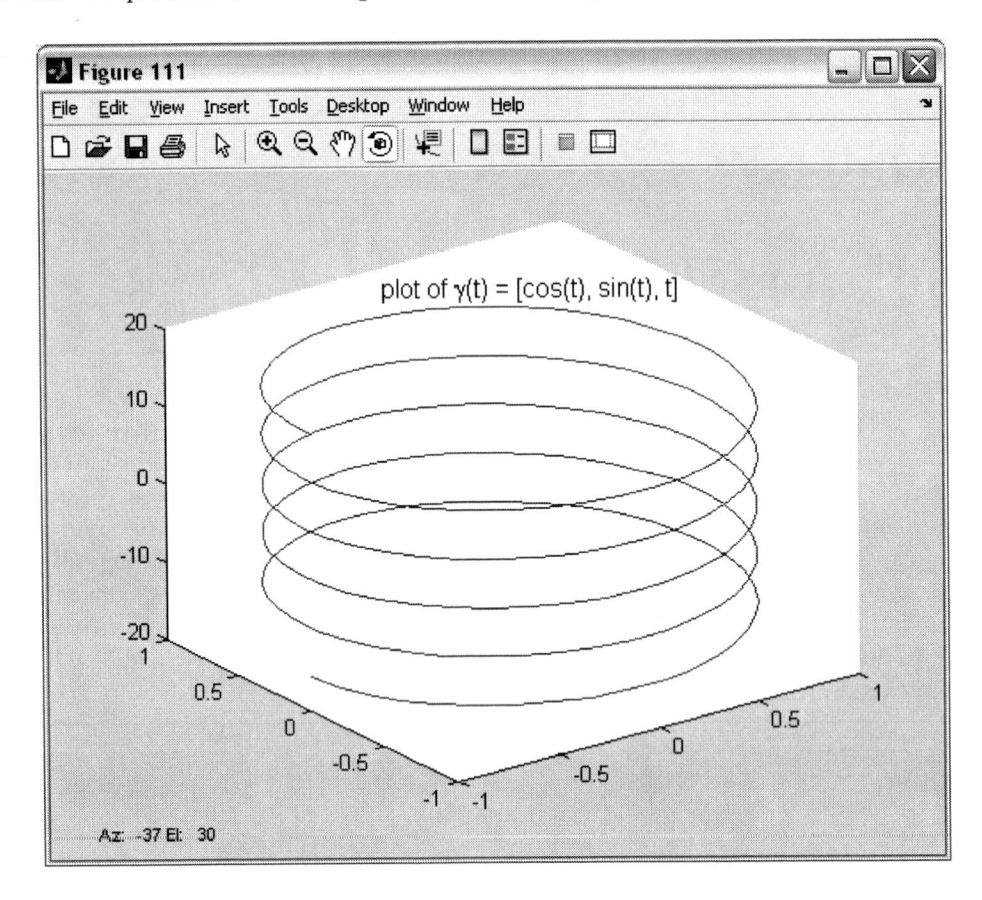

plot of γ(t) = [cos(t), sin(t), t]

We may also consider curves in three dimensions which are not obtained as the graph of a function $\alpha(t) = [x(t), y(t)]$, where $z(t)$ has simply been set to t. An obvious example is the path of a particle moving in three dimensions which can be represented by a vector-valued function
$$\gamma(t) = [x(t), y(t), z(t)], \qquad t \in [a, b].$$

Needless to say, plot3() is equally capable of displaying these more general curves. For example, suppose we traverse the helix ten times as fast (so $\gamma = [\cos 10t, \sin 10t, t]$) and then radially project[1] the curve onto the unit sphere (so $\gamma \to \gamma/|\gamma|$), obtaining the parametric equations
$$x(t) = \frac{\cos 10t}{\sqrt{1+t^2}}, \quad y(t) = \frac{\sin 10t}{\sqrt{1+t^2}}, \quad z(t) = \frac{t}{\sqrt{1+t^2}}.$$

---

[1] If, instead of a radial projection, we use a Mercator projection, then the resulting curve is call a spherical helix, or "loxodrome". See http://en.wikipedia.org/wiki/Loxodrome for more details.

The following code will plot this parameterized curve:

```
1 figure(200)
2 t    = linspace(-pi/2,pi/2,200);
3 x    = cos(10*t);
4 y    = sin(10*t);
5 z    = t;
6 r    = sqrt(x.^2 + y.^2 + z.^2);
7 plot3(x./r,y./r,z./r);
```

The resulting figure showing the radial projection appears below:

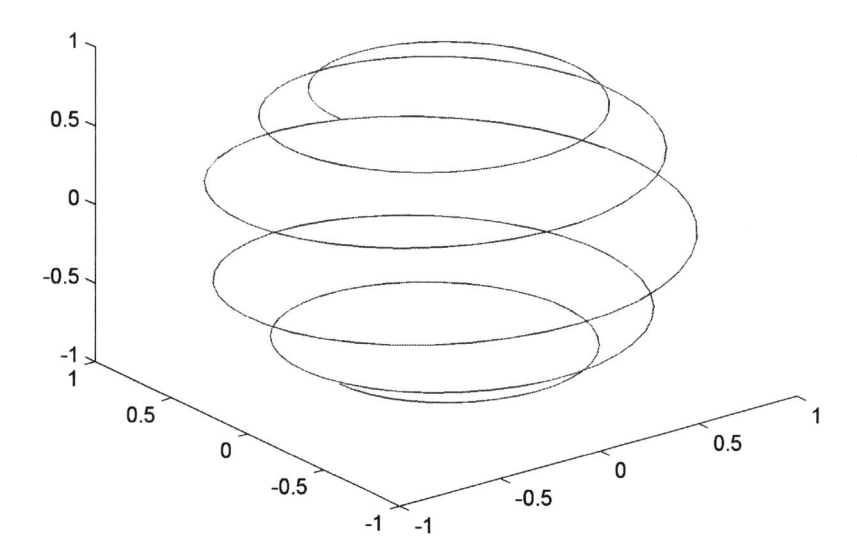

19.2 Rotations and Projections (HelixMain.m)

Now it goes without saying that any plot displayed to the computer screen is ultimately a two dimensional rendering. To what extent can we exploit the fact that MATLAB is actually keeping track of three dimensional data? We now discuss the "viewpoint" associated with a three dimensional plot.

Make sure that the Figure Toolbar is visible in your Figure Window, as shown in the plot displayed above[2]. Next, select the "Rotate 3D" tool located to the right of the hand icon, and

---
[2] If the Figure Toolbar is not displayed, go to the View menu and select "Figure Toolbar" to enable it.

204   Chapter 19. Plotting II

position the cursor over the body of the figure so the cursor icon changes to a circular arrow. By pressing the left button while moving the mouse, you can observe the view of the helix move around in three dimensions, while at the same time the "azimuthal and elevation" parameters associated with the changing view angle are displayed in the lower left. For example, the plot displayed above shows a viewpoint with `Az = -37, El = 30`.

Exercise 110

Lookup `azimuth` in the Help Browser, and read the discussion on the topic "Setting the Viewpoint with Azimuth and Elevation." Change the viewpoint with which the helix is initially displayed by adding the following lines to your code:

```
az = -37;
el = 60;
view([el, az])
```

Experiment with rotating the figure around using the Rotate tool. You should be able to reproduce the following plots corresponding to elevations of 2° and 90°:

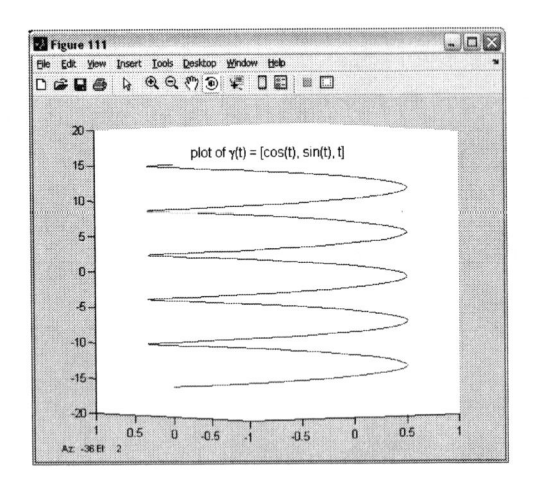

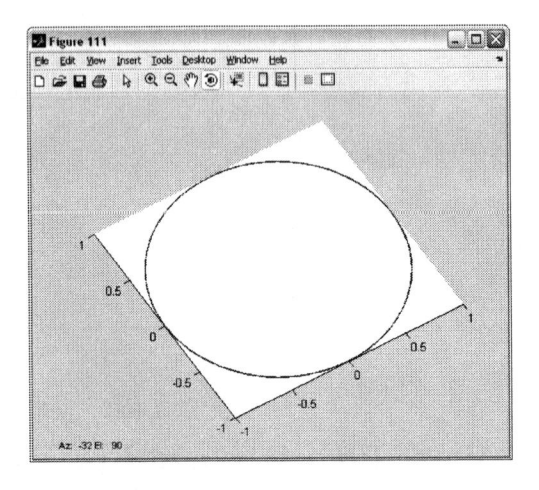

When discussing parametric equations in Calculus courses, one encounters the figure traced out by a point on the circumference of a rolling wheel, called a "cycloid". The cycloid has a noticeable "cusp" every cycle, and its equation is given by

$$x(t) = r(t - \sin t) \qquad y(t) = r(1 - \cos t), \qquad \text{constant } r > 0.$$

More generally, one may consider the track (also called the "locus") of a point interior to the rolling wheel, where the resulting figure is called a "curtate" cycloid. These more general

cycloids are described by the following parametric equations[3]:
$$x(t) = at - b\sin t \qquad y(t) = a - b\cos t, \qquad \text{constants } a, b > 0.$$

A family of figures similar to the cycloids can be obtained by projecting the helix onto a plane in three dimensions. More concretely, consider a plane Π passing through the origin whose perpendicular direction (unit vector denoted $\mathbf{v}$) forms an angle θ with the z-axis:
$$\Pi := \mathbf{v}^\perp \qquad \text{where } \angle(\mathbf{v}, \mathbf{e}_3) = \theta \qquad (\text{ so } \mathbf{v} \cdot \mathbf{e}_3 = \cos\theta \text{ }).$$

Then if we imagine the sun shining from the direction $\mathbf{v}$, the shadow cast by the helix on the plane Π will be a compressed cycloid. We will write a short program demonstrating this fact by first developing the mathematics to construct the appropriate projection operator, and then implementing a GUI which allows the user to adjust the angle θ at which the plane is inclined.

First, if $\mathbf{v}$ forms the angle θ with the z-axis, then a candidate for $\mathbf{v}$ is given by
$$\mathbf{v} = \begin{pmatrix} \sin\theta \\ 0 \\ \cos\theta \end{pmatrix}.$$

To verify this, it is enough to observe that $\mathbf{v} \cdot \mathbf{e}_3 = \cos\theta$. In other words, we will assume that $\mathbf{v}$ lies in the $\{x, z\}$-plane.

Second, observe that projecting onto the plane Π along the direction $\mathbf{v}$ is equivalent to rotating the entire three dimensional space by the angle θ about the y-axis, and then projecting into the $\{x, y\}$-plane by dropping the third coordinate. In other words, the desired projection is obtained by applying the following transformation:
$$P_\theta = \begin{pmatrix} 1 & 0 & 0 \\ 0 & 1 & 0 \end{pmatrix} \cdot \begin{pmatrix} \cos\theta & 0 & -\sin\theta \\ 0 & 1 & 0 \\ \sin\theta & 0 & \cos\theta \end{pmatrix}.$$

Exercise 111

Show that the parametric equations of the family of curves obtained via the projections P_θ applied to $\gamma(t)$ are given by:
$$x(t) = b\cos t - a t, \qquad y(t) = \sin t, \qquad \text{where } a = \sin\theta, b = \cos\theta.$$
Deduce that one obtains a circle when $\theta = 0$, a (squashed) cycloid when $\theta = 45°$, and a sinusoid when $\theta = 90°$. Since the *shape* is unaffected by re-parameterizations of t, as well as translations in x and y, we can rewrite these equations so their relationship with the cycloids becomes apparent:
$$x(t) = a\,t - b\sin t, \qquad y(t) = a - \cos t, \qquad a^2 + b^2 = 1.$$

---

[3]See http://mathworld.wolfram.com/ProlateCycloid.html for more information. If one tracks an exterior point then the resulting locus is called a "prolate" cycloid.

If we discretize the t-values using an array `t=linspace(-6*pi,6*pi,200)`, the $3 \times n$ array

```
[cos(t);sin(t);t]
```

can be thought of as either a triple of $1 \times n$ row vectors representing the discretization of each component of the helix, or as a collection of 3×1 column vectors (one for each value of t). Applying our 3×3 transformation P_θ defined above to the collection of points of the helix amounts to applying P_θ to each of the 3×1 column vectors in the second interpretation. The following code will therefore produce the desired collection of image points:

```
%%%%%%%%%%%%%%%%%%%%%%%%%%%%%%%
%%%% HelixMain.m, primary function HelixMain() %%%%
%%%%%%%%%%%%%%%%%%%%%%%%%%%%%%%
function HelixMain()
%create the helix as [x(t),y(t),z(t)] which is 3x200 array
t  = linspace(-6*pi, 6*pi, 200);
x  = cos(t);
y  = sin(t);
z  = t;

%specify hardwired value for the angle theta
th = 30;

%create P from the rotation matrix about y-axis
Ry = [cos(th) 0 -sin(th); 0 1 0; sin(th) 0 cos(th)];
P  = eye(2,3) * Ry;

%apply P to EACH of the [x(t);y(t);z(t)] column vectors (one for each t!)
%result XY is 2x200
XY = P * [x; y; z];

%plot image curve on plane
plot(XY(1,:),XY(2,:))
return
```

This above code correctly projects the points of the helix $[\cos t, \sin t, t]$ onto the plane $\Pi_\theta = [\sin\theta, 0, \cos\theta]^\perp$ when $\theta = 30°$. Of course, the code is perfectly adaptable to handling other values of θ, but our approach to addressing the hardwired nature of θ is sufficiently ambitious that we will devote an entire section its description.

19.3 Object-oriented programming (SliderGui.m)

In this section we solve the problem of allowing the user to adjust the value of θ in the program HelixMain.m. Our approach will expand on the GUI developed in OdeGui.m from

Chapter 17, except we will be somewhat "quick-and-dirty" in the interest of focusing on some new ideas. In particular, we create a single function SliderGui containing all of the GUI code, violating our emphasis on creating secondary functions (e.g. there is no separate `CreateText()` function, whose value was explained earlier). Also, our interface is somewhat sloppy in that we simply slap a slider control onto the figure without any static text control reflecting its value. Additionally, the user must exit using the figure's close box. On the other hand, our goal is to introduce some topics not covered in Chapter 17. In particular, `SliderGui()` has these important features:

1. Variables like `gRunning` and `gPlotProjection` are not globally shared with `HelixMain()`; when `HelixMain()` wants to know these variables it *interrogates* `SliderGui()` by calling it with a special value of the `cmd` parameter.

2. Variables that `SliderGui()` needs to share with its callbacks are made persistent variables; `SliderGui()` uses no global variables.

3. The function `SliderGui()` is sometimes called with one argument, and sometimes with two arguments; moreover, the return value is sometimes ignored by the caller, sometimes indicates a new value of the slider control (i.e. the angle θ has been modified by the user), and other times indicates that the interface is no longer running (i.e. the close box has been clicked by the user).

4. It demonstrates how a slider control works; the slider's built-in ability to enforce a range of values (in our case, a value of $\theta \in [0, 90]$) obviates the need to implement a filter.

5. It demonstrates how a figure's `CloseRequestFcn` property can be used.

These ideas play an important role in modern programming design, and can even be considered an introduction to so-called "object-oriented programming". In particular, `SliderGui` is already beginning to look like an "object" in that it has the following characteristics:

1. Encapsulation: interrogating `SliderGui()` for the value of an internal variable, rather than exporting variables as globals.

2. Polymorphism: the value of the first parameter `cmd` determines the presence and interpretation of the second argument, as well as the return value.

3. Constructor: calling `SliderGui('init',...)` to create a figure; the caller is burdened only with passing the initial θ to be used by the slider control.

4. Destructor: calling `SliderGui('close')` to internally issue the `delete(hFig)`; the caller is unburdened with manipulating the figure directly.

To be sure, `SliderGui()` does much more than just create and delete a figure handle. Though only a few instructions, the logic of the interaction between the variables `gRunning` and `gPlotProjection` is non-trivial. The point is that the subtle juggling of setting and clearing these internal variables is a private matter for `SliderGui()`, and any "consumer" of SliderGui's functionality need only interact with it through the four values of `cmd`:

208   Chapter 19. Plotting II

'init', 'isRunning', 'spin', 'close'.

In object-oriented parlance, this is referred to as the "interface" to the object.

```
%%%%%%%%%%%%%%%%%%%%%%%%%%%%%
%%%% HelixMain.m, primary function HelixMain() %%%%
%%%%%%%%%%%%%%%%%%%%%%%%%%%%%
function HelixMain()
%notice the absence of globals shared with SliderGui()

%create the helix as [x(t),y(t),z(t)]
t    = linspace(-6*pi, 6*pi, 200);
x    = cos(t);
y    = sin(t);
z    = t;

th       = 0;
thDeg    = 0;
SliderGui('init',thDeg);     %notice 2nd parameter
while SliderGui('isRunning')
    %project helix onto [cos(th),0,sin(th)]-perp
    P    = CreateProjMatrix(th);
    XY   = P * [x; y; z];

    %plot image curve on plane
    plot(XY(1,:),XY(2,:))
    axis ([-8 8 -2 2])
    axis equal
    %add some informative text
    str    = sprintf('projection of helix onto plane');
    str    = sprintf('%s [cos(\\theta), 0, sin(\\theta)]^\\perp', str);
    str    = sprintf('%s\n \\theta = %4.2f^o', str, thDeg);
    hText  = text(0.1, 0.85, str,'units','normalized','FontSize',12);

    %ask Gui for next value of theta
    thDeg  = SliderGui('spin');
    th     = thDeg * pi/180;
end
SliderGui('close');
return

%%%%%%%%%%%%%%%%%%%%%%%%%%%%%
%%%% HelixMain.m, secondary function CreateProjMatrix() %%%%
function P  = CreateProjMatrix(th)
```

19.3. Object-oriented programming (SliderGui.m)

```matlab
41     Ry = [cos(th) 0 -sin(th);0 1 0;sin(th) 0 cos(th)];
42     P  = eye(2,3) * Ry;
43     return
44
45 %%%%%%%%%%%%%%%%%%%%%%%%%%%%%%%%
46 %%% SliderGui.m, primary function SliderGui() %%%
47 %%%%%%%%%%%%%%%%%%%%%%%%%%%%%%%%
48 function retVal = SliderGui(cmd,thInit)
49 persistent  hFig hTheta gPlot gRunning
50 %only cmd='init' uses 2nd parameter thInit
51 %meaning of retVal depends on argument cmd
52
53 retVal  = 1;
54 switch cmd
55 case 'init'
56     hFig       = figure(200);
57     gRunning   = 1;
58     gPlot      = 0;
59     set(hFig,'CloseRequestFcn','SliderGui(''exit'');');
60
61     cmdText = 'SliderGui(''thetaSlider'');';
62     hTheta  = uicontrol('callback',cmdText,...
63         'units','normalized','position',[.2 .01 .6 .04],...
64         'style','slider','SliderStep',[0.01 0.10],...
65         'min',0,'max',90,'value',thInit);
66 case 'isRunning'
67     retVal  = gRunning;
68 case 'spin'
69     while ~gPlot & gRunning
70         pause(0.01);
71     end
72     gPlot   = 0;
73     retVal  = get(hTheta,'val');
74 case 'thetaSlider'
75     gPlot   = 1;
76 case 'exit'
77     gRunning   = 0;
78 case 'close'
79     delete(hFig);
80 end
81
82 return
```

Chapter 19. Plotting II

Exercise 112

Why does the program distinguish between "exiting" and "closing"? Why is it necessary that we use `delete(hFig)` rather than `close(hFig)`?

Exercise 113

Modify `SliderGui()` so that the second argument `thInit` is replaced with a structure containing the three fields `'min'`,`'max'`,`'initVal'`. Thus, `HelixGui()` would also be modified as follows:
`thInit = struct('min',0,'max',90,'initVal',thDeg);`

Some snapshots with different values of θ are displayed in the figures below.

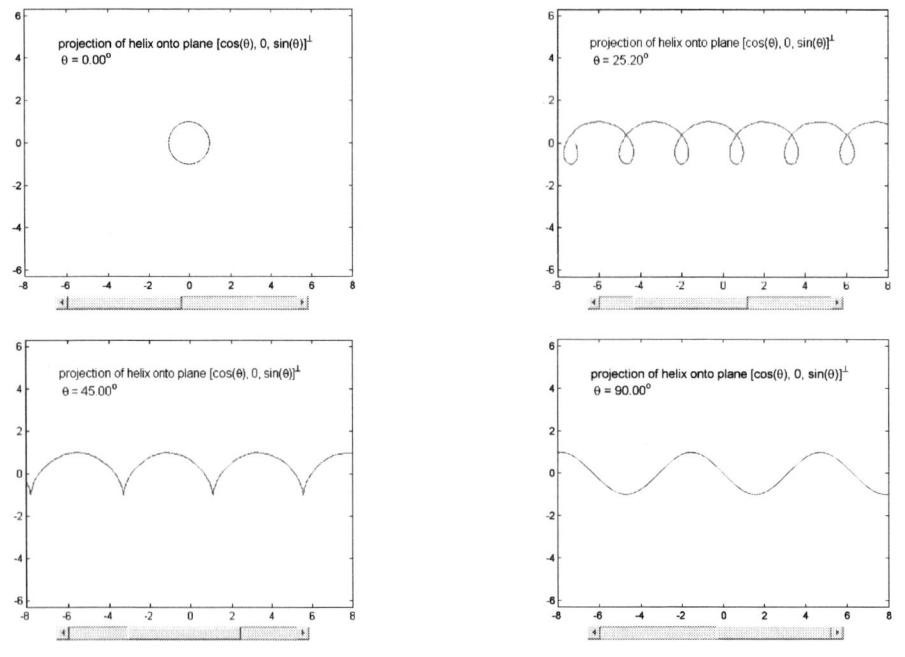

[figures showing projection of helix onto plane $[\cos(\theta), 0, \sin(\theta)]^\perp$ at $\theta = 0.00°$, $\theta = 25.20°$, $\theta = 45.00°$, and $\theta = 90.00°$]

Notice how this sequence of pictures gives some intuition concerning the development of the cycloidal cusp when $\theta = 45°$. Indeed, many examples of cusp singularities arise as "shadows" of perfectly smooth geometric objects[4].

---

[4] We recommend the beautiful book "Curves and Singularities" by J. W. Bruce and P. J. Giblin for more information on this topic. http://www.cambridge.org/catalogue/catalogue.asp?isbn=9780521429993.

Exercise 114

Explain the relationship between MATLAB's view angle parameter `elevation` and our inclination angle θ. Also, add a GUI to the original helix code which lets the user set the elevation, thereby mimicking the Rotate3D tool. In other words, when the user adjusts a slider control, you should reset a variable `el` and then execute the following commands:
`plot3(x,y,z)`
`view([el, az])`

19.4 Topics covered in this chapter

In this chapter we described how to create three dimensional plots of parametric curves. We continued to develop techniques of program design by reusing the slider GUI developed in Chapter 17, and also introduced some techniques of object-oriented programming. We described the following MATLAB functions and keywords:

1. Plotting curves given parametrically $[x(t), y(t), z(t)]$: `plot3()`, `view()`

2. Figure properties and uicontrol styles: `'CloseRequestFcn'`, `'slider'`

Chapter 20

Plotting III

In the previous chapter we described how to plot parameterized curves in three dimensions

$$t \to [x(t), y(t), z(t)], \qquad t \in [a, b],$$

and we motivated our discussion by using the example of a *graph* of a vector-valued function:

$$[x(t), y(t), t], \qquad \text{where } a \le t \le b.$$

If we explicitly make $z = t$ the independent variable, then we can write the above as $[x(z), y(z), z]$. Furthermore, by swapping the roles of x and z, we can proceed by pretending that x has been made the independent variable, and so we write:

$$[x, y(x), z(x)].$$

Lest this appear confusing, recall that the two dimensional version of this expression is the familiar graph of the function $x \to y(x)$ given by the curve

$$[x, y(x)], \qquad \text{where } a \le x \le b,$$

which is simply a special case of a parameterized curve in two dimensions:

$$t \to [x(t), y(t)], \qquad t \in [a, b].$$

Note that the curve $\gamma(t) = [x(t), y(t), z(t)]$ can equally well be described as a triple of scalar-valued functions defined on a common domain $[a, b] \subset \mathbb{R}^1$, hence MATLAB's representation of a curve as a *triple of row-vectors*.

In this chapter we will discuss plotting two dimensional *surfaces* in $\mathbb{R}^3$, which is a natural generalization of a one dimensional curve in $\mathbb{R}^3$. Just as many space curves are obtained as graphs $[x, y(x), z(x)]$, it is also the case that surfaces often arise as graphs. Specifically, if we denote by F a real-valued function of two variables

$$z = F(x, y), \qquad F : [a, b] \times [c, d] \to \mathbb{R}^1,$$

then the graph of F is the two dimensional collection of points in $\mathbb{R}^3$ given by

$$[x, y, F(x,y)], \qquad \text{where } a \leq x \leq b, \quad c \leq y \leq d.$$

Furthermore, analogous to our discussion of curves, these graphs are a special case of a *parameterized surface* given as a vector-valued function defined on a rectangular domain in $\mathbb{R}^2$:

$$(s,t) \rightarrow [x(s,t), y(s,t), z(s,t)], \qquad (s,t) \in [a,b] \times [c,d].$$

Further still, in analogy with the conclusion of the previous paragraph, one can view a surface given in parametric form as a triple of scalar-valued functions defined on a common domain $[a,b] \times [c,d] \subset \mathbb{R}^2$, hence MATLAB's representation of a surface as a *triple of rectangular-arrays*.

20.1 Graphing the function $z = F(x, y)$ (GraphZ.m)

We now develop these ideas more concretely. Suppose we are given the scalar-valued function

$$z = F(x, y).$$

In order to graph this function in three dimensions, we must first specify its domain as a subset of $\mathbb{R}^2$, which we always take to be a rectangle $[a,b] \times [c,d]$. In other words, we assume

$$a \leq x \leq b, \qquad c \leq y \leq d,$$

and so naturally construct the row vectors x = linspace(a,b,Nx) and y = linspace(c,d,Ny) where Nx is the number of points in the x-discretization, and similarly for Ny.

If we use the mathematical notation x_i and y_j to denote the MATLAB components x(i) and y(j), then the set of (x, y)-pairs comprising our rectangular domain can be organized into the array:

$$A = \begin{bmatrix} (x_1, y_1) & \cdots & (x_1, y_{N_y}) \\ \vdots & (x_i, y_j) & \vdots \\ (x_{N_x}, y_1) & \cdots & (x_{N_x}, y_{N_y}) \end{bmatrix}.$$

Our convention here is that the x-coordinate is associated with the vertical direction in the array, which is to say that as x increases we march down the rows of the above matrix; similarly, increasing y corresponds to marching across the columns. Although it may seem more natural to associate x with a horizontal direction in the array, there are advantages to adopting this convention, at least initially. We will eventually revisit this issue, but for now $A(i,j) = (x_i, y_j)$.

It is critical to observe that the "array" A is NOT a legitimate MATLAB array, since it is NOT an array of numbers - it is an *array of (x, y)-pairs*! Abstractly, the array A is a representation of the *vector-valued mapping* $[1, N_x] \times [1, N_y] \to \mathbb{R}^2$ given by

$$(i, j) \rightarrow (x_i, y_j).$$

20.1. Graphing the function $z = F(x,y)$ (GraphZ.m)

Now MATLAB *can* represent just the x-components of the array A, which is to say the *scalar-valued mapping*

$$(\texttt{i},\texttt{j}) \to [\texttt{x(i)},\texttt{y(j)}] \to \texttt{x(i)},$$

and similarly for the y-component. However, the above mapping should NOT be confused with the row vector x

$$\texttt{i} \to \texttt{x(i)}.$$

What kind of animal *is* $(\texttt{i},\texttt{j}) \xrightarrow{\texttt{X}} \texttt{x(i)}$? It is the following rectangular array of scalars:

$$\texttt{X} = \begin{bmatrix} x(1) & \cdots & x(1) \\ \vdots & \cdots & \vdots \\ x(N_x) & \cdots & x(N_x) \end{bmatrix}$$

In other words, the array X is defined by the following property:

$$\texttt{X(:,j)} = \texttt{x'} \text{ for } \texttt{j} = 1,\ldots,\texttt{Ny}.$$

Similarly

$$\texttt{Y(i,:)} = \texttt{y} \text{ for } \texttt{i} = 1,\ldots,\texttt{Nx}.$$

Although $\texttt{X(i,j)} = \texttt{x(i)}$ ignores the index j, it accomplishes something that the one dimensional vector x cannot - it assigns numbers to a two dimensional entity, namely the discretization of the rectangular domain $[1, N_x] \times [1, N_y]$. The need for the arrays X and Y is recognized by MATLAB, which accordingly provides the command `ndgrid()` which returns two $N_x \times N_y$ arrays from the $1 \times N_x$ and $1 \times N_y$ row vectors:

```
x      = linspace(a,b,Nx);
y      = linspace(c,d,Ny);
[X,Y]  = ndgrid(x,y);

%verify X(:,j) = x'
for j=1:Ny
    isequal(X(:,j),x')
end
%verify Y(i,:) = y
for i=1:Nx
    isequal(Y(i,:),y)
end
```

If you've found this discussion unduly pedantic, emphasizing the distinction between the mappings $\texttt{i} \to \texttt{x(i)}$ and $(\texttt{i},\texttt{j}) \to \texttt{x(i)}$, then rest assured that the worst is over. We now have all we need to generate a three dimensional plot of the graph of the scalar-function F on the domain $[a,b] \times [c,d]$, discretized with N_x points in the x-direction, and N_y points in the y-direction. In particular, after creating the array Z=F(X,Y), we can plot, for each (i,j) in

Chapter 20. Plotting III

[1:Nx] x [1:Ny], the triple of points [X(i,j),Y(i,j),Z(i,j)] using plot3(X,Y,Z). The program GraphZ.m implements this method:

```
%%%%%%%% GraphZ.m %%%%%%%%%%%%%%%%
function GraphZ(F,Fstr,a,b,c,d,Nx,Ny)
%Graph the function z=F(x,y)
% by plotting the points (x,y,F(x,y)) in 3-dimensions
%on entry, F is a function handle
%on entry, Fstr is the string version for use in legends
%on entry, domain is taken to be [a,b]x[c,d]
%on entry, Nx and Ny are discretizations in x and y directions
if nargin < 7
    Nx = 100;
    Ny = 100;
end

%create the X-array of x-coordinates, Y-array of y-coordinates
x      = linspace(a,b,Nx);
y      = linspace(c,d,Ny);
[X,Y]  = ndgrid(x,y);
%create the Z-array of z-coordinates
Z      = F(X,Y);

figure(100)
%for each (i,j) in [1:Nx] x [1:Ny], plot [X(i,j),Y(i,j),Z(i,j)]
plot3(X,Y,Z)
%add some informative text
str    = sprintf('Graph of function z = %s\n',Fstr);
str    = sprintf('%s on [%4.2f,%4.2f]x[%4.2f,%4.2f]',str,a,b,c,d);
hText  = text(0.2, 0.25, str,'units','normalized','FontSize',12);
az = 120;
el = 15;
view([az,el])
return
```

The following invocations of GraphZ produce the graphs shown below:

```
GraphZ(@(X,Y) sin(X.*Y), 'sin(xy)', -pi/20, pi/20, -3*pi, 4*pi, 9, 39);
GraphZ(@(X,Y) sin(X.*Y), 'sin(xy)', -pi/20, pi/20, 3*pi, 4*pi, 9, 39);
```

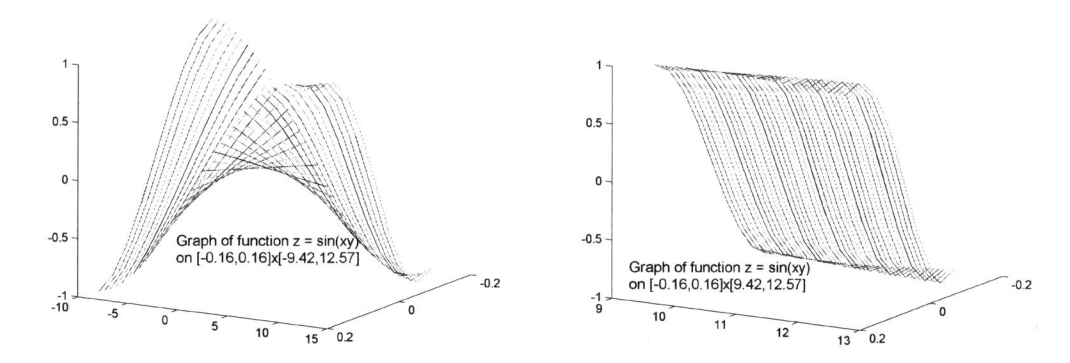

Observe from the figures how `plot3()` interpolates the points in the x-direction, but not in the y-direction. Our choice of parameters for the second plot is meant to enable one to easily distinguish the x and y directions.

Exercise 115

Confirm the assertion made above by using the Rotate3D tool, and also by modifying the code in GraphZ.m so `az=0, el=90`.

20.2 Plotting surfaces in three dimensions (Paraboloid.m)

Creating a plot of a surface that *looks* like a surface is a non-trivial and highly developed subject. Issues related to coloring, positioning of the light source, interpolating *surface patches*, not to mention shading and texturing, are some of the topics studied in computer graphics courses. For our purposes, using the `surf()` and `mesh()` functions instead of the simplistic `plot3()` function, serves well.

Exercise 116

Consult the Help documentation on the topic "Representing a Matrix as a Surface." Replace the `plot3()` code in GraphZ.m with `surf()`, and then with `mesh()`, and describe some of the differences.

Next, we revisit the convention we adopted concerning the correspondence between the graphical directions (horizontal vs. vertical) and the parameter directions (x vs. y). In some applications we may want to use the equally valid convention which swaps our choice of horizontal and vertical; in other words, `(j,i)` $\to$ `(x(i),y(j))`. This alternative convention amounts to replacing the matrix A from Section 20.1 with its transpose A^t. This swapping is achieved by using the following construct:

```
[Y,X] = ndgrid(y,x)
```

Notice `ndgrid()` will return two matrices, each of size $N_y \times N_x$. This comes up often enough that MATLAB provides the function `meshgrid()` to achieve the same result:

```
1  x    = linspace(a,b,Nx);
2  y    = linspace(c,d,Ny);
3  [X,Y]   = meshgrid(x,y);
4  [YY,XX] = ndgrid(y,x);
5  isequal(X,XX)
6  isequal(Y,YY)
```

In other words

$$[X,Y] = \text{meshgrid}(x,y) \iff [Y,X] = \text{ndgrid}(y,x).$$

Finally, in case you have found this chapter difficult to follow, be aware the MATLAB is not unsympathetic; the functions `mesh()` and `surf()` are designed to *also* accept the one dimensional vectors x and y directly as their first two arguments, thereby saving you the trouble of creating X and Y using the intermediate step [X,Y] = meshgrid(x,y). So why were we subjected to the torture of the last section giving such a detailed explanation of the `ndgrid()` and `meshgrid()` commands? One must still compute the array Z of function values, and this is most easily done with a vectorized expression like Z=sin(X.*Y). On the other hand, one could also compute the entries of Z manually. The following code compares these two approaches.

```
1  x  = linspace(a,b,Nx);
2  y  = linspace(c,d,Ny);
3  Z  = zeros(Ny,Nx); %x direction is horizontal, so Nx columns
4
5  %new technique - avoid meshgrid, but compute each Z(i,j)
6  figure(1)
7  for i=1:Ny       %rows are in vertical (y) direction
8      for j=1:Nx   %columns are in horizontal (x) direction
9          Z(i,j) = sin(y(i)*x(j));
10     end
11 end
12 mesh(x,y,Z);
13
14 %meshgrid technique - computation of Z less clumsy
15 figure(2)
16 [X,Y]  = meshgrid(x,y);
17 Z      = sin(X.*Y);
18 mesh(X,Y,Z);
```

There is actually a third approach which uses the `mesh(x,y,Z)` variant without computing the individual entries of `Z` in two nested for-loops. This approach is based on the concept of the "outer-product" of two vectors. Recall that the "inner-product" of row vectors `x` and `y` (each of length `N`) is defined to be the scalar quantity

$$\texttt{x*y'} = \sum_{i=1}^{N} x_i y_i.$$

Though we give this operation a distinguished name, it is simply a special case of matrix multiplication. Similarly, one may define the "outer-product" of a row vector `x` of length `Nx`, and another row vector `y` of length `Ny`, to be the $(N_x \times N_y)$-array of pairwise products

$$\texttt{x'*y} = \begin{bmatrix} (x_1)(y_1) & \cdots & (x_1)(y_{N_y}) \\ \vdots & (x_i)(y_j) & \vdots \\ (x_{N_x})(y_1) & \cdots & (x_{N_x})(y_{N_y}) \end{bmatrix}.$$

Like the inner-product, the outer-product is a special case of matrix multiplication (recall Exercise 83). Using the outer-product, we can also assert

[X,Y] = ndgrid(x,y) $\iff$ X = x'*ones(1,Ny), Y = ones(Nx,1)*y;

[X,Y] = meshgrid(x,y) $\iff$ X = ones(Ny,1)*x, Y = y'*ones(1,Nx).

Exercise 117

Verify the above assertion by creating arrays `XXX` and `YYY` as outer-products and using the `isequal(X,XXX)` and `isequal(Y,YYY)` statements.

Using the outer-product, our third variant of the above code fragment becomes:

```
19 figure(3)
20 %apply sin() to each entry of (Ny x Nx) matrix (y(i)*x(j))
21 Z   = sin(y'*x);
22 mesh(x,y,Z);
```

Chapter 20. Plotting III

Exercise 118

Explain the following code, excerpted from the built-in function `sphere.m`:
```
n       = 20;
theta   = (-n:2:n)/n*pi;         %1 x 21 row vector
phi     = (-n:2:n)'/n*pi/2;      %21 x 1 column vector
cosphi  = cos(phi); cosphi(1) = 0; cosphi(n+1) = 0;
sintheta = sin(theta); sintheta(1)=0; sintheta(n+1)=0;
x       = cosphi*cos(theta);     %21 x 21
y       = cosphi*sintheta;       %21 x 21
z       = sin(phi)*ones(1,n+1);  %21 x 21
surf(x,y,z)    %pass a triple of 21 x 21 arrays
```

Reproduced with permission of The MathWorks, Inc.

Type **sphere** at the command-line and observe the three dimensional plot created by MATLAB. We can investigate how this works by creating a file containing the single line **sphere** which invokes MATLAB's built-in function, and then use the "Step into" feature of the Debugger to single-step the code. Using tiled-windows and split-screens, we reproduce a snapshot of a sample debug session.

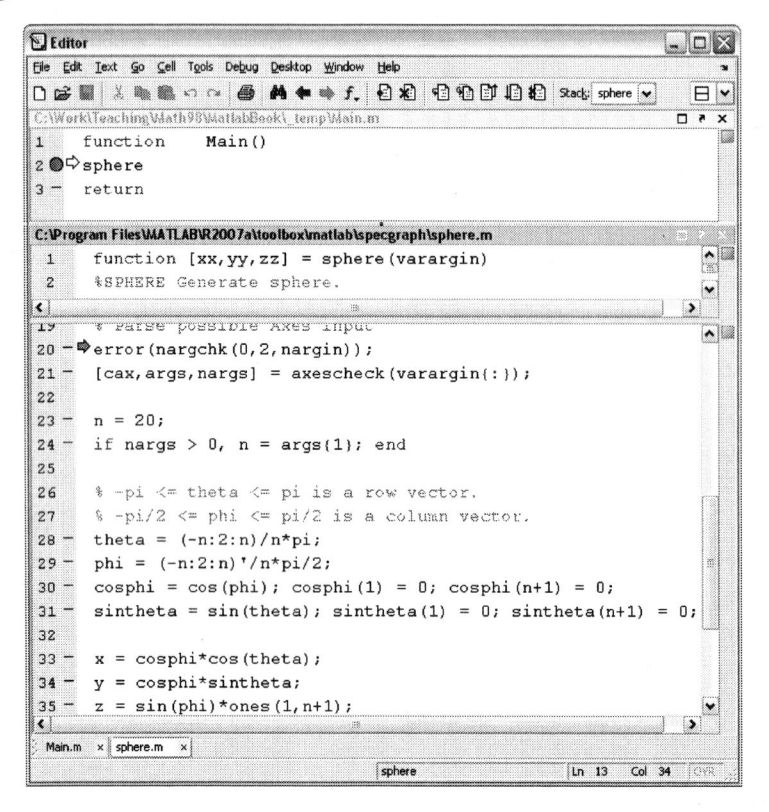

20.2. Plotting surfaces in three dimensions (Paraboloid.m)

If you attempted Exercise 118, then you should already have a sense that `sphere` does not create the surface plot as a *graph* of a function $z = F(x, y)$. In fact, its behavior is analogous to the methods used in Chapter 19 where we plotted *parameterized curves*. Indeed, this code gives an example of a *parameterized surface*, since (x, y, z) is a *triple* of $n \times n$ arrays:

$$(\theta, \phi) \to [x(\theta, \phi), y(\theta, \phi), z(\theta, \phi)], \qquad (\theta, \phi) \in [-\pi, \pi] \times [-\pi/2, \pi/2].$$

Exercise 119

Is it any more difficult for MATLAB to plot the surface defined by $x = y^2 - z^2$, than it is to *graph* the function $z = x^2 - y^2$?

We now undertake to write the program Paraboloid.m which will illustrate how the `mesh()` and `surf()` and `contour()` functions are used in practice. In analytic geometry one learns that the conic sections, namely parabolas, ellipses, and hyperbolas, have generalizations to three dimensions. The complete list of quadric surfaces (centered at the origin) is given in the following table[1]:

Name of Quadric	implicit equation	a, b, c characterized by:
ellipsoid	$ax^2 + by^2 + cz^2 = 1$	all positive
hyperboloid of one sheet	$ax^2 + by^2 + cz^2 = 1$	two positive, one negative
hyperboloid of two sheets	$ax^2 + by^2 + cz^2 = 1$	one positive, two negative
elliptic cylinder	$ax^2 + by^2 + cz^2 = 1$	one zero, other two positive
hyperbolic cylinder	$ax^2 + by^2 + cz^2 = 1$	one zero, other two opposite sign
cone	$ax^2 + by^2 + cz^2 = 0$	not all the same sign
elliptic paraboloid	$ax^2 + by^2 = z$	$ab > 0$
hyperbolic paraboloid	$ax^2 + by^2 = z$	$ab < 0$
parabolic cylinder	$ax^2 + by^2 = z$	$ab = 0$

We will focus on the last three quadric surfaces in the above list, namely the paraboloids:

$$z = ax^2 + y^2, \qquad a \in (-\infty, \infty).$$

In this form, we see that each value of a determines a specific paraboloid, and that the sign of a determines the "type" of paraboloid (elliptic, hyperbolic, or cylindrical). For example, when $a = 1$ we get the rotationally symmetric circular paraboloid $z = x^2 + y^2$, and when $a = -1$ we get the standard hyperbolic paraboloid $z = x^2 - y^2$. Our goal in this section is to consider the *family* of all paraboloids by imagining the parameter a varying continuously from $-\infty$ to ∞.

---

[1]For more information, see http://en.wikipedia.org/wiki/Quadric.

It turns out that the values of a of greatest interest, because they are most representative of the shape of the surface, are $a = -\infty^+, -1, 0, 1, \infty^-$; for this reason, we prefer to write the equation in the form
$$z = (\tan\alpha)x^2 + y^2, \qquad \alpha \in (-\pi/2, \pi/2).$$
In other words, we replace the parameter a with the parameter α, and now the values of interest become $\alpha = -\frac{\pi}{2}^+, -\pi/4, 0, \pi/4, \frac{\pi}{2}^-$. This change of parameter is also justified by ideas from projective geometry.

Next, recall the definition of the *level set* of a scalar-valued function on $\mathbb{R}^2$:
$$F^{-1}(C) = \{(x, y) \in \mathbb{R}^2 \mid F(x, y) = C\}, \qquad C \in (-\infty, \infty).$$

The concept of a level set provides yet a second example of a *family* of geometric objects, in the sense that we can imagine the constant C taking on values continuously varying between $-\infty$ and ∞. Typically, each level set of such a function consists of a finite collection (possibly empty) of continuous curves, also called the *level curves* of F. Understanding how the shape of the level curves $F^{-1}(C)$ changes as the parameter C varies is an important clue to understanding the behavior of the function F. As is well known, the level sets of the above quadric functions $z = F(x, y) = ax^2 + by^2$ are conic sections. This can be seen by setting $z = C$, which results in the level set equation $ax^2 + by^2 = C$. Whether this conic section is an ellipse, hyperbola, or pair of straight lines, will depend on the relative signs of a, b, and C.

Exercise 120

Whereas the graph of the function $z = F(x, y)$ is a *surface* in $\mathbb{R}^3$, the level sets of the function are *curves* in $\mathbb{R}^2$. Prove that the level curves corresponding to any particular value of C can be viewed geometrically as resulting from the intersection of a surface with a plane.

Solution 120

The surface is given by the graph
$$S = \{(x, y, z) \mid z = F(x, y)\} = \{(x, y, F(x, y))\},$$
and the (horizontal) plane is given by
$$\Pi = \{(x, y, z) \mid z = C\} = \{(x, y, C)\}.$$
The intersection corresponds to solving these equations simultaneously:
$$S \cap \Pi = \{(x, y, C) \mid F(x, y) = C\}.$$
The curves of intersection lying on the surface $S \subset \mathbb{R}^3$ can be plotted using the `contour3()` function. The level set $F^{-1}(C)$, which is the projection of $S \cap \Pi$ onto its first two coordinates, can be plotted using the `contour()` function.

20.2. Plotting surfaces in three dimensions (Paraboloid.m)

If we design Paraboloid.m to be passed the value of α as a parameter, then the following code will display three dimensional plots of the graph of

$$z = (\tan \alpha)x^2 + y^2$$

using the `mesh()` and `surf()` commands. An additional two dimensional plot is displayed which uses the `contour()` command to show the level curves

$$\{(x, y) \mid (\tan \alpha)x^2 + y^2 = C\}$$

for the specific values $C = -20, -16, .., 16, 20$.

```matlab
%%%%%%% Paraboloid.m, primary function Paraboloid()   %%%
function Paraboloid(alphaDeg)
%on entry, alphaDeg is angular parameter (-90 -> 90) used in function
% z = tan(alphaDeg) x^2 + y^2, whose graph we wish to plot

T       = 10;
t       = linspace(-T,T,41);
[X,Y]   = meshgrid(t,t);
Z       = tan(alphaDeg*pi/180)*X.^2 + Y.^2;

figure(100)
mesh(X,Y,Z)
MakeTitle('mesh',alphaDeg);

figure(200)
surf(X,Y,Z)
MakeTitle('surf',alphaDeg);

figure(300)
Cvals   = -20:4:20;
contour(X,Y,Z,Cvals)
MakeTitle('contour',alphaDeg);
return

%%%%%%% Paraboloid.m, secondary function MakeTitle()   %%%
function    str = MakeTitle(typePlot,alphaDeg)
cr  = sprintf('\n');
str = sprintf('%s plot of z = (tan \\alpha) x^2 + y^2', typePlot);
str = sprintf('%s %s \\alpha = %3.1f ^o',str,cr,alphaDeg);
title(str);
return
```

224   Chapter 20. Plotting III

Invoking `Paraboloid(-22)` produces the following output:

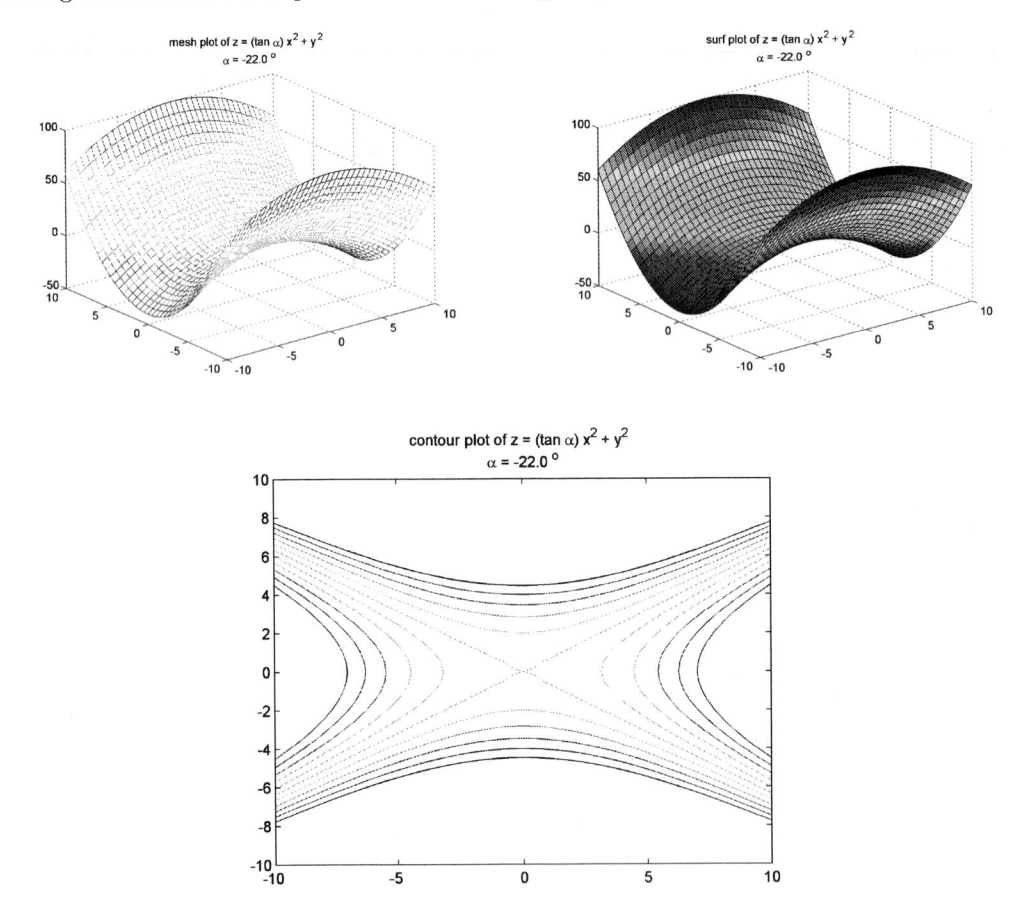

Naturally, one will want to explore the geometry of the three dimensional surface plots using MATLAB's `Rotate3D` tool. As for the contour plots, note that one may omit the list of C-values passed to `contour()`, in which case MATLAB will make its own choice about which values of C to use.

Our next version of Paraboloid.m will mimic OdeMain.m in that we will use a slider control to adjust the parameter α. Be aware that in this version the minimum allowed value of α will be $-90°$ rather than $0°$. Notice how `SliderGui()` is entirely reusable for this completely different application. This important observation is one of the principal justifications for the object-oriented approach to programming. We also display the graph of $z = F(x, y)$ and its level curves on the same plot.

```
%%%%%%% Paraboloid.m, primary function Paraboloid()   %%%
function Paraboloid()
```

20.2. Plotting surfaces in three dimensions (Paraboloid.m)

```matlab
3 %as alpha = angular parameter (-90 -> 90) varied by using slider control
4 % graph z = tan(alpha) x^2 + y^2, and show level curves
5
6 T        = 10;
7 t        = linspace(-T,T,40);
8 [X,Y]    = meshgrid(t,t);
9
10 alpha    = 45;
11 alphaInit  = struct('min',-90,'max',90,'val',alpha);
12 SliderGui('init',alphaInit);
13 while SliderGui('isRunning')
14     Z    = tan(alpha*pi/180)*X.^2 + Y.^2;
15     mesh(X,Y,Z)
16     hold on
17
18     %draw level curves in black
19     contour(X,Y,Z,'k')
20     hold off
21
22     %add informative text
23     str = sprintf('graph of z = tan(\\alpha) x^2 + y^2\n');
24     str = sprintf('%s where \\alpha = %4.2f \\pi',str,alpha/180);
25     text(0.35,0.15,str,'units','normalized','FontSize',12);
26
27     %ask Gui for next value of theta
28     alpha   = SliderGui('spin');
29 end
30 SliderGui('close');
31 return
32
33 %%%%%%%%%%%%%%%%%%%%%%%%%%%%%%%%%%%%%%%%%%%%
34 %%%%%%% Paraboloid.m, secondary function SliderGui()   %%%
35 function retVal = SliderGui(cmd,thetaInit)
36 persistent  hFig hTheta gPlot gRunning
37
38 retVal   = 1;
39 switch cmd
40 case 'init'
41     hFig       = figure(200);
42     gRunning   = 1;
43     gPlot      = 0;
44     set(hFig,'CloseRequestFcn','SliderGui(''exit'');');
45     cmdText = sprintf('SliderGui(''thetaSlider'');');
```

226   Chapter 20.   Plotting III

```
46        hTheta   = uicontrol('callback',cmdText,...
47            'units','normalized','position',[.2 .01 .6 .04],...
48            'style','slider','SliderStep',[0.01 1.0],...
49            'min',thetaInit.min,'max',thetaInit.max,'value',thetaInit.val);
50 case 'isRunning'
51        retVal   = gRunning;
52 case 'spin'
53        while ~gPlot & gRunning
54            pause(0.01);
55        end
56        gPlot    = 0;
57        retVal   = get(hTheta,'val');
58 case 'thetaSlider'
59        gPlot    = 1;
60 case 'exit'
61        gRunning   = 0;
62 case 'close'
63        delete(hFig);
64 end
65
66 return
```

By adjusting the slider control from $-90°$ to $+90°$ one gets an intuitive sense of "varying through the family of paraboloids" by the parameter α. The plots generated by Paraboloid.m for two specific values of α (± 0.2) are displayed below.

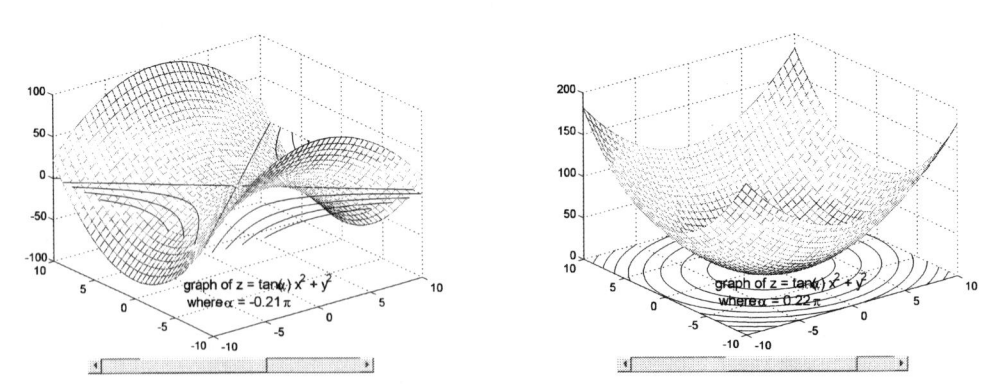

Mathematically, one can also take the point of view that the distinction between the *parameter* α and the *independent variables* x and y is somewhat artificial; indeed, can't we think of z as a function of three variables $z = f(x, y, \alpha)$? From this point of view, our slider control is helping us to visualize the graph of a function of three variables, which is to say a three dimensional hyper-surface in $\mathbb{R}^4$. We can also think of $\alpha = \alpha(x, y, z)$ as function of (x, y, z), in which case these plots are the "level-surfaces" $\alpha^{-1}(\pm 0.2)$.

20.3 Plotting trajectories of a constrained dynamical system (Gravity.m)

In this section we give an application of our plotting skills to simulating one of the earliest dynamical systems studied by physicists. Suppose a particle of mass M is positioned on the surface of a landscape specified as the graph of the function $z = F(x, y)$. Furthermore, we will assume that the particle's motion is determined solely by the force of gravity, whose magnitude is the constant G, and whose direction is vertically downward. The vector form of Newton's fundamental equation "Force = Mass · Acceleration" amounts to the following system of second-order ODE:

$$M \begin{bmatrix} \ddot{x} \\ \ddot{y} \\ \ddot{z} \end{bmatrix} = -\frac{G}{R^2} \begin{bmatrix} F_x \\ F_y \\ F_x^2 + F_y^2 \end{bmatrix}, \quad \text{where } R = \sqrt{1 + F_x^2 + F_y^2}.$$

To see this, let $\mathbf{F}$ denote the force of gravity, and $\mathbf{N}(\mathbf{x})$ denote the vector normal to the surface at a point $\mathbf{x}$. Then our assumptions imply

$$\mathbf{F} = \begin{bmatrix} 0 \\ 0 \\ -G \end{bmatrix}, \quad \mathbf{N}(\mathbf{x}) = \frac{1}{R} \begin{bmatrix} F_x \\ F_y \\ -1 \end{bmatrix}.$$

The formula for $\mathbf{N}$ is easily verified by virtue of its satisfying

$$\mathbf{N} \perp [1, 0, F_x]^t, \quad \mathbf{N} \perp [0, 1, F_y]^t, \quad \|\mathbf{N}\| = 1.$$

Furthermore, because the particle's position is constrained to the landscape $(x, y, F(x, y))$, only the component of the gravitational force *along* the surface can influence the particle's motion:

$$M \begin{bmatrix} \ddot{x} \\ \ddot{y} \\ \ddot{z} \end{bmatrix} = \text{component of gravitational force tangential to surface } z = F(x, y)$$

$$= \mathbf{F} - \text{normal component of gravitational force}$$

$$= \mathbf{F} - (\mathbf{F} \cdot \mathbf{N})\mathbf{N}$$

$$= \begin{bmatrix} 0 \\ 0 \\ -G \end{bmatrix} - (\mathbf{F} \cdot \mathbf{N}) \begin{bmatrix} F_x/R \\ F_y/R \\ -1/R \end{bmatrix}$$

$$= \begin{bmatrix} 0 \\ 0 \\ -G \end{bmatrix} - \frac{G}{R^2} \begin{bmatrix} F_x \\ F_y \\ -1 \end{bmatrix} = -\frac{G}{R^2} \begin{bmatrix} F_x \\ F_y \\ F_x^2 + F_y^2 \end{bmatrix}.$$

Exercise 121

In the special case when the surface is taken to be an inclined plane $z = -(\tan\alpha)x$, where α is the angle of inclination, show that the equation of motion for the z-coordinate obeys $M\ddot{z} = -G\sin^2\alpha$. In terms of the quantity $s =$ "distance travelled by the particle along the surface", show that this reduces to the famous formula of Galileo $M\ddot{s} = G\sin\alpha$. Understanding motion along an inclined plane was essential in the sixteenth century when clocks were too inaccurate to measure free-fall motion in the vertical direction.

Clearly, if we solve the smaller system of equations for just x and y, namely

$$M\begin{bmatrix}\ddot{x}\\\ddot{y}\end{bmatrix} = \frac{G}{R^2}\begin{bmatrix}F_x\\F_y\end{bmatrix},$$

then we can reconstruct the $z(t)$ coordinate from the constraint equation $z(t) = F(x(t), y(t))$. This assertion relies on the observation that the right hand side of the ODE involves x and y only. Needless to say, the resulting function $z(t)$ will automatically satisfy the second-order ODE

$$M\ddot{z} = -G(F_x^2 + F_y^2)/(1 + F_x^2 + F_y^2).$$

Exercise 122

Show that the ODE system for the point $\mathbf{x}(t) = (x(t), y(t))$ can be re-expressed as
$M\ddot{\mathbf{x}} = -G\dfrac{\nabla F}{1 + |\nabla F|^2}$. Is the sign consistent with what you know about ∇F pointing in the direction of *increasing* z?

Exercise 123

Can the ODE system be reduced further to a one dimensional ODE? The ODE in just the z-coordinate appears problematic, since the right hand side involves x and y. More fundamentally, to know how the height of the particle's position evolves will not completely characterize its trajectory. On the other hand, there may be other candidates for a one dimensional parameter whose evolution determines the motion.

Now we have already become acquainted with using MATLAB's `ode45()` function to solve the first-order ODE in one unknown variable $y(t)$:

$$\dot{y} = Ay + B.$$

20.3. Plotting trajectories of a constrained dynamical system (Gravity.m)

In the present problem we have two unknown variables $x(t)$ and $y(t)$. Furthermore, we have a second-order ODE system, which is to say that second-derivatives are specified rather than first-derivatives. The good news is that any second-order ODE system can be transformed into a first-order ODE system in twice the number of variables. The trick here is to artificially introduce variable names for $\dot{x}$ and $\dot{y}$, say

$$u = \dot{x}, \qquad v = \dot{y}.$$

In the problem at hand, the resulting first-order system in x, y, u, v becomes

$$\begin{bmatrix} \dot{x} \\ \dot{y} \\ \dot{u} \\ \dot{v} \end{bmatrix} = \begin{bmatrix} u \\ v \\ \ddot{x} \\ \ddot{y} \end{bmatrix} = \begin{bmatrix} u \\ v \\ \frac{G}{R^2} F_x \\ \frac{G}{R^2} F_y \end{bmatrix}.$$

As for the question of solving an ODE system involving several unknown variables, there is more good news; it is no more difficult for `ode45()` to solve the first-order *vector* differential equation $\dot{\mathbf{y}} = \mathbf{F}(\mathbf{y})$, than it is to solve the scalar ODE $\dot{y} = F(y)$.

An additional point needs to be made concerning initial values. We know our first-order system in x, y, u, v will require the four initial conditions $x(0), y(0), u(0), v(0)$. Since the variables u and v were artificially introduced, how do we interpret their initial values? By definition, $u(0) = \dot{x}(0)$ and $v(0) = \dot{y}(0)$, so specifying these quantities amounts to specifying an *initial velocity* $\dot{\mathbf{x}}(0)$. This is an expected state-of-affairs, since different initial velocities will result in distinct motions of the particle. That we need to specify an initial velocity is due to the fact that Newton's equations are second-order differential equations. Perhaps the u and v are not so artificial[2].

The program Gravity.m, which we present below, will simulate the trajectory followed by a particle constrained to move along the surface of a landscape under the force of gravity, and whose initial position and velocity are specified as input parameters. Additionally, the mass M of the particle is assumed to be 1, and the gravitational constant G is passed as an additional parameter. Finally, the function $z = F(x, y)$, whose graph specifies the landscape surface, is hardwired by the formula:

$$z = F(x, y) = x^2 + y^2.$$

The implementation details are as follows: The landscape is plotted using the `mesh()` command. We specify the mesh discretization in the variable `h`, and we will reuse this quantity to illustrate the `gradient` command. Our plot of the particle's path will be drawn *on* the constraint surface.

---

[2]There is another approach to mechanics, due to Sir William Hamilton, in which u and v are put on the same footing as x and y. In Hamiltonian mechanics the first-order ODE system (called "Hamilton's equations") plays the central role.

Chapter 20. Plotting III

Furthermore, a second figure is created which shows the projection of the particle's path onto the (x, y)-plane, i.e. we plot $(x(t), y(t))$. On this two dimensional plot we also show the level curves of $z = F(x, y)$ giving a topographical representation of the landscape, as well as the gradient vector field $[F_x, F_y]$ which is always perpendicular to the level curves. In this regard, we prevail upon the reader to consult the Help Browser concerning the MATLAB functions gradient() and quiver().

```
%%%%%%%%%%%%%%%%%%%%%%%%%%%%%
%%%% Gravity.m, primary function Gravity() %%%%
function Gravity(x0,y0,vx0,vy0,G)
% M=1, G; z=F(x,y), r2=(1 + Fx^2 + Fy^2)
% x'' = -G(Fx/r2), y'' = -G(Fy/r2)
global G

%final time
Tend    = 1400;

if nargin < 5
    G   = 0.005;
end
if nargin < 1
    x0  = 1;
    y0  = 1;
    vx0 = 0;
    vy0 = 0;
end

%create grid
h       = 0.1;
xvals   = 1.5*(-x0:h:x0);
yvals   = 1.5*(-y0:h:y0);
[X,Y]   = meshgrid(xvals,yvals);
[Z,Zx,Zy]  = gradF(X,Y);

%solve ODE using MATLAB's built-in ode45
[t, sol]   = ode45(@OdeFunc, [0 Tend], [x0,y0,vx0,vy0]);

%plot results
close all
x       = sol(:,1);
y       = sol(:,2);
[z,zx,zy]  = gradF(x,y);

```

20.3. Plotting trajectories of a constrained dynamical system (Gravity.m)   231

```
37 figure(100)
38 %plot space curve in 3d
39 mesh(X,Y,Z);
40 hold on
41 %plot landscape in 3d
42 plot3(x,y,z,'linewidth',2.5)
43
44 cr   = sprintf('\n');
45 str1 = sprintf('Particle rolling on surface z=x^2+y^2 by force of gravity');
46 str2 = sprintf('Initial Position: x_0=%4.2f  y_0=%4.2f',x0,y0);
47 str3 = sprintf('Initial Velocity: Vx_0=%4.2f  Vy_0=%4.2f',vx0,vy0);
48 str4 = sprintf('%s%s%s',str1,cr,str2,cr,str3);
49 title(str4);
50
51 figure(200)
52 %plot level-curves in 2d
53 contour(X,Y,Z)
54 hold on
55 %plot gradient-vectors in 2d
56 [Px,Py] = gradient(Z,h,h);
57 quiver(X,Y,-Px,-Py);
58 %plot (x,y)-solution in 2d
59 plot(x,y,'linewidth',2.5);
60
61 return
62
63 %%%%%%%%%%%%%%%%%%%%%%%%%%%%%%%%
64 %%%% Gravity.m, secondary function OdeFunc() %%%%
65 function ydot   = OdeFunc(t,y)
66 global  G
67
68     [F, Fx, Fy] = gradF(y(1),y(2));
69     r2      = 1 + Fx^2 + Fy^2;
70
71     ydot    = zeros(4,1);
72     ydot(1) = y(3);
73     ydot(2) = y(4);
74     ydot(3) = -G*Fx/r2;
75     ydot(4) = -G*Fy/r2;
76 return
77
78 %%%%%%%%%%%%%%%%%%%%%%%%%%%%%%%%
79 %%%% Gravity.m, secondary function gradF() %%%%
```

Chapter 20. Plotting III

```
80 function [F, Fx, Fy]    = gradF(x,y)
81     F   = x.^2 + y.^2;
82     Fx  = 2*x;
83     Fy  = 2*y;
84 return
```

The following two invocations of `Gravity()` will produce the plots displayed below.

`Gravity(0.9,0.9,0,0.008);`   `Gravity(0.9,0.9,-0.03,0.03);`

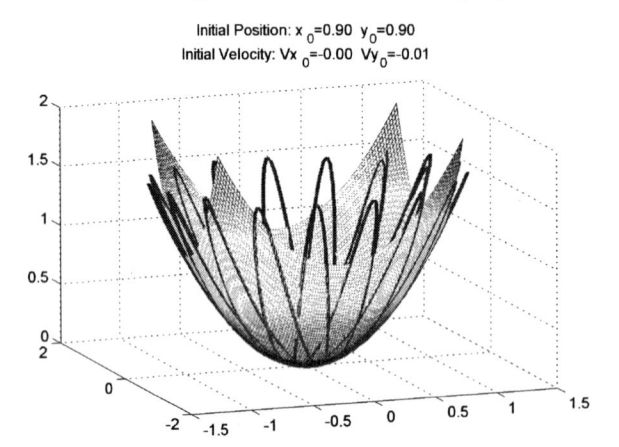

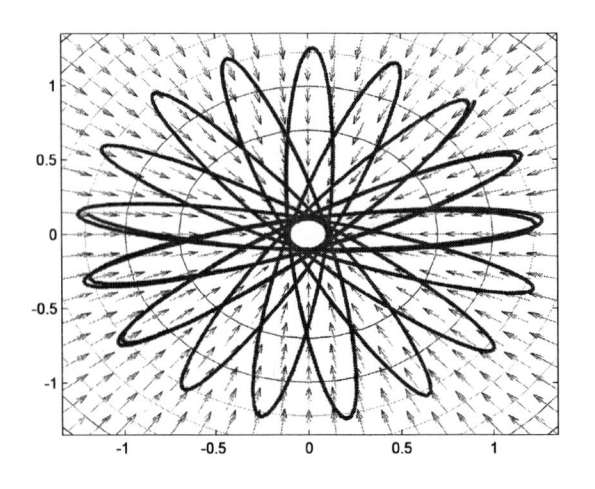

Particle rolling on surface $z = x^2 + y^2$ under force of gravity

Initial Position: x_0=0.90 y_0=0.90
Initial Velocity: Vx_0=-0.00 Vy_0=-0.01

20.3. Plotting trajectories of a constrained dynamical system (Gravity.m)

Particle rolling on surface $z = x^2 + y^2$ under force of gravity

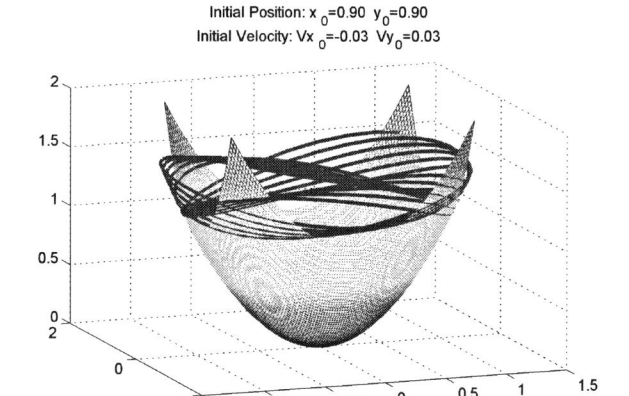

Initial Position: x_0=0.90 y_0=0.90
Initial Velocity: Vx_0=-0.03 Vy_0=0.03

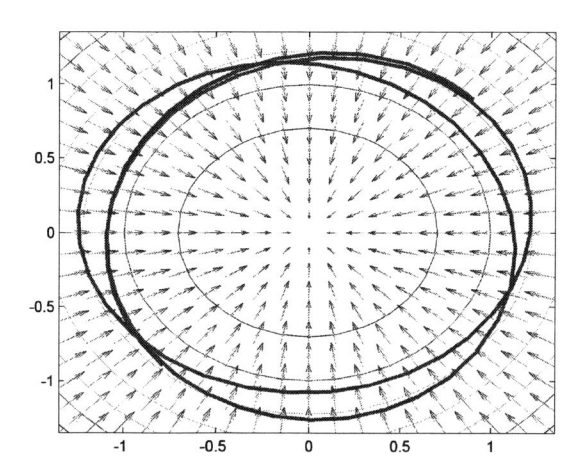

Exercise 124

To observe the particle's motion, replace `plot3()` code with the following:
```
for k=2:length(z)
    plot3([x(k-1),x(k)],[y(k-1),y(k)],[z(k-1),z(k)],...
        'linewidth',2.5)
    pause(0.05)
end
```
Add to `Gravity.m` an input parameter `realtime` which selects between the two implementations of plotting the trajectory.

> **Exercise 125**
>
> Compare the numerically computed gradient determined by the `[Px,Py]=gradient(Z,h,h)` command, with the theoretically computed gradient determined by `[Z,Zx,Zy] = gradF(X,Y)`.

> **Exercise 126**
>
> Does changing the value of G affect the "shape" of the particle's trajectory? Experiment with a variety of initial velocities, and comment on which of the following behaviors are possible:
> 1. The particle "escapes to infinity", i.e. leaves the region and never returns.
> 2. The particle eventually stops at a (local) minimum of the surface.
> 3. The particle never returns to its initial position.
> 4. The particle never returns to its initial height.
>
> It will be instructive to investigate the idea of a "conservative dynamical system". Also, experiment with a variety of landscapes $z = F(x,y)$ by modifying the code in `gradF(x,y)`.

20.4 Topics covered in this chapter

In this chapter we explained how to graph a scalar function of two variables, and create three dimensional plots of parametric surfaces. We described the following MATLAB functions:

1. Creating grid arrays for surface plotting: `ndgrid()`, `meshgrid()`

2. Plotting a surface in three dimensions: `mesh()`, `surf()`

3. Plotting level curves of $z = F(x,y)$: `contour()`, `gradient()`, `quiver()`

Chapter 21

Systems of nonlinear equations

Recall that in the first chapter we attacked the problem of numerically computing the square root of five by applying Newton's root-finding algorithm to $f(x) = x^2 - 5 = 0$. Though it fully took all of Part II and the first three chapters of Part III covering functions, NewtonAlg1.m eventually evolved to the "general purpose scalar root-finder" implemented in Section 14.2. In this chapter we will apply some techniques of matrix algebra to generalize the Newton algorithm to higher dimensions.

21.1 Generalizing scalar equations

It may appear that solving $x^2 = 5$ must be the simplest problem with which to begin this course, but a still simpler problem would have been to solve a *linear* scalar equation such as $5x = 2$. We make this point only to explain that graduating from $f(x) = 5x - 2 = 0$ to $f(x) = x^2 - 5 = 0$ is only one direction of generalization. Another direction of generalization is to consider a *pair* of equations, such as

$$\begin{cases} 5x = 2 \\ 3y = 1 \end{cases}, \quad \text{or more challenging} \quad \begin{cases} 5x + 2y = 7 \\ 3y - 7x = 1 \end{cases},$$

and to seek the pair (x, y) which solves the pair of equations *simultaneously*. Our point is merely that there are two directions of generalization:

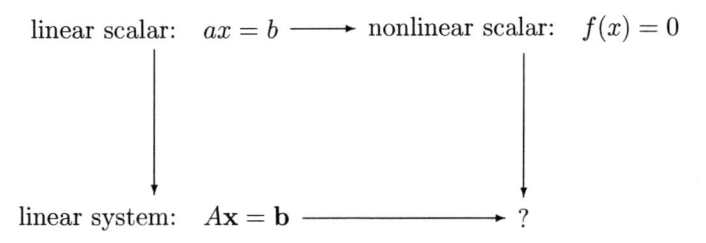

$$\text{linear scalar:} \quad ax = b \longrightarrow \text{nonlinear scalar:} \quad f(x) = 0$$

$$\downarrow \qquad\qquad\qquad\qquad\qquad\qquad \downarrow$$

$$\text{linear system:} \quad A\mathbf{x} = \mathbf{b} \longrightarrow \quad ?$$

From a purely notational point of view, one might guess that the lower-right corner of this diagram should read $\mathbf{F}(\mathbf{x}) = \mathbf{0}$. After explaining what it means to solve n simultaneous nonlinear equations in n unknowns, we will see that this guess is, in fact, the correct generalization.

Chapter 21. Systems of nonlinear equations

> **Exercise 127**
>
> Write the two linear systems in our example above in the matrix form $A\mathbf{x} = \mathbf{b}$. When each equation of a system can be solved independently, as in the first pair of equations on the left, the system is said to be "completely uncoupled". What property of the matrix A characterizes a system that is completely uncoupled? Likewise, if one or several equations can be solved independently of the others, then one says that the corresponding variables can be uncoupled from the other variables. What property of the matrix A characterizes a system that is partially uncoupled? Needless to say, techniques for *uncoupling* systems into smaller systems play a role of enormous importance, which explains the significance of reducing matrices to block-diagonal and other *canonical* forms in Linear Algebra courses.

In this section we consolidate these generalizations by considering *nonlinear systems*:

$$\begin{cases} f_1(x_1, \ldots, x_n) &= 0 \\ \vdots & \vdots \\ f_n(x_1, \ldots, x_n) &= 0 \end{cases}.$$

If, as usual, we indicate vector-valued quantities in bold-face, then finding the roots of a nonlinear system amounts to solving the vector equation:

$$\mathbf{F}(\mathbf{x}) = \mathbf{0}, \qquad \mathbf{F} : \mathbb{R}^n \to \mathbb{R}^n.$$

Here, $\mathbf{x} = (x_1, \ldots, x_n)$ will be the vector solution in $\mathbb{R}^n$, and $\mathbf{0} = (0, \ldots, 0)$ is the origin in $\mathbb{R}^n$. This notation helps us appreciate the generalization of $f(x) = 0$, but in practice we will work mostly with the n-components of the vector-valued function $\mathbf{F}$, namely the n scalar functions $f_k(\mathbf{x})$:

$$\mathbf{F}(\mathbf{x}) = \begin{bmatrix} f_1(\mathbf{x}) \\ \vdots \\ f_n(\mathbf{x}) \end{bmatrix}.$$

Two examples of nonlinear systems in two variables are given by

$$\begin{cases} x^2 - y^2 &= 1 \\ x - 2y &= 3 \end{cases}, \quad \text{or more challenging} \quad \begin{cases} x^y + \sqrt{x}\cos y + y \sin x &= 1 \\ e^{(-x^2 - y^2)} + \tan(2x - 3y) &= -1 \end{cases},$$

> **Exercise 128**
>
> Solve the first system on the left. Draw the solution curves for each of the two scalar equations of the system, and show how the solutions can be realized as the geometric intersection of the these curves.

21.2 Vectorizing the Newton algorithm for systems (VectorNewton.m)

One might imagine that the problem of solving systems of equations simultaneously will require new techniques that are *at least* as complicated as solving a matrix equation on the one hand, and solving a scalar nonlinear equation on the other hand. It is an impressive testament to the genius of the MATLAB language that this is not the case:

> A general nonlinear solver for systems is syntactically the same code as the scalar solver ScalarNewton.m.

First, recall the idea behind the scalar Newton algorithm. We are sitting at the point $(a, f(a))$ on the graph of $y = f(x)$, and we want to arrive at the point ('root of f', 0). We therefore make a move in the x-direction (from a to $a + \Delta x$) such that the corresponding move in the y-direction will bring us from $y = f(a)$ to $y = 0$. But a move in the x-direction by Δx results *approximately*[1] in a move of $f'(a) \cdot \Delta x$ in the y-direction. Furthermore, if the function is linear, then this formula is exactly correct. Thus, $\Delta x = $ ('new x' $- a$) is chosen according to

$$f'(a) \cdot (\text{'new } x\text{'} - a) = \text{'new } y\text{'} - f(a) = 0 - f(a).$$

In other words,

$$\text{'new } x\text{'} = a - \frac{f(a)}{f'(a)}.$$

To change notation slightly, let's consider a to have been the nth approximation $x^{(n)}$, and the 'new x' to be the $(n+1)^{th}$ approximation $x^{(n+1)}$. Thus

$$x^{(n+1)} = x^{(n)} - \frac{f(x^{(n)})}{f'(x^{(n)})}.$$

Next, let's consider the scalar function of several variables $y = f(x_1, \ldots, x_n)$, and we wish to locate a root $\mathbf{a} = (a_1, \ldots, a_n)$ at which $f(\mathbf{a}) = 0$. Again, pretend we are currently sitting at the point $(a_1, \ldots, a_n, f(\mathbf{a}))$ on the graph of f. Then to bring the y-value of f from $f(\mathbf{a})$ to 0, we should make a move (in analogy with a truly linear f) in the **x**-direction of $\Delta \mathbf{x}$ where

$$\nabla f(\mathbf{a}) \cdot \Delta \mathbf{x} = -f(\mathbf{a}).$$

For those needing a quick review of the basics of the Calculus of several variables, recall $\nabla f(\mathbf{a})$ is defined to be the row vector $[\partial f/\partial x_1, \ldots, \partial f/\partial x_n]$. The above result follows from the fact that a move of size h in any of the x_k-directions will produce a move in the function's value by *approximately* $(\partial f/\partial x_k) \cdot (h)$, and therefore a move of size Δx_k in each of the x_k-directions will result in a cumulative change in the function's value by:

$$\sum_{k=1}^{n} \frac{\partial f}{\partial x_k} \Delta x_k = \nabla f \cdot \Delta \mathbf{x}.$$

---

[1] By approximately we really mean "to first-order".

Now, there are many "moves $\Delta \mathbf{x}$" which will accomplish this, since generally $y = f(\mathbf{x})$ will intersect the $\{y = 0\}$-plane in a curve or surface, rather than a point. For example, if $n = 2$ and $y = f(x_1, x_2) = x_1^2 - x_2^2 - 1$, then the $\{y = 0\}$-plane intersects the graph of y in the hyperbola $x_1^2 - x_2^2 = 1$. In other words, $\nabla f(\mathbf{a}) \cdot \Delta \mathbf{x} = -f(\mathbf{a})$ has many solutions - typically $(n-1)$ dimensions worth! On the other hand, this equation is nonetheless a *requirement* we want $\Delta \mathbf{x}$ to satisfy when determining the 'new $\mathbf{x}$'.

Finally, when dealing with the system

$$\begin{cases} f_1(x_1, \ldots, x_n) &= 0 \\ \quad \vdots & \vdots \\ f_n(x_1, \ldots, x_n) &= 0 \end{cases},$$

we do not want just $f_1(\mathbf{x}) = 0$, but indeed all $f_k(\mathbf{x}) = 0$, giving us the n *simultaneous* requirements

$$\nabla f_k(\mathbf{a}) \cdot \Delta \mathbf{x} = -f_k(\mathbf{a}), \qquad k = 1, \ldots, n.$$

In other words, for fixed $\mathbf{a}$, we wish to solve the linear system (only the components of 'new $\mathbf{x}$' are unknown):

$$\begin{pmatrix} \nabla f_1(\mathbf{a}) \\ \vdots \\ \nabla f_n(\mathbf{a}) \end{pmatrix} \left(\text{'new } x\text{'} - \mathbf{a} \right) = \begin{pmatrix} -f_1(\mathbf{a}) \\ \vdots \\ -f_n(\mathbf{a}) \end{pmatrix}.$$

Recall that the $n \times n$ matrix of numbers (or column vector of gradients) given by

$$D\mathbf{F}(\mathbf{a}) := \begin{pmatrix} \nabla f_1(\mathbf{a}) \\ \vdots \\ \nabla f_n(\mathbf{a}) \end{pmatrix}$$

is called the "Jacobian matrix" of the vector-valued function $\mathbf{F} : \mathbb{R}^n \to \mathbb{R}^n$ evaluated at $\mathbf{a} \in \mathbb{R}^n$; it is the n-dimensional generalization of $f'(a)$.

We can now state the n-dimensional version of Newton's root-finding algorithm:

$$D\mathbf{F}(\mathbf{a}) \, (\text{'new } \mathbf{x}\text{'} - \mathbf{a}) = \mathbf{0} - \mathbf{F}(\mathbf{a}).$$

To solve this matrix equation for the 'new $\mathbf{x}$', we need to move the $D\mathbf{F}(\mathbf{a})$ to the right hand side, which is to say we must apply a *left-inverse* of $D\mathbf{F}(\mathbf{a})$ to both sides of the equation[2] Happily, MATLAB does not require us to compute the left-inverse $D\mathbf{F}(\mathbf{a})^{-1}$ to solve this matrix equation; using the "left-divide matrix operator" described in Chapter 15, we can assert $\Delta \mathbf{x}$ solves

$$D\mathbf{F}(\mathbf{a}) \, \Delta \mathbf{x} = -\mathbf{F}(\mathbf{a}),$$

---

[2] Needless to say, we are ignoring the numerically important issue of the invertibility of the Jacobian at each of the iterates $\mathbf{x}^{(n)}$. For our purposes we will assume, as we did in the scalar case, that $\mathbf{x}^{(n)}$ is never a critical point of $\mathbf{F}$.

21.2. Vectorizing the Newton algorithm for systems (VectorNewton.m)

and therefore
$$(\text{'new } \mathbf{x}\text{'} - \mathbf{a}) = -D\mathbf{F}(\mathbf{a}) \backslash \mathbf{F}(\mathbf{a}).$$
In terms of the nth approximation $\mathbf{x}^{(n)}$, we therefore restate this matrix equation as
$$\mathbf{x}^{(n+1)} = \mathbf{x}^{(n)} - D\mathbf{F}(\mathbf{x}^{(n)}) \backslash \mathbf{F}(\mathbf{x}^{(n)}).$$
If we transpose this matrix equation so that $\mathbf{x}$ and $\mathbf{F}$ become row vectors (a change of convention which we will adopt in the code), the Jacobian DF becomes transposed into DF^t, and left-divide is replaced with right-divide, then we have:
$$\mathbf{x}^{(n+1)} = \mathbf{x}^{(n)} - \mathbf{F}(\mathbf{x}^{(n)}) / DF(\mathbf{x}^{(n)})^t.$$
Obviously, the implementation of the functions F and DF must change to accept a row vector argument instead of a column vector.

As promised, this formula for the nth iterate is identical to that found in the scalar version. Are there any other changes required of NewtonAlg.m? Only a small one which arises when measuring how close our approximations come to falling within tolerance. In particular, we must replace the $|x_{n+1} - x_n|$ (i.e. `abs(x(n+1)-x(n))`) used to measure the distance between two scalars with the vector norm $\| \ \|$ (i.e. `norm(x(n+1)-x(n))`). Note that the latter construct agrees with the former when applied to scalars, and could have been used from the beginning. Our pièce de résistance is a general nonlinear solver for systems:

```
1 %%%%VectorNewton.m, primary function VectorNewton()
2 function [y, success]    = VectorNewton(x0, maxiter, tol, f, df)
3 %f = [f1,..,fn] is vector-valued function on Rn
4 %solve simultaneous system f(y) = f(y1,..,yn) = (0,..,0)
5 % x0 = (y1(0),..,yn(0))'
6 % on return, y(:,end) is best approximation of root (y1,..,yn)'
7
8 y         = zeros(length(x0),maxiter);
9 y(:,1)    = x0;
10 xold     = x0;
11 err      = inf;
12 k        = 1;
13 while (err > tol) && (k < maxiter)
14     xnew    = xold - feval(f,xold)/feval(df,xold);
15     err     = norm(xnew - xold);
16     k       = k + 1;
17     y(:,k)  = xnew;
18     xold    = xnew;
19 end
20
21 y(:,k+1:end)= [ ];
22 success    = err < tol;
23 return
```

21.3 A root-finder for two dimensional systems (Nonlinear2dSolver.m)

In this final section of Part III, we compose a "wrapper" or "shell" to VectorNewton. We name this file Nonlinear2dSolver.m, since it is specific to a system of two equations in two unknowns. The basic functionality of this program is to:

1. Specify (i.e. hardwire) the system $\mathbf{F}(\mathbf{x}) = [f_1(\mathbf{x}), f_2(\mathbf{x})]^t$.

2. Invoke `VectorNewton` to return a sequence of approximations to a root of $\mathbf{F}(\mathbf{x}) = 0$.

3. Display the approximations $\mathbf{x}^{(n)} \longrightarrow \hat{\mathbf{x}}$ in a table.

4. Display a two dimensional plot of the level curves of f_1 and f_2, with each contour curve labelled with its corresponding z-value.

5. Plot the approximations $\mathbf{x}^{(n)}$, demonstrating their convergence to the intersection of the $\{f_1 = 0\}$ and $\{f_2 = 0\}$ level curves.

```matlab
%%%%%%%% Nonlinear2dSolver.m, primary function VectorNewtonMain %%%%
function    Nonlinear2dSolver()

%%%%%%%%%%%%%%%%%%%%%%%%%%%%%%%%%%%%%%
%%%%%%% initialization section %%%%%
x0      = [1.4, 2.3];
maxiter = 1000;
tol     = 1e-5;

%function handles to simultaneous system F and Jacobian DF
f  = @Fnonlinear;
df = @DFnonlinear;

%%%%%%%%%%%%%%%%%%%%%%%%%%%%%%%%%%%%%%
%%%%%%% algorithm section %%%%%
%call vectorized Newton solver for systems
[approxRoot, success]   = VectorNewton(x0, maxiter, tol, f, df);

%%%%%%%%%%%%%%%%%%%%%%%%%%%%%%%%%%%%%%
%%%%%%% output section %%%%%
if success
    DisplayRoots(approxRoot);
else
    fprintf('Failed to converge within \%e in \%d iterations', tol, maxIter);
end

return
```

21.3. A root-finder for two dimensional systems (Nonlinear2dSolver.m)

```
28
29 %%%%%%%%%%%%%%%%%%%%%%%%%%%%%%%%%%%%%%%%%%%%%%%%%%
30 %%%% Nonlinear2dSolver.m, secondary function DisplayRoots %%%%
31 function    DisplayRoots(approxRoot,hFig)
32 %on entry, approxRoot = array (row vector) of approximations Xn
33 % until tolerance achieved
34 %on entry, hFig = handle to figure in which to do subsequent plotting
35
36 root     = approxRoot(end,:);
37 %display solution to Command Window
38 fprintf('root = [%g,%g]\n', root(1), root(2));
39
40 %plot sequence of approximations converging
41 figure(200)
42 hold on
43 plot(approxRoot(1,:),approxRoot(2,:),'ro','MarkerFaceColor','r')
44 plot(root(1),root(2),'ro','MarkerSize',15)
45
46 %two contour plots with 8 (cmsize) level curves each
47 % and we label every other one using clabel()
48 x        = linspace(-3,3,41);    %odd #points so cusp visible on z2=0
49 y        = linspace(-3,3,41);
50 [X,Y]    = meshgrid(x,y);
51 [Z1,Z2] = FnonlinearPlotting(X,Y);
52
53 cmsize   = 8;
54 [C,h] = contour(X,Y,Z1,-[0:cmsize]);
55 clabel(C,h,-[0:2:cmsize]);
56 [C,h] = contour(X,Y,Z2,[0:cmsize]);
57 clabel(C,h,[0:2:cmsize]);
58 colormap(lines(cmsize))
59
60 %display functions z=f(x,y) whose level curves are plotted
61 cr   = sprintf('\n');
62 str = sprintf('Level sets of %sz_1 = x^2 + y^2 - 10 %sfor z=0,-1,..,-8',...
63              cr,cr);
64 text(0.02,0.9,str,'FontWeight','demi','units','normalized');
65 str = sprintf('Level sets of %sz_2 = x^3 - y^2 %sfor z=0,1,2,..,8',...
66              cr,cr);
67 text(0.37,0.52,str,'FontWeight','demi','units','normalized');
68
69 return
70
```

```
71 %%%%%%%%%%%%%%%%%%%%%%%%%%%%%%%%%%%%
72 %%%% Nonlinear2dSolver.m, secondary function Fnonlinear %%%%
73 function z   = Fnonlinear(y)
74 %on entry, y = two dimensional (row or column) vector
75    z(1)     = y(1)^2 + y(2)^2 - 10;
76    z(2)     = y(1)^3 - y(2)^2;
77 return
78
79 %%%%%%%%%%%%%%%%%%%%%%%%%%%%%%%%%%%%
80 %%%% Nonlinear2dSolver.m, secondary function FnonlinearPlotting %%%%
81 function [Z1,Z2]  = FnonlinearPlotting(X,Y)
82    Z1     = X.^2 + Y.^2 - 10;
83    Z2     = X.^3 - Y.^2;
84 return
85
86 %%%%%%%%%%%%%%%%%%%%%%%%%%%%%%%%%%%%
87 %%%% Nonlinear2dSolver.m, secondary function DFnonlinear %%%%
88 function dz = DFnonlinear(y)
89 %on entry, y = two dimensional (row or column) vector
90 %on exit, dz = Jacobian of F evaluated at y
91    %1st row is grad Z1
92    dz(1,1) = 2*y(1);
93    dz(1,2) = 2*y(2);
94    %2nd row is grad Z2
95    dz(2,1) = 3*y(1)^2;
96    dz(2,2) = -2*y(2);
97 return
98
99 %%%%%%% VectorNewton.m, primary function VectorNewton %%%%
100 function [y, success]    = VectorNewton(x0, maxiter, tol, f, df)
101 %on entry, x0 = initial guess to start Newton algorithm
102 %on entry, maxIter = maximum number of iterations to execute
103 %on entry, tol = tolerance
104 %f   = handle to function whose roots we seek
105 %df  = handle to derivative function
106 %call with F = inline('x^2-5'), DF = inline('2*x')
107 % or call with F = @MyFunc, DF = @MyFuncDer
108 %on exit, success = 1 if tolerance achieved
109 %on exit, y = matrix of column vectors of approximations Xn
110
111 y       = zeros(length(x0),maxiter);
112 y(:,1)  = x0;        %initial value is first column
113 xold    = x0;
```

21.3. A root-finder for two dimensional systems (Nonlinear2dSolver.m)

```
114 err      = inf;
115 k        = 1;
116 while (err > tol) && (k < maxiter)
117    xnew     = xold - feval(f,xold)/feval(df,xold)';
118    err      = norm(xnew - xold);
119    k        = k + 1;
120    y(:,k)   = xnew;
121    xold     = xnew;
122 end
123
124 y(:,k+1:end)= [ ];
125 success  = err < tol;
126 return
```

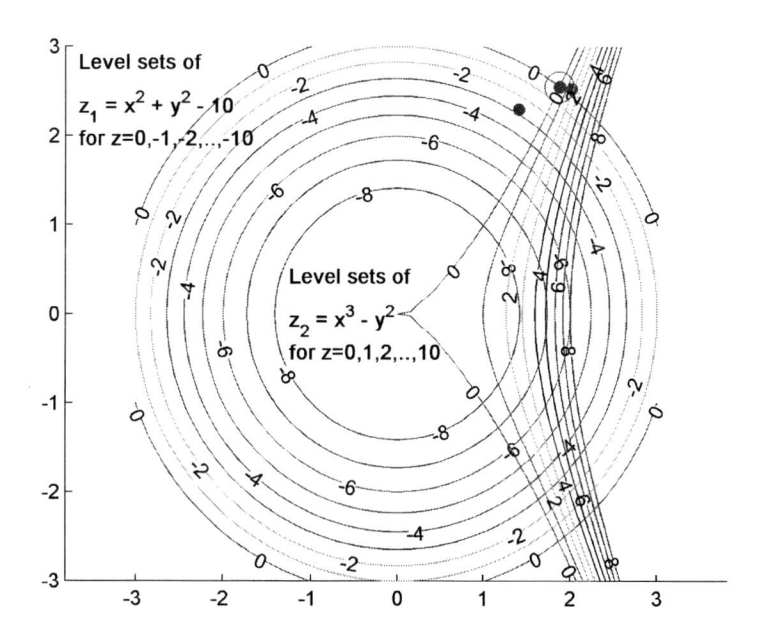

Notice that the $\{z_1 = 0\}$ level curves are *drawn* for $z_1 = \{0, -1, \ldots, -8\}$ and *labelled* for $z_1 = \{0, -2, -4, -6, -8\}$, while the $\{z_2 = 0\}$ level curves are *drawn* for $z_2 = \{0, 1, \ldots, 8\}$, and *labelled* for $z_1 = \{0, 2, 4, 6, 8\}$. This reduces some of the clutter from the labels, making the intersection

$$\{z_1 = 0\} \cap \{z_2 = 0\},$$

more transparent.

The figures below show an enlarged view of the approximations $\mathbf{x}^{(n)}$ approaching the intersection of the $\{z_1 = 0\}$ and $\{z_2 = 0\}$ level curves.

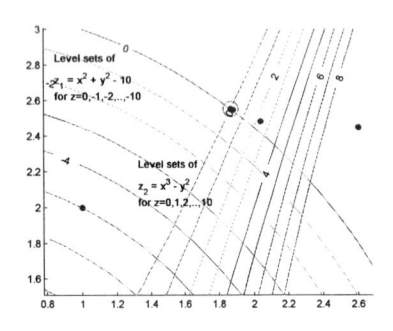

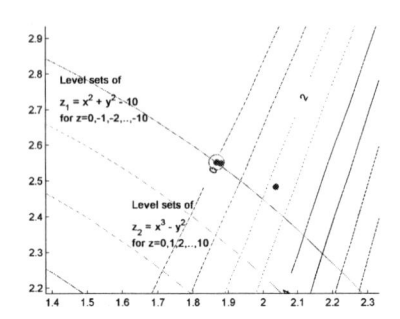

> **Exercise 129**
>
> Show that the x-coordinate of the solution (x, y) satisfies $x^3 + x^2 = 10$.

> **Exercise 130**
>
> Improve the modularity of the code by removing from Nonlinear2dSolver the hardwired specifics of the vector-valued function $\mathbf{F}(\mathbf{x})$ and its Jacobian $D\mathbf{F}(\mathbf{x})$. In other words, create a separate file which implements the three functions Fnonlinear(), FnonlinearPlotting(), DFnonlinear().

Note that if we are only interested in returning the (approximate) root, and are not interested in analyzing the sequence of approximations, then VectorNewton can return a value rather than an array. In this case, it is quite remarkable that the following implementation could have worked as our original NewtonAlg for scalar equations!

```
%%%%%%%%%%%%%%%%%%%%%%%%%%%%%%%%%%%%%%%%%%%%%%%%%%%%%%
%%%%%%%% NewtonAlg.m, primary function VectorNewton %%%%%
function [xnew, success]    = VectorNewton(x0, maxiter, tol, f, df)
%on entry, x0 = initial guess to start Newton algorithm
%on entry, maxIter = maximum number of iterations to execute
%on entry, tol = tolerance
%f   = handle to function whose roots we seek
%df  = handle to derivative function
%on exit, success  = 1 if tolerance achieved
%on exit, y = matrix of column vectors of approximations Xn

```

```
12 xold    = x0;
13 err     = inf;
14 k       = 1;
15 while (err > tol) && (k < maxiter)
16    xnew = xold - f(xold)/df(xold)';  %works for scalar or matrix division!
17    err  = norm(xnew - xold); %equivalent to abs(xnew - xold) for scalars!
18    k    = k + 1;
19    xold = xnew;
20 end
21
22 success = err < tol;
23 return
```

21.4 Topics covered in this chapter

In this chapter we have seen the major themes of Part III, namely Arrays, Functions, Sharing Data, and Plotting come together. Based on the Newton algorithm from Chapter 2 used to find roots of scalar equations, we described an algorithm for solving systems of nonlinear equations. We implemented this n-dimensional algorithm by vectorizing NewtonAlg.m, which required the techniques of Chapter 15. We organized our program into functional units using callbacks, which required the techniques of Sharing Data I and the chapters on Functions. Finally, we applied techniques of Plotting III to visualize the convergence of the iterations to the intersection of the $\{z_1 = 0\}$ and $\{z_2 = 0\}$ level curves. The following MATLAB functions related to contour plotting were also utilized:

1. Contour plotting: contour(), clabel(), colormap(), lines()

Further Reading

[1] George Lindfield and John Penny. *Numerical Methods Using MATLAB*. Prentice Hall, Upper Saddle River, New Jersey, 2000.

[2] Patrick Marchand. *Graphics and GUIs with MATLAB*. CRC Press, Boca Raton, FL, 1999.

[3] L.F. Shampine, I. Gladwell, and S. Thomson. *Solving ODEs with MATLAB*. Cambridge University Press, Cambridge, UK, 2003.